W9-BJC-787

Kasher in the Rye

Kasher in the Rye

The True Tale of a
*White Boy from Oakland Who Became
a Drug Addict, Criminal,
Mental Patient, and Then Turned 16*

Moshe Kasher

GRAND CENTRAL
PUBLISHING

NEW YORK   BOSTON

Grand Central Publishing
Hachette Book Group
237 Park Avenue
New York, NY 10017

www.HachetteBookGroup.com

Printed in the United States of America

Binder's code: RRD-C

First Edition: March 2012
10 9 8 7 6 5 4 3 2 1

Grand Central Publishing is a division of Hachette Book Group, Inc.
The Grand Central Publishing name and logo is a trademark of Hachette Book Group, Inc.

The publisher is not responsible for websites (or their content) that are not owned by the publisher.

Library of Congress Cataloging-in-Publication Data

Kasher, Moshe.
   Kasher in the rye : the true tale of a white boy from Oakland who became a drug addict, criminal, mental patient, and then turned 16 / by Moshe Kasher.—1st ed.
      p. cm.
   ISBN 978-0-446-58426-5
   1. Kasher, Moshe.   2. Jewish comedians—United States—Biography.   I. Title.
PN2287.K26A3 2012
729.7'6028092—dc23
   [B]
                        2011027140

For my mother. I wouldn't be here without you.

Acknowledgments

I didn't even know this thing was a book, and without the help of many, it probably wouldn't have been. Many thanks are due. First and foremost to my manager, Josh Lieberman, for having the vision to crush my dream of putting on a one-man show while building a new vision for me that became this book. To the master, Richard Abate, for handing me the building blocks and teaching me how to stack them. To my editor, Ben Greenberg, for his faith in me and for putting my manuscript and talents to the whetstone. Together we made something razor-sharp. To Flag Tonuzi, for designing the perfect cover for this book. To everyone else at Grand Central. To all the kids I grew up with in Oakland, for teaching me how to survive. Thanks to Oakland Public Schools, OPD, every therapist I ever had, every adult I ever hated, and everyone who made a mistake with me. I ain't mad acha. To everyone at the Gersh Agency and to Dave Becky and everyone at 3arts. To every stand-up who inspires me. To everyone I forgot: I didn't mean it. To every gangster rapper, ever (especially those whose songs made my chapter list). To all my dear friends, especially my brother from another mother, Mr. Moon, for allowing a sliver of his story to be told by me, and for living his life with me all these years. To Jeremy Weintraub, for his help and support. To John Rose, for helping me untie the knot. To the chief conductor, for all the music. To Arlene and John. To Larry Wilhoit, the finest step entemologist I could have asked for. To my entire wild, insane, brilliant family: Kashers, Swirskys, Sterns, Worthens, etc. A very special thanks to my brother from the same mother, David Kasher, the world's sexiest rabbi, for the constant patience, feedback, love, and criticism, and for helping me name this book. And finally, always, to Oakland.

Author's Note

About the Artwork

Each of the inserts you see throughout the book demarcating its different sections was drawn by Oakland artist and graffiti legend Eskae aka Ezra Li Eismont. I first met Ezra when I also used to write graffiti back in the day, and when I hung up my paint can due to a lack of any measureable artistic talent, Ezra did the world a favor and kept painting. He is now an internationally recognized artist and a real good guy. Check out his work at www.ezrali.com.

Also, all of the calligraphy you see was hand drawn by Emily Snyder, a master calligraphy artist and owner of the business www.queenofquills.com. Have her write something for you.

About My Name

The names in this book have been changed to protect the guilty and the innocent. With one odd exception. The documents that

I have included throughout the book are, you might notice, describing someone named "Mark Kasher." Yes, that's me. Like many American Jews I was given a "slave name" in order not to arouse suspicion should the Gestapo ever make a resurgence here in the USA. Mark is the Toby to my Kunte Kinte. At about sixteen, I began going full-time by my middle name, Moshe. I was feeling a desperate need to re-create myself with a new identity. Read the book and you'll soon see why.

Kasher in the Rye

Introduction

Memoirs are inexact things, messy around the edges and distorted by the twists and turns of memory. Sometimes details get lost or hazy and confusing. I've been in the middle of telling a story only to realize, "Oh shit, this didn't happen to me, this is a Steven Segal film plot." Although, strangely, I did once rescue the President from hijackers on a plane. See, there we go again. You'll never know if that last part is true.

As you go back through the creaky secret rooms of your memory, you find places damaged by time and neglect. You can dust them off, but often you want to present them in a form that is understandable to people, and I can imagine polishing a corroded memory and making it prettier or more compelling than it deserves to be.

Under the weight of all of that, I would like to offer you my memoir: a drug-filled journey through the harrowing years of my youth. I have tried as best I can to give it over with honesty and accuracy. But you'll be shocked to realize that a drug-addicted, mentally ill journey of violent insanity is a bit of a hazy cat's-cradle to untangle. Hazy or not, this is my life.

I even found, at points, when diving into my memory that *I* was surprised at how bad things had gotten when I was young. Surprised by my own memories. Do you remember that scene from the movie *The Princess Bride* when, after Princess Buttercup is swallowed by the Snow Sands in the Fire Swamp, Westley cuts a vine from a nearby tree and dives in after her? He's in there, breathless, blind, feeling around for what's important. That's how I felt the entire time I was swimming around in my memories. I felt swallowed by them, and only the lifeline of my adult brain made me feel safe and like I'd emerge again, able to breathe.

Writing this book was painful and illuminating, exciting and emotional. I can only hope that reading it makes you feel that way, too. When I was a very young man I remember reading books like *Catcher in the Rye* and *The Basketball Diaries* and thinking secretly, "Look, here are people who are just as broken as me." It gave me a private thrill to know that I wasn't the only piece of damaged machinery out there. So I suppose I'd like to say to the person who's reading this book who feels like I did when I was young— like a factory defect from the human being plant: I get it. You'll be okay. Hell, maybe someday you'll even write a book about it.

PART ONE:
Genesis

Chapter 1

"The Dayʒ of Wayback"
—NWA

I was born ugly. Babies are ugly. At least I've always thought so. Little pruny creatures. Shooting down the birth canal, the final seconds of prelife bliss tick to a sudden stop and a gross little *thing* is bungeed into the world. Leaving behind the vaginaquarium floating bliss of yesterday, it pops into the world. Here comes Baby, covered in gel and matter, wrinkles and blood, shit and life juices. I've always imagined a mother looking down and in the first millisecond thinking, "Goodness, *what* is *that?*" But before she even has a chance for that thought to shoot up her synapses and reverberate in her mind, the doctor smacks Baby's bottom and the little one shrieks its first cry. That cry, quick as sound, quicker, jams itself into its mother's ears, derailing that first repulsed thought. It circumvents her brain. It shoots into her heart. Mommy forgets all about that first thought when she hears that wail. Her only thought now is, "My son!"

My mother never heard that wail. My mother is deaf.

My shriek flew up to her ears and, finding two broken, swollen drums, ricocheted back and meandered around the hospital room looking for somewhere to roost before it impotently spilled onto the hospital floor.

And though her second thought no doubt was a loving one, I've always wondered if that first "Eww, gross," thought didn't make it to my mother's brain and, planting itself deep inside her, make her ask, years later, "What is wrong with this kid?"

My earliest memories are of flying fingers. Flesh-colored strings zapping through the air, signifying meaning. I didn't realize my first word was "spoken" in sign language. How would I have known that wasn't just how everyone talked?

I didn't realize my mother was deaf, but I did realize that if I cried when she wasn't looking, it made no difference to her. If I wept in view of her, her face would screw up in compassion and she would reach down and scoop me up to make me feel okay again. I took this information and imprinted it into my brain.

As early as I can recall, adults have been telling me there was something wrong with me. I was passed around, adult to adult, each one throwing their hands up and declaring, "I don't know what's wrong with him either!" Adults talked about me like that, right in front of me, all the time, as if my mother's deafness somehow applied to me by association. I'd spend time in the mirror, trying to figure out what was looking back at me, what weird alien thing I was.

According to my mother, I was born out of control, a feral kid, wild at heart and physically unable to handle the energy and ferocity of my own body. If you could see my little Jew body now, you would find that very difficult to believe.

I'd snarl and snap, I'd bite and foam, I'd shake with anger when the slightest thing didn't go my way, and my body would seize in convulsions of rage and uncontrollable emotion.

Frightened, my mother sent me to a therapist. I was four years old. That is a demarcation point in my life. I was booted into the therapeutic garden and left to wander, entering an old rusty gate guarded by the ghosts of Freud and Jung. Being told, still wet from the womb, that you need therapy, it almost makes a boy feel broken.

Oh, and my mother and father are both deaf.

People are always fascinated when I tell them that.

"They are *both* deaf?" they ask, winding up for a dumb question: "What are the odds of that?"

I suppose they imagine two lost deaf people wandering across the land with a sign in hand reading: DEAF LONELY HEART SEEKS MATE!

Having no experience with deaf people, folks usually assume they are rare as unicorns and that only magic could bring two of them together.

The real story is less magical, more practical.

In 1967, the World Games for the Deaf preliminary trials were held in Berkeley, California.

All the way in Brooklyn, New York, Steven J. Kasher, my father, the deaf, sickly son of two Jewish communists, was determined to make those games. Lord knows why. My father was hardly an athlete. He was a slight, scrappy, monkey of a boy, a shock of jet-black curls wrapped around his head like Art Garfunkel's long-lost evil, dark-haired cousin. Nonetheless, my father walked into the living room and announced to his family that he was hitchhiking to Berkeley and that he'd be leaving that afternoon.

His mother, my baba, Helen Kasher, wrung her hands with worry.

She hated when he left New York. She hated when people left her.

Baba was raised in Hungary, the first of five children raised by a mighty Chassidic patriarch, my great-grandfather Zeidi. Zeidi was the undisputed leader of the family, a chicken butcher by day, a Torah scholar by night, a saint by apocryphal family history. Zeidi isn't a name, by the way. *Zeidi* is just the Yiddish word for "grandfather." But in my family, Zeidi wasn't just someone's grandfather, he *was* Grandfather. He *was* Zeidi. As far as I know, everyone called him that, including his wife. Sounds like their sex life was rockin'. Give it to me, Grandpa!

His daughter, Helen, seemed to be the only one who was not convinced of his beneficent grandfatherness. Sometime in the 1920s, Zeidi sailed to America alone, waving good-bye from a ship's bow vowing to send for everyone soon. I imagine a sad man with patches holding together his oversized suit playing a plaintive song on the fiddle behind Zedi as he yelled down to my baba and the rest of the family.

"I'll see you all soon!" he'd cry as the ocean brined the sides of the ship. "In the meantime, there will be some really exciting news coming from Germany soon that should keep you guys busy!"

For years Zeidi struggled alone in Brooklyn to kill enough chickens to send for the family. Unfortunately for him, every chicken throat he slit further cut the cord of connection to his oldest child, my grandmother.

And as she saw the world around her fall into ashes and all of

Europe go septic with anti-Jewish infection, all she was able to see was that her father left her.

By the (nick of) time that Zeidi brought the family over, the gulf between them was more profound than the space between New York and Hungary.

To the shock and horror of the family, the second they stepped onto American soil, my grandmother threw a pair of pants on and declared herself free of the shackles and poison of religion. She cursed the Torah. She decried Judaism and all other faiths as divisive and archaic. She joined the American Communist Party and marched for civil rights. She vowed never to have anything to do with Judaism again. Then she married my grandfather, a Jewish, Yiddish novelist, Duvid Kasher.

Hardly the huge anti-Jewish rebellion she'd been planning.

My grandfather was a quiet, thoughtful man whose hands shook with the reverberation of the things he'd left behind in Poland. He was a writer who had chewed on Yiddish prose in coffeehouses in Warsaw with legends like Sholem Aleichem. He moved to America to escape the horrors and left behind the linguistic fluency that defined his career. He left a scholar; he arrived an immigrant.

When they had my father, their endogamic, muddied, closed-circuit DNA code zapped my father's nervous system, leaving him deaf and addled with Gaucher's disease, a rare disorder that strikes eastern European jews almost exclusively. An ironic proof to my baba that Judaism literally *was* poison.

Nonetheless, my father was born a fighter. Not expected to live past the age of six, he gave everyone the finger and did what the fuck he wanted. A scrappy firecracker, my dad took control of every room he was ever in. He sparkled with charisma. He was electric. My father was like a king.

The Deaf King.

So when the king stepped out onto the field of the World Games for the Deaf trials and dusted his hands off, my mother's jaw dropped.

A week later she left a note on her mother's kitchen table: *I moved to New York. I'll be okay.*

And that is how two deaf people met and made me.

Seven years later, an old brownstone co-op building in Queens housed a family on the edge. In a one-bedroom apartment were my mother, my father, my big brother, David, almost four years old at the time, and a nine-month-old baby, handsome and charismatic as hell for an infant, but simmering with latent drug addiction, learning disabilities, and violent tendencies.

I was lying in my crib wondering when I could get out and start smoking and listening to hip hop when my older brother leaned in to say hello. I smacked him in the face.

"Why did he hit me?!?" David wailed.

"He must be angry already." My father laughed.

Oh, Ha Ha, Father.

When no one was looking, I somehow made my way out of the crib and climbed down into the bathroom.

In there I found an array of pretty things: brightly colored makeup kits and glittery perfume bottles. My hand stopped on a Liz Taylor's "White Diamonds" bottle. I grabbed it and wrenched the labial cap off the thing. I took a gulp of perfume. I kept gulping. The fact that I took a sip of perfume makes some sense to me. A baby smells a pretty thing and tries to see if it tastes pretty, too. The concerning detail is that I polished off the bottle. That night was my first night in a hospital due to out-of-control drinking.

Out of control. That's how my mother always described me. She'd sign, "You were just always out of control."

Apparently my father was, too. My mom told me stories of how scared she was, of how he threw her around, but to be honest, I never believed her. It wasn't until years later, when I started throwing her around myself, that I thought there might be something to the story.

My father, the charismatic lightning rod of our family, sometimes burned, sometimes exploded.

Sometimes, according to my mother, lightning struck.

My father would spend hours in his studio, painting enormous canvases with rich oils, trying like hell to get his demons out in the painting. He'd gone to art school and was an emerging talent. The deaf beatnik painter from Brooklyn. It was a backstory gallery owners salivated over.

But my dad also raged. He also fumed and yelled. He also grabbed my mother by the hand so hard he broke her fingers. Seems like my dad might've been born angry, too.

In the spring of 1980, when I was almost a year old, my mom took us on a two-week vacation to California. We never returned. These days, stealing your children away across the country like that would be considered an abduction. But back then the Fathers' Rights Movement was barely gaining steam, and my dad was mostly powerless to do anything but sit there and wait for us to come home.

Twenty years later, after his body caught up with him and he sickened and died, I found a wall calendar in a pile of his stuff as my family and I did that sick divvying of the loot that happens when someone dies. There in the square for April 18 was my father's unmistakable handwriting, packed with flourishes and loops. Even his scribble had pizzazz. The box read:

April 18th: Bea and the boys leave to California

Each day we were gone was crossed with a big X. Each day ticked off in anticipation of seeing his family again. Eventually, I imagine, he realized, sick to his stomach:

"They aren't coming back."

Eventually, the X's stopped. When the X's stopped, my life in Oakland began.

We moved in with my grandmother straightaway. My mother's mother, Hope. There was never any question of going back. In my family, divorce was a kind of sacred rite, passed down from matriarch to matriarch. My mother is a third-generation divorcée, which means that my great-grandmother left her husband. Divorce in 1917 was likely to turn a respectable woman into the town harpy, but the holiness of the divorce rite was so deeply embedded in her genetic code that even witch burnings and convents couldn't keep my great-grandmother married.

My grandmother's heart fluttered when she saw us tumble onto her doorstep, bags in hand.

"Finally," she said, "you've come to your senses and left that fucking man. I've said it a thousand times, all men are pigs." She looked down at my brother and me, "Except you boys, of course."

My mother had come home.

My grandmother burned all of her life with unceasing resentment toward my grandfather, a man named, appropriately, depending on who you ask, Dick.

Anytime his name would come up, my grandma's knuckles

would go white with rage. "That bastard, that piece of shit. *An abuser that's what he was, an ABUSER.*"

My little soft-palate mind registered, *"Do not be an abuser."* Check.

Despite the endless fires of hatred that burned for Dick the Dick, my grandmother seemed to nonetheless have another flame burning for him. As far as I know, she was never with another man the entire forty years of her life after leaving him. She arranged her life neatly to live without romance, replacing it with poisonous resentment. That resentment bubbled over and then trickled down onto my brother and me, anointing us with holy oils, crowning us the princes of a man-hating coven.

About the time we arrived in Oakland, my mother started to notice there was something wrong with me. Or perhaps that was when my mother started looking for something to be wrong with me. Most likely it was a combination of the two. My grandmother had found the courage to leave Ol' Dick through the support of a therapist she'd seen in secret for a year prior to her divorce. She impressed upon my mother that the only way through the trauma of her relationship with my father was to find a therapist.

She went, and that cemented my mother's deep and abiding belief in the power of analysis. My mother believed in therapy the way that people believe in Jesus. It was simply infallible. It contained all of life's answers. It was perfect. So when I began showing signs of the rage that would later come to define me, there was only one thing to do. Send me to therapy.

Therapy became, in my house, more than just a source for answers. It became a third parent. It was the pant leg of the father that I didn't have around to tug on and ask for something when my mother refused me. When my mother's characteristic franticness kicked in, she was intractable. If she decided something was correct, it would remain correct until the peacemaker of a therapist would step in. My mother, tired of being told what to do and when to do it by my controlling father, became addicted to being right. She was sure she was right, even when she knew damn well she was wrong.

If my mother and I were engaged in an argument about, say, the blueness of the sky, and she swore with gasping incredulity that it was, in fact, green, all I had to do was wait until we went to family therapy to settle the score.

I'd begin, "Dr. Therapist, my mother insists the sky is green."

"It *is* green," my mother would snarl.

"You see what I mean?" I'd point to my mother helplessly.

Dr. Therapist would step in. "Now, Bea, you know that the sky is blue. It is blue."

"It is blue," my mother would repeat like she had been hexed by Obi-Wan Kenobi.

And *that* is how we found the truth in my family growing up.

My first therapist was a man named Ruben, who had white hair and an extensive collection of turtlenecks. To this day I cannot think of psychoanalysis without picturing turtlenecks.

Therapy for a four-year-old is different from regular therapy. Mainly, it involved Ruben sucking my penis while convincing me not to tell my parents. Just kidding. Ruben therapy was actually Nerf sword fighting: a Ruben-invented form of play therapy or, as it is commonly known, bullshit.

Six-year-old therapy looked like this: Ruben would hand me a Nerf sword and I would beat him as savagely as I could around the legs, buttocks, and genitalia. Then I would leave and Ruben would, I assume, take notes on my form:

WEEK ONE: Subject Moshe Kasher. The boy seems to have acute aggression issues and takes immediately to the swords. One note, he is slightly better than me at Nerf swords. Must remember to protect groin.

WEEK TWO: Forgot to protect groin. Aggression continues. Subject will likely calm down by next week's session if past participants' behavior is any predictor. However, if the aggression continues at this level, I will exert myself physically in order to show the boy that I, too, am a man with power. Therapeutically this is known as alpha exertion.

WEEK THREE: No change in aggression. Alpha exertion unsuccessful. MUST PROTECT GROIN!

WEEK FOUR: Pain. Only pain.

Ruben eventually told my mother that I was beyond help and I was too angry for therapy to work. What bullshit. I wasn't too angry. I should have killed him for saying so.

To combat my anger and energy, my mother and I never left the house without her first strapping a leash around my torso. I wish I were kidding.

Every morning, when it was time to leave the house, my mother would strap a four-point harness on my back and explain to me how the day was to go.

"No running in the streets, no hitting strangers, no hitting me, got it?" she'd repeat infinity times over infinity days. *I didn't got it.*

Most days, we'd leave the house and immediately my mother would have to yank me back from playing in traffic or biting a woman's vagina or whatever other mess I got myself into. I was unusually horny as a toddler.

As a result, there was a lot of yanking on the leash. The heavy resistance of the weight of my young body at the end of the leash gave my mother confidence and assurance that I was there, and as a result, she paid a little less attention to me with every tug.

But one should never doubt the tenacity of a four-year-old boy with severe behavioral issues. Or at least, one should never doubt the behavioral issues of a four-year-old boy with behavioral issues.

I'd chew on the leather of the strap, enjoying the tangy "almost jerkyness" of the thing. One day, after being ignored too long and gnawing a bit too much, I broke the leather in two. Freedom. I stared at the two ends of the thing with giddy excitement. This was my chance to ruin everything. I *loved* doing that.

I scanned the traffic to see how likely getting run over would be should I break across the street. I eyed the strangers to see if any of them looked enough like snatch-and-grab kidnappers to take the risk of running toward them, screaming, "Quickly, to your van! Take me, I'm yours!"

This was my only chance to make a break for it, and I needed to maximize the amount of trouble I could get into in one movement. All the passersby looked benign and boring so I decided to dash into the streets. I shot out from behind my mother and hurled myself toward the street where the bliss of oncoming traffic awaited me.

I could almost feel the impact of the car, the screams of horror, the looks of pity. Everyone would be nice to me. Women, or at least busty young girls, would throw themselves at me. People would pay attention to me! This was my moment. I was close, twenty yards, then ten, when the one sound that could've put a stop to my freedom run stabbed through the air: my mother's hyena-like, piercing, unintelligible scream. Like a garbled banshee, my mother shrieked and everyone stopped. Pretty young couples looked at each other with disgust. Dogs yelped and ran in circles as if an earthquake were coming. Old men's eyeglasses shattered. Young men clutched their throbbing heads in agony. The deaf wail stopped me in my tracks. I don't even know why she used the fucking leash.

I felt tied to her even when the leash wasn't on. My job as the son of deaf parents was not just to be a son but, rather, also an ambassador of deaf culture to all of the boundary-less idiots of the world.

"Now, can your mother read?" a ranger asked us once as we pulled into a state park, handing me the maps she was sure would baffle my mother.

"Yes," I replied, handing them back over to my mother defensively, "she is deaf, not retarded."

It seemed, though, like everyone else was. Some people shot me looks of pity when they saw me walking down the street, signing to my mother. I got looks of heroic admiration from other people.

People would ask me questions about my mother and my childhood right in front of her as if she didn't exist.

"Is she speaking English when she talks?" they'd ask, blissfully unaware that I might not be interested in answering their trivia about what my life was like.

"No, actually, it's Crypto-Cyrillic. My mother is from the far-away past, sent here to warn us all!"

People we didn't know at all would come up to us and ask about our home life like it was their right to know and my duty to tell them. My entire life was like a cute baby that complete strangers could coo over and play peekaboo with. I didn't know what to make of any of it. I just knew it was not normal.

When your parents are deaf, nothing is normal. Everywhere you go, you are treated like retarded royalty. I walked around in a constant state of embarrassment, mortified when my mother was speaking, anxiety ridden that she would begin speaking when she wasn't.

My mom's voice humiliated me. It made everyone uncomfortable when they heard it. I hated everyone. Even the lady at Taco Bell.

I loved Taco Bell more than anything, and my mother used it as a bribery tool for good behavior. She couldn't afford to take us out to eat, but she would offer me Taco Bell as a kind of desperate bargaining chip, especially after the little debacle at her friend Dimitri's house when, upon discovering a small hole in the seat of my pants, I ripped it wide open and then ran into the living room, bent over, with my head between my legs, and exposed my anus to a group of her friends while screaming, inexplicably, "Cat! Cat! Cat! Cat!" After that, the money for Taco Bell was made manifest by the sheer desire to avoid such humiliation. Poverty shrank in the face of the anal cat dance.

As she harnessed me up for another outing, she'd make the big offer, "Now, we are going to go out, okay? If you behave yourself and don't piss on anything, or take off any clothing, I'll take you to Taco Bell afterwards."

Mostly this wouldn't work because as soon as I arrived where I was going, I would forget about the promise of zesty ground beef and pull my pants down to expose my zest instead.

But sometimes it did work and I waited to hear the magic words, "Welcome to Taco Bell, can I take your order?"

I'd step forward to order for us both, but my mother is a proud woman, unwilling to let me do for her what she felt she could do herself. She'd push me back and start ordering in her *deaf voice*.

Deaf voice is, in fact, speech. Years of intensive speech therapy are required to turn the primal scream ejaculations of deaf people into the approximation of actual words that well-educated deaf people bring to the table.

I understood my mother perfectly. The only problem is that when deaf voice meets *hearing ear*, the hearing ear gets afraid that chimpanzees are attacking it and cannot distinguish the words. Every word sounds to them like a scream: "RAAAAAAAAAAAAAR!"

"Welcome to Taco Bell, can I take your order?"

"RAAAAAAAAAAAAAR!" my mother replied, a confident smile on her face.

"I'm sorry, what?" The poor minimum wager looked a little scared.

"RAAAAAAAAAAAAAR!" my mom yelled again.

At this point the girl just tried to guess.

"Okay...um...three chicken burritos? Is that it?"

Humiliated. Taco Bell was *my* place, but I just wanted to run away. I pushed to the front and blurted out the order, to the consternation of my proud deaf mother.

"Three beef tacos and cinnamon twists."

My mother grabbed a handful of bills from her purse and pushed them onto the counter.

Ms. Taco Bell looked down and her face scrunched up in confusion. "Um...I'm really sorry, but we don't take food stamps here."

"RAAAAAAAAAAAAAR?"

The girl behind the counter shifted uncomfortably and looked at the line forming behind us. "You know what? Just take it. It's on me."

Like I said: royalty.

Chapter 2

"Under Pressure"
—Tupac

We were alone in Oakland, the three of us sleeping in my grandmother's living room. My mother couldn't get work. The whole system is stacked against deaf people. Would you hire one?

Every woe my mother had, she found a way to blame on my father. Vocally. Loudly. He was responsible for her every difficulty. My mother would feed us a shitty meal or say no to us when we wanted candy and she would point east and sign, "Your father!" This kind of poisoning of the parental well had little effect on my brother, who had a pretty clear memory of his relationship with my dad. But for me, my mother was able to morph the image of my father into a kind of evil specter, floating behind us at all times, snatching fun things from our fingertips.

When my father would send holiday gifts to my brother and me, my mother would itemize them, and if David received even one more chocolate than I did, my mother would hold them out and yell, "See? Your father loves your brother more than he loves you!" Those words would gut me. Unable to understand the little pettiness of ex-lovers (having hardly taken any at that point), I just assumed my mother was telling the truth. I didn't understand why he loved David more. Well, I guess David always did have a stronger chin than me.

Really, David had a stronger everything than me. He was the firstborn son in a Jewish family, and he played the hero right, according to biblical character arc. Somehow, my big brother was born with the tools to navigate right down the churning white water of my parents' river of anger. I just drowned. He was born a quiet statesman, perfect. The perfect son. The perfect student. The perfect Jew. He was everything I wasn't. While people looked at me with microscopes trying to figure out what was wrong with me, they only ever pointed to what he was doing just right. It wasn't his fault. He was playing the role that made him feel safe in the insane world we were both born into. In fact, on quiet nights, David and I would huddle together and wonder how this was our life.

Meanwhile, my mother's resentment against my father grew the worse our circumstances got.

The poorer we became, the more she openly slandered him, the more she hated him. When his mother, my baba, Helen Kasher, got sick with Parkinson's, my father wrote my mother pleading with her to let me come to New York to visit and see her before she became too far gone to speak. My mother wrote back informing my father that no visitation had been agreed to and, therefore, I would not be coming for a visit. As a result, I have no memory of my baba. No memory. Just wisps and phantoms.

Eventually the imaginary enemy of my father held us back so

badly financially that we got on welfare. That's where those food stamps came from. Food stamps and government assistance. Jews on welfare. That's rare. Like seeing a leprechaun. If you could've caught us in the wild, we would've granted you wishes. By the way, this was *old* welfare. Back before it had been filtered to prevent shame. These days the food stamp is just an allusion to a bygone era. Poor families nowadays are simply issued a discreet-looking card, impossible to differentiate from a credit card in order to maximize dignity. What bullshit. Underprivileged, poverty-stricken youth have it so easy these days. In my day, the food stamp was an actual stamp, humiliating and bold. Light colored so as never to be mistaken for actual money (we poor people didn't have that). It was larger than a regular dollar—like a Confederate note. MC Hammer's face was on the twenty-dollar stamp, looking back at you, grinning with huge white teeth. Every time my mother busted them out, it was a trail of tears, the white note screaming to everyone, "Poor family here! Sneak a glance while you can! They can't even afford foooooooood!"

It might as well have been Kermit the Frog hopping out of my mother's wallet in a top hat, dancing a soft shoe, singing "Welfare!" What a travesty. When the public assistance department found out that we were Jews, we were assigned a counselor to deal with the trauma. Then we were given a plaque and a private entrance to the back of the welfare office in order to avoid being seen by other members of the Jewish community.

Of course I wasn't just Jewish; I was mega-Jewish. I was *Yiddish*. When I was seven, my father and the justice system informed my mother, to her smoldering disappointment, that she would have to allow my brother and me to return to New York for visitation.

I reluctantly returned to the city of my birth to visit the man who abused, the man who didn't love me like he loved my brother. I was angry, of course I was. I also worshiped him a bit, of course I did.

I went back to New York to find out that, in my absence, he had become a member of a Chassidic sect, the Satmars. My father had always been enamored of the Chassids. His childhood was marked by weekend trips to Zeidi's house, staring at his gnarled, arthritic hands as they swept across the pages of the Talmud, looking for secrets hidden in the deep codex of the law.

Somehow, the order and austerity of Zeidi's world seemed pure and righteous to my father even when he was just a boy. So, when all the order left his life overnight, when his entire family slipped through his fingers, my father turned deeply into the religion his mother had thought she'd neatly left behind.

He had gotten remarried to another deaf woman, named Betty Drummer, who had been raised behind the steep religious walls of the Satmar community.

The Satmars are among the oddest and most insular of all the Chassidic groups. I'll say that again. Of all the Yiddish-speaking, society-rejecting, gown and fur hat–wearing Chassidic groups, the group my father married into was the most bizarre and outside the lines of society. It would be like being among the fattest groups of Walmart shoppers.

Normally, a person from my stepmother's family would never have been allowed to even consider marrying a person like my father—a beardless painter who didn't read Hebrew, much less speak Yiddish.

But Betty had been married before and not to a nice man, so the fact that my dad was Jewish and increasingly observant was good enough for the odd Council of the Elders of Zion, who approved of the match. Betty, unlike my mother and father, has a powerful strain of hereditary deafness that shot straight through her genetic code. Betty and her sister, Barbara, are both deaf, as are all of their children and grandchildren. Their brother, Heshy, can hear, as can all of his children and grandkids. Painted down the female line of the Drummer family was a deaf gene. In the Satmar community, the pool of eligible men willing to marry a divorced deaf woman, guaranteed to birth other deaf kids, was a little small, and thus, my father was happily welcomed into the family.

As soon as they married, my father found the order he'd been looking for, the order he remembered. The 613 laws of the Torah explained everything to him, kept him whole, kept his volatility in check.

Now my father wasn't exactly a full-on Satmar Chassid. To be that, he would have had to dive into the deepest of deep pools of religiosity. He was more like an affiliate. Like a fella who does work for the Mafia but isn't a made guy. Regardless, my father quickly became a very, very religious man. He put down his paintbrushes and never touched them again, his artistic desires sated by religion. Or who knows, maybe his spiritual needs were just being fulfilled by painting while they waited for the Torah. All I really know is my dad turned into a Chassid.

And so six weeks a year I would have to become a Chassid myself.

My father drove me straight from LaGuardia Airport to the Chassidic Jewish barber in the Borough Park district of Brooklyn and plopped me in front of him with a look that said, "Fix this." The fat Russian Gulag barber looked at my head with disgust.

"Why you cut off your payos?" he asked, contempt in his voice.

Payos, the Chassidic side locks, are very important to the Satmars. It's through those wacky sideburns that God is made aware of how abjectly devoted you are to him. I mean, you are willing to make yourself look completely ridiculous for him. This pleases the Lord.

"I'm sorry," I explained to the complete stranger/barber. "You see, my family is in a complex religiosocial situation. In my mother's household, I'm mostly secular, thus the payos make little sense. But when I come to New York, I feel a deep shame that I'm not aesthetically pleasing to you, a bewarted pogrom survivor that I've never met before, and the rest of your judgmental ilk."

Actually what happened is, I'd mutter, "Dunno," through red-faced shame and wait for my spiritually painful haircut to be over and to receive the closest approximation of a biblical hero hairdo possible from my California bowl cut.

Then we'd jump back in the car and drive to Sea Gate, my hell away from home. If you get off the F train at the last possible stop and then walk past all the Coney Island fun and past all the people of color (yikes!) and through a gate, then through a time portal to pre-Nazi Europe, you get to Sea Gate. A little shtetl in Brooklyn. There I lived among first-language Yiddish speakers who, despite their families having been in America since the 1930s, spoke with European accents. *They* never spoke to *anyone* who was not Jewish. I, *Moshe Kasher*, was as close to a non-Jew as any of them had ever met. *They* pleasure-read in Yiddish. *I* didn't even know the Hebrew alphabet.

Sea Gate was a citadel of isolation, a strange village of identical penguins waddling around, looking busy. Chassids are always busy. No matter what, they are in a hurry. I was a secular kid from laid-back California, takin' it slow. Of course, that was when I wasn't freaking out with angry temper tantrums. Everyone looked and acted the same, and thus, I stuck out, hard. Around me swirled the world of the ultrareligious, and I tried desperately to stay on the ride, to look cool and collected, to not scream with difference. I tried to make friends.

In Sea Gate, the Ultra-Orthodox kids and the *really* religious kids played dodgeball games. Essentially, English speakers versus dead-language enthusiasts. The pasty old-worlders should have been rather easy to bean, as their legs were slightly atrophied from years of study in the yeshiva by day and high-chicken-fat meals by night.

This is the part of the story where I'm supposed to become a local hero because my secular sports skills made us neighborhood champs. But I was chubby and out of shape. I got winded and then I got blasted by the ball while cries of "Hit the goy!" reverberated in my mind.

Somewhere around that time I found a well of fear to jump into. I felt so different, I ached. I'd been in therapy for years at that point and I was only seven; I just knew something was fundamentally wrong with me. I became obsessed with the fear that someone would figure all of this out and expose me for the broken piece of human machinery that I was. I was terrified of everything. My feral snarling slowly started to give way to a pool of fear. I transitioned smoothly between angry out-of-control kid into frightened out-of-control kid. I was seven years old and I was sure I was shit.

My father didn't help much. When he saw how lost I was in Sea Gate, he sent me to a Chabad (another, slightly more user-friendly sect of Chassidism) day camp to "learn the ropes" of Chassidic Judaism. This is the equivalent of sending your illiterate, developmentally disabled child to Yale rather than Harvard and grinning at the concession you've made. He just didn't get it.

"Don't worry about the kids making fun of you, just act like you know what you are doing."

"But Dad, I *don't* know what I'm doing. I can't pray in Hebrew, if I don't *know* Hebrew," I'd shoot back, hoping against all odds that logic could save me from another day of mouthing along to Hebrew prayers, my prayer book upside down, hoping no one noticed I wasn't saying anything at all.

"I don't *know* how to be hearing either, but I fool people every day. You just act Jewish like I act hearing."

My dad had a kind of pet obsession with how "undeaf" he appeared to be. Until the day he died, he was convinced—no matter how many times his questions and queries were answered with "Huh?"—that he was fooling them; that despite his mangled Charlie Brown's teacher voice, no one ever noticed he couldn't hear.

He always had a sort of odd resentment toward the deaf community, rolling his eyes at the sincerity of its struggles for equality. They were, to him, more or less naive bumpkins who wished they could be as smart as he was. Yes, he was deaf, but he wasn't deaf like *that*. He considered himself above essentially every deaf person in the world. My king-like father had a king's ego, too. One of his favorite jokes was to hold his face in shock when he looked in the mirror and scream, "I'm *beautiful*!"

Well, he sort of *was* beautiful. At least his wives thought so. While I had been in Oakland, my father had been busy. I met my two new siblings on my first visit back to New York. My brother Aron and my sister Hinda were born in quick succession after my father and Betty had married. They were respectively three and four years younger than I, and both deaf. I was, at this point, essentially surrounded by deaf family. My brother and grandmother were the only hearing people I knew. Your normal was my abnormal. I spent my early childhood being "not quite." I was Jewish, but not quite. I was hearing, but not quite. I belonged in my family, but not quite. However, back in Oakland, I *was* quite white.

To most of the students in the Oakland Public School System, I was *white boy*. That was my nickname at school. Well, to be fair, that wasn't my nickname, it was *our* nickname. I and every other white male student, and there weren't very many, shared the well-thought-out, hypercreative moniker: *white boy*. That was on the good days. On the bad days, when things weren't going as well at home for my black buddy, or maybe because I was being just a little too white, I became *honky* or *cracker* or *white bread* or *white chicken bread* or *bitch*.

I tried calling a kid *nigger* once. Once. I was in third grade and was fighting with a kid named Darryl, who was yelling out a rapid-fire machine-gun assault of:

Honkycrackerwhitebreadwhitechickenbreadbitch!

Honkycrackerwhitebreadwhitechickenbreadbitch!

Honkycrackerwhitebreadwhitechickenbreadbitch!

So I got mad. A man's not perfect, especially when he's a boy. It seemed only fair at this point for me to let loose the rumbling slur from the recesses of my nonexistent Confederate roots. *Nigger.* All activity stopped.

Darryl's face fell; he looked more sad than mad.

"You can't say that, dog. You'll get killed!" Darryl seemed to be warning me more than he was threatening me.

"But what about all that honkycrackerwhitebreadwhitechickenbreadbitch stuff?" I asked, confused.

Darryl welled up with compassion and he explained the rules to me.

"That's different," he said. "You're white."

Then he punched me in the stomach.

"I guess that's true," I admitted, groaning in pain.

I felt like shit and slumped off the playground, determined that I'd rather be a honkycrackerwhitebreadwhitechickenbreadbitch than a racist bitch. So that was my first and last time calling someone a nigger.

Later, when I became black, I would often call people *nigga*, but that was affectionate and a reclamation of the word. Actually, technically it was a re-reclamation of the word, as it had already been reclaimed by actual black people. My people, whites who wished they were black, then re-reclaimed it from them and used it among ourselves, proving that white people could use the word in a cool, friendly way.

Speaking of words, it was around then that I figured out what my main and only weapon would be from that point out. My big fat mouth. I slowly started sharpening my tongue on the whetstone of Oakland Public Schools. If I couldn't win all the fights, I'd certainly win all the rounds of verbal sparring. People fucked with me so I learned how to fuck right back. I started to hone the questionable skill set of the class clown. In short, I became an asshole.

❧

I met Richard Lilly in first grade. He was one of the only white kids in my class, and we became best friends instantly. How kids become friends in that personality-less time in their lives is beyond me. What did we find in common?

"Hey, I have an incredibly small white penis; do you?"

Somehow we forged a connection and were inseparable from then on. Maybe our connection was subconscious. His family was as fucked up as mine, but we never talked about it like that.

Richard lived with his grandmother, too. His dad was an alcoholic, his mother was a crackhead prostitute. We were two deeply troubled white kids trying to keep our heads above water.

Richard's dad was that kind of handlebar-mustached, fluffy-haired, Cadillac alcoholic who would drive us around, smoking with the windows up as we gagged and coughed, overdramatizing our disdain for smoke just like the antismoking campaigns at school had taught us to.

"I'm literally dying back here," Richard choked, grabbing his throat, his tongue lolling out the side of his mouth.

"You kids shut it, or we don't get dinner tonight."

We shut it.

We stopped by a transient hotel on Martin Luther King Street in West Oakland, and Mr. Lilly turned to us with a smoking cigarette butt hanging from his lip. "Wait here."

He got out of the car and crossed the street to a strung-out blonde in a miniskirt who was pacing back and forth like she was in a hurry, but she clearly had nowhere to be.

"That's my mom," Richard said flatly. I could tell questions were out of the question.

I peered across the street to see Richard's dad yelling at her. Richard turned red. I watched as his dad pulled out his wallet and handed her some cash, which she snatched and then scurried away. Then we went to McDonald's.

Richard never quite got around to telling me about how his mother's life affected him, but in retrospect, I realize it played out in his antidrug bravado. He was the poster D.A.R.E. child—he drank the antidrug Kool-Aid and preached the gospel. A success case.

"I think drugs are disgusting and I'm never fucking doing them," he told me out of nowhere, under the covers at a sleepover later that night. I nodded and suggested we throw things at cars from his grandmother's balcony.

We collected eggs and oranges from his kitchen and crouched behind the balcony, hurling stuff at cars as they drove by, him with increasing ferocity, me with my best friend's interests at heart.

Chapter 3

"Get In Where You Fit In"
—Too $hort

Oakland in the mid-eighties was a very interesting place to be white. The real murderfest was just about to begin there, and East Bay gangster rap was about to hit. In a few years, rappers like Too $hort, Spice One, Tupac, E40, and the Dangerous Crew would become my mentors, my Eckhart Tolle, my Rilke. Rather than *The Power of Now*, I would study the power of *Freaky Tales*, the filthy anthem of Too $hort explaining the ins and outs of male-female love relations:

"I knew this girl, her name was Tina, bitch so dumb we named her misdemeanor. Cuz it had to be a crime to be that dumb, I took her to the house and she let me cum in her mouth."

So my mother and grandmother hated men, and my philosopher kings and mentors hated women. With no one left not to hate, I spent my early years reading Gloria Steinem while imagining ejaculating on women's faces in disdain.

Of course, I never would have been allowed to listen to Too $hort when I was eight and nine years old had my mother not been deaf. Luckily she was, though, so for all she knew, I was listening to Brahms.

Richard would sneak over and he, my brother, and I would blare X-rated rap albums with my mother in the room, unaware of a thing, often turning to us and exclaiming, "I can feel the bass, I love it!"

We grinned as Too $hort explained how Nancy Reagan had given him a blow job:

"She licked my dick, up and down, like it was corn on the cob."

"I like the bass, too, Mom," I'd snicker.

Those songs were how I learned about the birds and the bees. Or rather, they were what I chose to listen to. In typical Bay Area hippie mother fashion, my mother was hardly shy about teaching us about sex. The harsh "we don't talk about that" boundaries of the 1950s were supplanted by porous, "I'm your buddy" parenting. I'm not saying I would have preferred an emotionally distant mother who never told me anything about sex other than that masturbating would make hair grow over your eyes and make you go blind, but it would have been nice to have had it as an option. My mother would be much more likely to cheer me on if she caught me jerking off, delightedly signing, "It's natural!" as I came.

Tuesdays were sex talk nights. Every horrid Tuesday, my mother would call my brother and me away from whatever we were doing and gather us for a humiliation session.

"Boys, come in here!" my mother would yell from the kitchen.

We'd run in breathless, hoping for something cool.

Shit. The blue book.

Boys and Sex was the name of the blue-covered manual from which my mother would read to us. For hours every Tuesday, we would pray for comets to hit the house and take us out of our misery as my mother droned on about "orgasms" and "rectal insertion." As she talked, our disgust turned to a buzzing sleepiness. Somehow, she took all the fun out of it. Never has a nine-year-old been so thoroughly bored by sex.

At the end of every chat was the same question, "Are either of you gay?" If there is such a thing as being too supportive of homosexuality, my mother had it. We got the distinct impression that not only would it be *okay* if we were gay, it would be preferred.

"Are either of you gay?"

"No, Mom," we'd explain again, "we still aren't fucking gay."

Swearing around my mother was nothing but a thing to us. We'd just wipe at our faces like we were dabbing barbecue sauce away and mutter the F word from behind the veil of our hands. If she didn't see it, she didn't know it happened. Mostly we did this for each other, to see how many swear words we could add into our conversations without being caught. My mom had some kind of preternatural ability to know when we were doing this, though. She was like the blind superhero Daredevil whose other senses were heightened when he went blind. But rather than using her powers to lock up criminals, my mother used hers to bust us when we were being assholes.

"David *does* like sucking an occasional dick, though." I laughed from behind the back of my hand.

My brother and mother slapped me at the same time.

"Stop with the cussing-behind-your-hands crap." My mom was about to begin a familiar admonishment.

"Being gay isn't funny. It's not a joke. It's just like me being deaf. Would you like it if people laughed at me for being deaf?"

"No, Mom," we'd repeat as one, "we wouldn't."

"Now"—she'd settle back in—"are either of you gay?"

"No, Mom, we aren't," we'd chant, "but we wish we were."

It was at this point that I'd just zone out and stop listening. I would transcendentally leave my body and float to East Oakland and imagine Too $hort telling me all about pussy. Now *that's* sex ed.

I learned to jerk off, too. A couple of years after my mother first cracked the blue book, I got my hands on a copy of Jim Carroll's *The Basketball Diaries*. In it, I read about how he would steal away to his hot New York roof and stare at the silhouette of his neighbor's body while he played with his dick in bliss. Up until that point, despite all the long-winded lectures from my mom, I thought masturbation, or "touching yourself," was when you put your hand down your pants while watching TV, à la Al Bundy. But I could sense, in my reading of the passage in *The Basketball Diaries*, that he was doing something different and I studied it carefully, again and again, until I found that ancient bit of limbic, instinctive wisdom that tells man to constrict his hand into the shape of a vagina. I stole away to the bathroom for hours daily to try my new trick. I was eleven years old and unaware that there was such a thing as ejaculating. Quite happy with the sensations I'd found from using my new "pussy hand," I'd simply lube up and jerk off for a while and then pack my little dick back in my pants and go on about my day, awaiting the next time me and me could be alone together again.

Richard was kept apprised of all these sessions as he had recently learned the wisdom of the "tube hand" as well. We would talk on the phone about different techniques. It was very gay, which would have made my mother proud, but we were too young to know it so it hardly counted.

Then, one day, I was happily in the midst of my stroking when something started to go very wrong. My arm started to tingle and then go numb. My latent Semitic hypochondria immediately rang alarm bells. "Oh my God, I'm having a stroke. The bad kind, not the good kind."

I wanted to stop but I couldn't as the terror and the ecstasy rushed into me. Trickling waterfalls of electric sand filled my arm and then back to my dick and then back to my arm. It shot through every square inch of my body and set my scalp on fire. My toes curled. My world changed.

I CAAAAAAAAAAAAAAAAAAAAAAAAAAME!!!!

I called Richard immediately to report the results.

"Dude, you just keep going until it happens. I'm not sure if it's good for you or not but it feels . . . I can't describe it."

Richard was excited to try. "Hold on the phone, I'm gonna go into the bathroom and try it, I'll be right back."

I waited as I wanted to hear his supplications as he thanked me for changing his world. Ten minutes later I could hear him bray from the background:

"I caaaaaaaaaaaaaaaaaaaaaaaaaaaaaaaaaaaaaaaaaaaaaaaaaaaaame!"

He returned to the phone, "Wow, dude. Wow. I'm gonna go do that again, but my grandma wants to know if you want to come over for dinner."

"What, was she there when you did it? 'Oh, now that you're done jerking off, ask if he wants dinner.' "

"Shut up, dude, she told me to ask you earlier. Yes or no, I really want to go try again."

"Yeah, okay, perv, I'll see you tonight, have fun jerking off in front of your grandma."

"Fuck you." He laughed and hung up.

Dinner over there was always pretty good. They were American gentile-type people, not Jewish hippies on welfare, and therefore, the meals were a lot cooler. Meat and potatoes kind of things with Jell-O for dessert, contrasting with the tempeh rice torture device waiting for me at home with a side of cool disappointment for dessert. I leapt at the invitation.

After gentile dinner ended, Richard's dad lit a cigarette and his grandmother looked at me and said, "Richard, don't you need to tell your friend something?"

I looked around, confused. "Uh-oh, are you gay, Richard? I'm okay with it if you are."

Richard's dad coughed. "I told you there was something wrong with the kid, Mom."

She looked at me with compassion, turned to Richard, and said, "Tell him."

Richard shifted in his seat guiltily. "We are moving to Lafayette."

"Lafayette?"

Lafayette was a suburb of Oakland but was so phenomenally wealthy that you'd never know by looking at it. Apparently, Richard's grandmother had liquidated her assets and bought a home there to set Richard up for success and, I suspect now, to get him away from his mother.

"But we'll still be best friends. I mean, you can come over all the time."

I paused, considering. This sucked.

"Well, fuck, man, now I'll be the *only* white kid at Claremont. Oh. Sorry I cussed, Mr. and Grandma Lilly. My mom lets me."

❧

I'd been looking forward to middle school for a long time. A strange thing when you consider that middle school is one of the most horrible environments on earth. In terms of torturous social environments the order goes:

1. Holocaust (various)
2. Siberian Gulag
3. Middle School
4. Iron Maiden (torture device or concert)

I had enrolled in Claremont Middle School filled with excitement and hope after having come precariously close to failing fifth grade. I was on my way into uncomfortable prepubescent adolescence. The world looked like my underdeveloped oyster. But now, with Richard gallivanting with wealthy cheerleaders (I imagined), I was suddenly alone, friendless, and about to get exiled into a social no-man's-land.

I saw pretty quickly that Claremont was deeply divided into racial and class strata. The semi-equality of elementary school dissipated the second it touched the blacktop at Claremont. The roles here were quite clearly demarcated. I just didn't know where I fit yet.

At Claremont Middle School, there were three kinds of white people. There were the white people who made it to the popular group (a multiethnic power clique brought together by their sheer disdain for others), the nerds, and the fuckups.

A word on the nerds. These aren't the classic nerds you may see in your mind's eye. They aren't bespectacled losers with acne so thick you don't notice their Dungeons and Dragons customized pocket protectors. I'm not defending them, I'm just clarifying. Mostly, *nerd* just meant *white*. For some reason, *white* just conjured images of squares and losers in the imagination of Claremont's consciousness. So the nerds, who would've just been "people" at another school, became the lowest rung of the social ladder at the watering hole that was Claremont.

Among the black people, there was diversity. There was the square, the churchgoer, the clown, the thug, the ladies' man, the crack dealer, the oft-flunked, the gay dude, the African, big-ass muthafucka, retard, rapist, nice to whites, hella tall, half Asian, knows karate, has a twin, black with freckles, going to college and more, and more and more. But if you were white, you were just white.

Unless you were a fuckup. Fuckups weren't white, they were fuckups. It was like you didn't even notice their whiteness because the dysfunction was screaming so loud that you couldn't pay attention to anything else. They were the kids people's mothers told them to avoid. The kids who you can find at the back of any school campus. These were Claremont Middle School's white boy terrors.

The first fuckup I saw was Joey Zalante. Joey was an eighth grader when I first entered Claremont and was one of the most badass motherfuckers I ever saw. Early in the sixth-grade school year I saw him do the impossible. He won a fight with a black kid.

At Claremont watching fights was a sort of holy ritual. As soon as anyone started squaring off, everyone, from the biggest to the smallest, from the toughest gangster to the dorkiest white boy, immediately dropped whatever they were doing and ran, streaming across the blacktop toward the conflict. We would gather around the gladiators, forming a kind of makeshift human Colosseum while the familiar but rather crude chant would begin.

"A fight! A fight! A motherfucking fight!"

To show you the odds Joey was up against, I will tell you the rest of this chant reserved only for interracial fights:

"A fight! A fight! A nigga and a white! If the nigga don't win, then we *all* jump in!"

These calls would spread across the yard, calling onlookers like a pied piper, and we would gather hoping for a show.

Something like this would happen almost every day, but to everyone's disappointment, most of these conflicts would end without much violence. Often what we watched was just a sort of odd human version of two animals in the wild, puffing themselves up, presenting the equivalent of their bright red baboon assholes to one another in an attempt to frighten their foe away.

Most fights looked exactly like this. The two "warriors" would walk around one another with their arms raised, screaming at each other. As the action got more intense, they would walk in concentric circles, closer and closer to one another until they were literally shoulder to shoulder engaging in a sort of alpha male waltz. Contact. Tensions would rise to the point of physical conflict. Not the good stuff, though; the fighters would shoulder-check each other and then back up to continue the dance. Usually this went on and on until a teacher came and broke it up. Of course, the moment a teacher took away the threat of an imminent beat-down, the circlers would go mad with rage, swearing that they were just about to beat the other's face in. "You're lucky this teacher is holding me back or that'd be your ass, motherfucker!"

"What about the twenty minutes of slow dancing you guys just did?" I'd yell, too funny for my own good. "What was holding you back then?" Often this would earn me a death threat from both fighters, their mutual disdain for me providing a common ground for reconciliation. People called me the Gandhi of the playground. Wait, no they didn't, they called me white bitch.

Once in a while, though, our dreams came true and actual fists would fly, violence would ensue, and the masses would be sated.

One of those times, Joey Zalante bent time and space. At least it looked that dramatic to me. He was standing in line for the poor kids' lunch.

The poor kids' lunch line was a humiliating place to be. A separate line reserved just for the kids who couldn't afford to select from the horrific smorgasbord that awaited students on the inside of the cafeteria, the poor kids' line stacked kids up outside, huddled in the cold like the lines for the food kitchens the school no doubt expected these students to end up frequenting in the years to come.

I stood in it every day that my mother didn't pack me a horrible brown bag of hippie gruel: thick grainy slices of wheat bread with gritty natural peanut butter slathered on, pineapple juice, and fruit leather. Not Fruit Roll-Ups, mind you, fruit leather. A kind of actual leather made from whatever the brownest, most fecal-tasting parts of a fruit were. I imagined the factory workers at the Fruit Roll-Up plant sweeping the remnants of their work off the floor and dumping them into a bucket marked FRUIT LEATHER SCRAPS FOR TORTURING BAD CHILDREN.

My brown bag lunches were so awful I prayed for the poor kids' line.

A snapshot of the poor kids' lunch line would serve as a kind of predictive criminal lineup for Oakland's future. The John

Dillingers and Bonnies and Clydes of the world always waited in the poor kids' lunch line. I was there standing in the back, waiting to get my juice cup and nacho cheese fries alongside a mealy pizza slice and an egg roll. Anyone who thinks welfare is an awesome meal ticket for undeserving people ought to be forced to eat one actual meal from below the poverty line. Following the most intense diarrhea of their lives would be the realization that being on government assistance sucks balls.

Ahead of me in line was Joey, whom I would soon gaze upon lovingly as a prince among men. In front of him was Sean The Bomb.

Sean The Bomb had fists of dynamite. At least so he told everyone who would listen. "I'm Sean The Bomb with the strength of King Kong. I got fists of TNT and my dick is long!"

Sean was simply enormous for an eighth grader. Who knows how old he actually was, but he stood more than six feet and was thick as a wall. Sean was not smart, but if you were, you would avoid pissing him off. He carried himself with the air of the pimp that I'm sure he has since become. A rule with pimps is to never step on their shoes.

At Claremont the crack-dealer kids could be spotted by their ever-changing Nike Cortez shoe collection. They called the shoes "Dougies," and the cooler you were, the more pairs you had. If you wore a red shirt, you *had* to have matching red Dougies. Black shirt, black Dougies, and so on. But the poorer you were, the fewer pairs of shoes you had to work with. Sean The Bomb had yet to figure out how to monetize his explosive fists and, as a result, had only one pair of white Dougies. Joey made the mistake of stepping on them.

"Get the fuck off my shoes, you dumb white motherfucker!"

Sean exploded, pushing Joey back into the line behind him, food flying everywhere.

"I ain't white, you big-lipped bitch, I'm Italian."

Joey just spat this back, almost as if he wasn't scared of Sean's bombs at all.

Sean tackled Joey without any pretense, no dancing, no chanting, no nothing. I held my breath.

Gravel flew everywhere as the two rolled back and forth scraping, scrambling, beating the shit out of each other. Somehow, though, Joey managed to flip Sean on his back and to sit on his stomach, pummeling him from the top. Sean The Bomb was not conscious long. He got knocked the fuck out.

I panicked.

WHAT JUST HAPPENED?

Joey got up and started dusting himself off as campus security ran over, too little too late. I looked around at the other people watching, flabbergasted.

"Did you see what just happened?!? What does this mean!?! Is this the End Times?" I screamed with jubilation.

All of the Caucasian kids at Claremont danced the hora together to celebrate. We cooked an ox in sacrifice and promised to name all of our firstborn sons Joey.

Just before Joey disappeared into the swirling masses, slipping out of sight of campus security, I could have sworn he winked at me, as if to say, "Yeah, that *was* pretty cool, huh?" He winked at me! Not bad. I thought to myself that a fuckup seemed like a pretty cool thing to be. It was like a little Post-it note reminder that I stuck to the inside of my head.

Note to self: Fuckups are afraid of nothing. You are afraid of everything. This information might come in handy someday.

Somewhere along the line, I figured out that the more I made people laugh, the less of a loser I would appear to be. I shucked and jived for my classmates, hoping like hell no one would figure out how scared I was. When an in-class lecture confused me, I'd make fun of the shoes of a kid poorer than me. At the end of the lecture, the teachers would only remember me mocking the kid's plastic Moon Boots, not that I had been unable to answer a single question on dividing fractions.

This kind of behavioral distraction technique kept me feeling safe but made every day at school one where I fell incrementally behind without anyone really noticing, and as a result, when my final grades came in, everyone scratched their head and pointed at one another, trying to assign blame for the failure.

It was a lesson in consequences. Shortly after school started in the seventh grade, I was sent to the retarded portable. A fat teacher/clinician combo meal of a woman approached me in class and pulled me aside with the private solemnity of an army officiant charged with the job of delivering the heartbreaking condolences to the next of kin.

"You have learning disabilities," she began, far too earnest for my comfort level. "LEARNING DISABILITIES."

She stared down at my puzzled face. "Do you know what that means? It means you learn differently than other students. Everyone learns differently and there's nothing wrong with that. Some people learn better with their ears." As she talked, she pointed to her ears just in case I wasn't aware of what an ear was.

"Some people learn better with their eyes."

She pointed to her fat eyes.

"We can't figure out what you learn best with. It seems like something might be wrong with your brain."

She pointed to her fat head.

"So we are going to bring you to a special classroom to help you learn. It's called Portable Three."

Portable Three. The retard portable.

"But isn't that where the retarded kids go?" I asked.

She was shocked. "We don't use that word anymore. Differently abled."

"Do you use the word *Down syndrome*? Because the kid with Down syndrome goes to Portable Three. Do I have Down syndrome?"

I never got an answer. To this day I'm not sure I don't.

Every day after fourth period, I would begin the long slog to the Portable Three DMZ at the back of the school. The first day there, I expected the door to open to a scene from an antebellum hospital for the mentally infirm. I expected young women chained to the door and people rocking in the corner picking at scabs. A woman with madness in her eyes would jump on top of me gasping, "Leave now . . . you'll never escape this place."

What I got was much different. Portable Three looked a lot like a regular classroom. The fourth-period class was specifically for people like me, regular kids with an appropriate amount of chromosomes but an inappropriate amount of F's on their report cards. The more severely disabled students were given classes earlier in the day and then sent home to lift heavy things for the carnival or eat paint chips or whatever.

What I was expecting was a caricature of a special education classroom, but what I got was so innocuous that neither I nor any of the other students in there realized the real insidiousness of what was happening to us. It wasn't Portable Three itself that would ruin you. It was the subtle left turn that your life makes when the public school system enrolls you in a special education classroom.

The special ed classroom is an open door with a friendly face beckoning you in, smiling, telling you, "Come in, come in! In this room is the help you've been looking for!"

The moment you step in, the door locks behind you. The smiles disappear; your name glows white hot on their forms. You aren't going anywhere.

The second your name is written into the blank space marked "Student" on the form for the Individualized Education Program, or IEP, you have been kicked down a trapdoor into the sick wonderland of special ed. Every special ed student gets an IEP, and in it, the "plan of action" for your future is outlined. Every detail about your past failures is listed. Every goal for your future is put down on paper. Your plan is set.

Every mistake you ever make again will be attributed to a "lack of educational support" or an "indication of unchanged educational deficiencies." An inch at a time, you become a product of the system. You slide down that tunnel like Alice chasing a rabbit, slowly and cautiously at first, thinking you are after something nice and cute like Peter Cottontail or, as they put it, "a more appropriate educational modality," but pretty soon you look back in the direction you came from to find that you have become quite lost. You couldn't make it back if you tried. A while later you realize the bunny ahead of you has long since disappeared and you are surrounded with people as mad as hatters. Adults with their Cheshire grins assure you that you are "right where you need to be." No one needs to shout, "Off with your head!" because they have been slowly taking your head away from you the whole time. A psychiatric guillotine has shaved your head away one thin slice at a time like a deli slicer. In three years I would find myself stuck, fucked up, and my life becoming curiouser and curiouser every second. That's the wonderland of Portable Three.

Of course, I realized none of this at first. All I knew was that Portable Three had a distinct corrosive effect on your social life. As soon as people find out you go there, you are out. No one likes a retarded friend.

Through the entire sixth grade I had managed to stay mostly socially neutral. I was almost popular. I had kept the weirdness of my home life to myself and tried very hard to make fun of the losers when it seemed appropriate in order to ingratiate myself with the cool kids.

I knew that I, too, was a loser, but as long as they didn't know, I figured I'd be okay. I was such a ball of social anxiety and so desperate to fit in that I wasn't quite accepted into the cool-kid club, but I wasn't exactly rejected either. I clung to that with the hope that someday, I, too, could be a vapid shallow dickhead. Ahh, to be popular.

Then came Portable Three, and all of a sudden they just iced me. I had been summarily dismissed.

Early in the year of seventh grade, one of the leaders of the popular pack, a kid named Jono, was having a birthday party and I had *not* been invited. It burned my little twelve-year-old heart. I was crushed. Then, to my delight and shame, I found an invitation to the party that had been discarded underneath someone's desk. I quickly snatched it up and stuffed it into my pocket and ran home. I didn't know what to do.

On the one hand, this invitation was my ticket to the coolest party in seventh grade, sure to be chock-full of awkward protosexual tension and manipulative shame games. On the other hand,

I hadn't been invited. Well, not officially. I could *choose* to look at my chance discovery of an invite as God himself inviting me. "Fuck it. I'm gonna go," I decided. "Ride or die."

Then I did something even more repulsive. I bought Jono a birthday present. That was the first time I snatched a ten-dollar bill from my mother's purse.

This motherfucker hadn't even invited me to his shit, and I was stealing from my mother's lean wallet and picking him up a gift certificate to Amoeba Records. I was pathetic and I knew it, but I ignored the voice in my head chanting, "Stay home, save your money, they don't want to hang out with you anyway." I charged forward, desperate to make this work, to make sure the class assholes or "classholes" didn't fall out of love with me due to the suspicion of mild retardation. I went. Berkeley Iceland.

More than just a skating rink, Berkeley Iceland was the home of much of the romantic hows and whys of local East Bay youth. Your love life for the next six months could be made or broken at Iceland. It was so important a social playground, its name belied its significance. It should have been called "FallontheICEandbea-loserforlifeLAND."

Like any skating rink, you'd start by shoving your foot into a little hepatitis-exchange boot and clip-clopping your way toward the ice. I crouched, just off the ice, and gave myself a little pep talk.

"You can do this," I told myself, absolutely sure that I couldn't. "No one will notice you weren't invited. Hell, maybe you *were*! Maybe that *was* your invitation on the ground. It must've fallen out of your desk and somehow been kicked into another classroom to land under Sarah Blakley's desk. Then maybe she doodled her name on the envelope and redropped it. You know how girls doodle!"

Yeah! I *had* been invited. At any rate, at least I could skate. My grandmother had sent me to figure-skating classes, determined, I imagine, that if she *had* to have a man in the family, she'd need to make sure that he wasn't in any way man*ly*. I zipped out onto the ice toward the section where the kids from class were. And I saw her. Naomi. Jewess. Woman. Popular. A real twelve-year-old knockout. All legs and flat chest and braces. Mmmmm.

I liked her even though I'd once happened to look at her right when she exhaled a bit too forcefully and shot a green grossness out of her nose. It was the kind of thing that makes your romantic memory bank scream, *"Nooooooo!!!"*—but I shoved the memory down and kept liking her.

I skated up to the Claremont kids and tried to look "cool and invited." So far so good. Jono was nowhere to be seen, but Naomi, in her silence, seemed to have agreed to let me skate the slow jam next to her as long as I didn't speak or make eye contact with her.

The slow jam was the epic romantic crescendo of the skating experience. Skating behind Naomi, staring at her flat little child butt, I finally knew what love was. Bell Biv Devoe crooned over the crackling loudspeakers, and I wrote a song in my mind about what I imagined someday would be the R&B-level love between Naomi and me:

And I wanna thank you, for letting me a-skate a-next to you.

Some-day, I'd like to have a-sex with you.

It was perfect. Then from all the way across the ice, I saw a grimacing monster. Jono was making double time, speed skating up to me. He slid to a stop, covering me in teenager-flavored shaved ice.

He looked me up and down, confused. "What are you doing here?"

"Hey, happy birthday, Jono! I'm just partying, you?"

Jono snarled, "I didn't invite you to my party, what the fuck are you doing here?"

"What?" I asked, in that way people say "What?" while they scramble to think of a good lie to say.

"But... you did invite me." That oughta do the trick, I thought.

"I did? When?" I wasn't expecting such a sophisticated comeback.

"You know, that time, when you did?"

That didn't work.

"Get the fuck out of here." I could see Jono moving from "confused" to "I'm gonna kick this white boy's ass."

This was bad.

"But I was just skating with Naomi." I turned to Naomi for confirmation, but she had skated off long ago to her girlfriends and was mouthing what my expert "son of a deaf kid" lip-reading picked up as, "He just wouldn't stop skating behind me, it was so gross."

I wanted to yell, "Gross? *Gross!?!?* What about that green snot thing, you *asshole?!?*"

I thought better of it, though, because I really saw a future between us, and you don't talk to your future wife that way.

Don't be an abuser.

Anyway, I had bigger problems to contend with: Jono.

I pulled out the gift certificate and meekly bleated, "I got you something."

Then something happened. Jono looked down at the impotent little envelope in my hands and realized that I'd bought him a gift. I looked into his eyes and I saw something shift. A little of the ice and the callousness in him melted. In that moment, we stopped jockeying for position and trying desperately to be accepted by our peers and we became who we truly were, just two of God's kids trying to make it in this world. Jono took the envelope out of my hand, looked into my eyes, and said, "Get the fuck out of here, you retarded motherfucker."

I started smoking that night.

I left Iceland on foot, close to tears. I started rapid-fire calling to mind the various horrible things that had happened to me, to date, just kind of diving into humiliation. My mind went into a "people suck" spiral. The good thing about my indulging in memories of people being cruel to me was that I had a lot of source material from which to draw. I remembered Conoy the crack-addicted fourth grader telling me I could eat my fucking freckles when I asked him for a piece of licorice. He made fun of my mother's voice, and when I protested, someone told me his brother had been murdered so I couldn't be upset.

I remembered a kid named Armando calling me fat in front of everyone. I remembered my brother and me being taken hostage for hours at my elementary school while two kids threatened to beat our heads in with baseball bats. "This is our get back for slavery, motherfucker!" My brother begged them to let me go and kick his ass instead, but they weren't really interested in kicking ass, just humiliating us. They made my brother kiss their shoes to win my safety. It didn't work. They convinced us, in our terror, to let them into our house and stole David's prized Gary Carter rookie card.

I remembered my mother telling me my father loved my brother more than me. I remembered believing her. I remembered all that shit and I needed a smoke. When I got home, I was covered in sweat and tear-streaked. I slipped on my trench coat.

I had this supercool trench coat back then. I had just turned twelve years old and was not too savvy on fashion versus costume. It was the last item left in my "It's cool to look like a 1920s crime fighter" repertoire. The bad news was it made me look like a gigantic loser. The good news was I was too big of a loser to know, and it had a trapdoor in the sleeve.

That trapdoor changed my life. After that first night, when my shame spiral led to a successful tobacco heist, I made a ritual of walking into Safeway intent on stealing some smokes. I wore my trench coat convinced that the trapdoor made it the perfect shoplifting accessory. I thought I was slick as hell, a boy-child slinking my way into a grocery store wearing an ankle-length trench coat. The fact that there is not a look that more conspicuously screams "SHOPLIFTER!" was totally lost on me.

I stole whichever pack my trembling hands brushed against first. Some days it was Virginia Slims, and I smoked like a gay playwright for a week. Thank God, the day I met Donny, I brushed against Marlboro Reds.

It was about a month after Jono's party and I'd just finished a trenchcoat raid on Safeway. I walked outside in my supercriminal coat with my plunder weighing heavy in my pocket. As soon as I got far enough away, I pulled out my smokes to see what I'd gotten. Marlboros...cool. I think cowboys smoked those. I'm a fuckin' cowboy, why not?

Just then someone approached me from the left. "Hey, man, where'd you get those cigarettes?" Shit! Someone had seen me even with the trench coat on. I didn't even know that was possible.

I turned to my left, expecting to see a security guard. It was Donny Moon, the king of the fuckups. Joey Zalante, the mythical black giant-killer, and his crew had moved on to high school and seemed to have vetted a group of badass kids in the grades below them to succeed them in terrorizing the school. Donny was their choice for leader. Nobody would've said so out loud, but it was obvious. Donny was just like Joey in a lot of ways—tough, fearless, charismatic, and capable of being scary as hell. Donny was short, but he had so much bravado and self-confidence that no one, including him, ever noticed.

He wore a Starter jacket and walked around without fear of it being stolen. Starter jackets were these hooded puffy coats with the emblem of your favorite sports team gaudily embossed on their back. They were the pinnacle of hood style in Oakland. If you had a pair of Nike Air Jordans (a shoe even more coveted than the Dougie) and a Starter jacket, you were essentially a deity in Oakland. You could simply nod at any woman and receive an obligatory blow job.

At the time, a popular pastime of black kids was to run up behind white boys with Starters and grab the hood, strip it from them, and run off. No one ever did that to Donny, though. He had grown up in the Bushrod Park area—the grimiest, most murderous part of North Oakland. He was buddy-buddy with the Bushrod boys, which gave him a kind of "ghetto pass" that allowed him to liaise between the white kids and the toughest kids in school. This was a privilege that commanded respect.

And here was this dude, approaching me, asking me about my smokes. Fucking badass.

"Where'd you get the smokes?" he repeated, staring at me as if he were trying to figure me out.

"I took them. See, I have this trench coat and—"

"Uh, yeah, I noticed the trench coat, dork. So you stole 'em?"

"Yeah...totally," I stammered, trying to figure out how to sound even cooler.

"Lemme buy half of them from you. I need some smokes bad, man."

"Yeah, cool, I know how that can be, I've been smoking a little while now and I've even inhaled a couple of times."

I took out the pack and split it in half. I gave Donny one extra. I guess I didn't know it at the time, but that eleventh cigarette was my admission fee to the fuckups.

Donny took the cigarettes and stared at the handful I'd given him. He looked up at me, lit one right there, and smiled. "That's pretty cool you stole smokes, man, you should come kick it with us sometime."

I kept it chill. "Sure, sounds cool."

I told you I was a fucking cowboy.

Chapter 4

"The Chronic"
—*Dr. Dre*

I called Richard the next night and told him what happened.

"I dunno, man, it was a weird night," I explained to him.

"This Donny dude sounds sketchy to me," Richard said, tossing his suburban wet blanket on the fire of dangerous excitement I was feeling.

"Yeah, he *is* sketchy! That's what's so awesome. He's like us, y'know, fucked up, but cooler."

There was a silence on the other end of the line.

"Richard?"

"I'm not fucked up," Richard said, hurt.

"That's not what I meant. I just meant like how we throw stuff at stuff and stuff, Donny and his friends do things like that, too, whatever, he's the only potential friend I've got right now."

A pause.

Richard said, "Hey, I gotta get going."

"What, do you have a varsity football match or something? A sock hop?" I resented his escape from Oakland, even though I thought Lafayette sounded boring as hell.

"Something like that, I got invited to a birthday party tonight, gimme a call tomorrow."

"Oh. All right, man, talk to you later." I slunk down into my chair and hung up the phone.

A birthday party. That suburban motherfucker.

Back in Oakland, Donny started bringing me around the guys. A jalopy little group of true-blue fuckups. Together they made up the P.A.G., a little proto–street gang that stood for the "Pure Adrenaline Gangsters." It was such a faggy name that it probably should have been named the Pure Hard-core Adrenaline Gangsters. P.H.A.G.

It was a broken group of boys. All of them, and I mean every single one of them, came from divorced homes. Most from fucked-up, abusive ones. Donny introduced me around.

There was DJ and Corey, a pair of brothers so incongruously proportioned they looked like Arnold Schwarzenegger and Danny DeVito from the movie *Twins*. DJ was enormous and incapable of having a violent thought without enacting it immediately with his fists. He carried penny rolls around with him wrapped in duct tape to increase the force and weight that his fists bore. He was the Luca Brasi to Donny's Don Corleone.

Corey, on the other hand, was kind of the Joe Pesci of the group. Little, obnoxious, loud, and always instigating things. He was a couple of years older than us but a couple of years less mature, so everything worked out just fine.

Terry Candle, or as he was more well known, Monk, was a

half-Japanese kid with a meticulous mind and a mother who had deep connections to pot farmers in Northern California. He got the nickname *Monk* because he could never be seen without a thick hooded sweatshirt pulled up over his head, making him look like a very small Benedictine drug dealer. I didn't know it at the time, but his mother's relationship to those pot-growing hippies up north made him the main weed peddler to the white-under-thirteen set in North Oakland.

And then there was Jamie. Jamie James was a kid so ridiculous he seemed like he must have been concocted by a screenwriter; bright orange hair and a preposterous pubescent peach fuzz mustache, Jamie looked like a clown. He acted like one, too. He was a pathological liar. It was impossible ever to know if he was telling the truth about anything. The victim of frequent, severe, man-sized beatings at the hands of his father, eventually his personality fractured into so many pieces that he just picked them up and shaped them into whatever fit the situation best. Unfortunately he did it poorly, and the result was a guy that only the P.A.G. could love.

Having a pathological liar as a friend scars you. To this day, if I ever meet anyone who tells too many crazy stories, I assume they are lying and I start to imagine a soft orange halo glowing about their countenance like a patron saint of dishonesty.

Guess who else was sometimes around? Joey! Imagine! The Italian giant slayer. He who fought a black kid and lived to tell the tale. This was like a Jewish kid in the sixties getting to hang around Sandy Koufax. I was hanging out with my hero. I tried not to swoon.

Little by little, the guys got used to me being around. I'd walk through the halls at Claremont and DJ would nod his head at me, "'Sup?" I felt like I'd been let in on a secret.

⁂

After a few weeks of infrequent invitations to steel off across the street during lunch and smoke cigarettes with the guys, I guess I had been promoted. Donny came up to me and told me to meet him at his house that day after school.

If I'd known what I was getting myself into that day, I'm not sure I would have had the courage to show up, but then again, I'm not sure I would have had the courage not to.

I approached the back of Donny's house and unlatched the gate to his backyard.

"Donny?" I called.

I rounded the bend into the backyard and saw everyone standing there—DJ, Corey, Joey, and the crew.

Donny grabbed me by the arm and announced to everyone that I'd decided to join the P.A.G. I'd done no such thing.

I looked over at Donny. "Uh, Donny, uh ... we haven't really discussed this in depth." I was a bit nervous, not sure I was ready to take the plunge into being a full-fledged baby gangster.

Donny just winked at me.

I looked around at this little ragtag group of white bad boys and gulped a deep gulp.

These were the kids mothers said to avoid, and I was being asked to jump into the deep end with them.

"It ain't nothin', homeboy," Jamie reassured me, speaking in the lilt of a character from a seventies blaxploitation film.

DJ rolled his eyes and muttered, "He's too fucking scared."

Jamie slipped his arm around me and said, sounding more

58

like an old-school traveling hippie this time, "Just be cool and go with it."

Joey, not really a member of the gang himself, but more like an outside consultant, just smoked and watched me.

I had seen this before. I was being tested. Much like Kevin Costner in *Dances with Wolves*, the tribal warriors were trying to see if I was brave enough to be one of them. I knew what I had to do.

I stepped forward, crouched into Tae Kwon Do horse stance, took a deep breath, and announced, "I am ready to join."

Everyone laughed hysterically. No one asked me to leave, though. Joining was not easy. Over the course of the next few weeks, I had to join like five fucking times. The thing about the gang was that it wasn't really a gang at all, rather just a name for the group of fuckups that I had fallen into. In fact, the name was the last little piece of youthful innocence in us. It was a juvenile name, like a little clubhouse, akin to the "He Man Woman Haters Club" from *The Little Rascals*. It wasn't the name that mattered, but the affiliation. The problem with it not being a "real" gang, however, was that the rules were rather undefined. Especially the rules concerning how to join.

Every P.A.G. initiation ritual I went through was somehow deemed insufficient afterward and then they'd ask me to perform some other pain ritual or sexual humiliation in order to be accepted in. I stuck my finger up my ass and tried to write my name on the wall in shit; I whacked my little pubescent dick against an ice-cold school bench; I drank a dead goldfish, and I put out a cigarette on my arm.

It was a Camel wide. I fucking remember that—believe me, you would, too. As this new group of guys gathered around, I jammed the lit end of this cigarette into my forearm and shook in pain while my flesh bubbled and smoked. All the guys cheered and slapped me on the back for what at the time felt like the best decision I'd ever made.

The burn got infected quickly, but unwilling to ask for help, lest the FBI be called in to investigate the P.A.G., I just slapped a Band-Aid on it and hoped for the best.

A month later it was putrescent and crusted gold and my arm felt like a fifty-pound water balloon. It only hurt when I moved it or laughed or talked or pointed it downward or upward or breathed, so I figured it was probably okay.

A few weeks later, I flew home for a visit with my dad in Brooklyn. After eyeballing it for a while, he finally said something about the Band-Aid that never came off. He forced me to show him and then immediately vomited on my arm. Maybe that didn't happen. He did, however, make me go to the hospital and save my arm from gangrene or amputation. What a square my dad was.

Worst of all, two months after my trial by fire, the P.A.G. disbanded. Not like anything whatsoever changed, not like we stopped hanging out or doing the exact same things we did before the end of the P.A.G. era; they just decided that the gang was lame and that it was over. I guess I should've been grateful. There was talk of ritual rape as my next induction ceremony. Despite it all, I never regretted the burn. I would look down at the scar over the years and grin a little, remembering the time I burned my way to fuckup.

It doesn't sound like much, but when you've never been admired for anything, being admired at all—even if it is for being the world's biggest fuckup—feels pretty good.

I sighed a sigh of deep relief when they took me in. These were the first people in my life who weren't asking me what was wrong with me. They didn't give a fuck. There was something wrong with them, too. But more to the point, they *got* that the true problem was that there was something deeply wrong with everyone else. The world of adults and rules was fucked. Our parents were hypocritical shit bags. The police were corrupt bastards. Our teachers were incompetent assholes. Only we got it. Only I and this group of lost boys understood. We weren't really in a gang so much as holding each other up. I had people. I wasn't alone.

I realized, after hanging out with these guys for a while, that they were smoking pot. *Pot.* Our parents called it grass, they called it dank. If it was really good, they called it The Chronic. The D.A.R.E. program called it a gateway drug.

I made a decision that I'd smoke with those guys if they asked me. Fuckin' weed! Bill Clinton said he didn't inhale and the nation laughed at him. I didn't. The first time I smoked weed, I related more to Bill Clinton than the black community did. I fucking tried. I'd been smoking cigarettes for months at that point, but the only time I'd inhale was when I accidentally swallowed a mouthful of smoke. I imagined that that was how people got lung cancer, just one too many accidental inhalations. I mean, it couldn't be what you were *supposed* to be doing, right? I wanted nothing more than to look cool in front of those guys, but I didn't have a clue what I was doing. I propose, with zero knowledge of anatomy or anything scientific, that it's an unnatural act for your lungs to allow smoke *in*. That's why people die of smoke inhalation. So when Donny invited me to the bushes to smoke some weed and I didn't get high, it was my lungs being a bitch, not me. I meant business. My lungs pussied up.

I wanted to do it right lest I not be invited to the fuckup birthday party. Little did I know the fuckups don't have parties, they fuck up other people's parties. They also don't tend to get rid of friends. Friends leave but not because they are asked. It takes a lot to be one of these guys. You gotta be willing to get robbed and beat up and have your parents' house sacked and all that kind of shit.

In exchange, though, you get a group of motherfuckers who will rob or beat the shit out of someone on your behalf at a moment's notice. That meant a lot to me. That meant the world.

So, when my pansy-ass lungs wouldn't submit to my will, I freaked out a little. I needed these guys to know I was serious. So, like none of the women I've ever been with, I faked it.

To be fair, I wasn't positive I wasn't high. I mean, maybe this was it, maybe pot felt exactly like not smoking pot, you just felt cool and tough for doing it.

I walked from that bush to my grandma waiting in the car to pick me up after school and I tried to convince myself that I was a changed man, that I had gotten high. But it wasn't until the next time I fired up that I realized how wrong I'd been.

The first time I got high for real was at Tommy Klark's house. His older brother passed me a joint and my lungs opened up to the smoky gateway through which I passed into a new world. The THC drip-dropped its thick syrupy coating over my brain and I floated away. So this is what it's like to be high...

I smoked and smoked and every hit chipped away another part of my life...puff puff...gone were my worries. What was there to worry about, it's Ganja Time! Puff puff, gone was my retardation; I could puff away the extra chromosome and feel my Down syndrome become more of a Down Situation...puff puff, shit I was smart! And even if I wasn't, fuck smart! Puff puff, gone was my fat! I had smooth, sculpted muscles under there somewhere.

Puff puff, gone was my fear of being rejected by the cool kids. I'd jumped through a Mario warp zone way past the cool kids. Fuck those square pieces of shit. I didn't need to be popular, I didn't want to be popular, I didn't want to be anything. All I wanted was to kick it with these guys and stay high for the rest of my life.

I'm not sure if there's a heaven, but if there is, I'm pretty sure it's gotta look something like Tommy's backyard.

After that, things get hazy. We started drinking Everclear margaritas. Everclear, for the uninitiated, is essentially potable rubbing alcohol. It's 99 percent alcohol and you can feel your suffering trachea disintegrate while you drink it. I ate a Popsicle and sprinkled salt on it. It was the most delicious thing I'd ever tasted. Somebody put on the song "While the City Sleeps," by Mc 900 Foot Jesus, and we all slam danced around the room until we collapsed in a heap. I've never had a better night.

Before I got high, I had no idea that's what had been wrong the whole time. It wasn't that I had deaf parents. It wasn't that I had a frantic angry mother or a fanatic absent father. It wasn't that I was fat and retarded or crazy, angry, Jewish, or anything else. I just needed to get high. That's the secret no one tells you when you're a kid. That it feels fucking great. They tell you that you feel loopy and disoriented, but no one tells you that it crawls through your skin, filling in every place of deficit, every gaping crack where your humanity didn't fuse. The thick warm lava of euphoria fills in the crevices of your psyche, and you realize your soul was an electric blanket that hadn't been plugged in until just then. Parents and shrinks never tell you that you will forget all the reasons you had to hate yourself. They don't tell you that shit because then everybody will want to get high.

It's that feeling—the numbing bliss of self-medication—that

makes people become drug addicts. Lots of people get high; only some become addicts. It's not the getting high that makes you an addict, it's what the getting high does for you. If you start low and you get high, you make it up to normal for the first time. Getting loaded feels good; but if it's the first thing that's ever felt good in your life, you're in trouble. That's what I chased. It wasn't the high, it was the feeling that I was all right. All right?

Getting high that first time was like seeing for the first time. It was as if I'd been wearing blinders my whole life, and with that first hit, they shot off and I saw the world in its full repose for the first time. The world had seemed so small and myopic before that first hit, and as I exhaled, I inhaled the new scene before me. The world expanded forever. It was bright and clear and I wasn't afraid of anything. I felt like I could see forever. My life had, until that point, been a dark, small, little place, the rules and dynamics of which had been set by all of the people who controlled me. I had no power over anything. And then, just like that, my world popped open. I could see for miles.

Right about the first time I got high, the famous thespian/professional wrestler "Rowdy" Roddy Piper had just graduated from the Royal Shakespeare Academy and body slammed Andre the Giant. (The Royal Shakespeare thing was a lie.) He was at the peak of his fame and thus got a starring role in the seminal classic *They Live*. (The seminal classic thing was a lie.)

I loved that movie. In it, Piper is a blue-collar schmo who happens across a pair of unremarkable-looking sunglasses. But these are no ordinary sunglasses. As soon as he puts them on, an entire secret alien world is revealed to him. There are aliens everywhere and apparently they have been here awhile. Billboards that to the naked eye seem to be Coca-Cola ads are shown to have messages for the alien occupiers. Famous actors have been aliens this whole time, their freaky alien faces revealed once Roddy slips the sunglasses on. A whole alien world had been running right under our noses, just beneath the surface. I felt like Rowdy Roddy Piper after that first joint. Not like, I want to wear a kilt and beat up the Macho Man Randy Savage, but like, I knew about a secret fucking world that had always been there and mindless victims had been walking around it for years, pretending it didn't exist. I saw the brave new world.

I'm not sure what happens to normal people when they get high for the first time. I assume that they get high, feel delighted, and think, "That was soul stimulating. I feel enlightened but not over-whelmingly so. I await another appropriate occasion for mind expansion in a reasonably far-off time, when I will make a conscious and mature decision to take a mood-altering substance again."

Not me. I realized in that little high sambo slam-dance circle, right before I melted into hemp butter, that I never wanted *not* to be high again. I would do whatever it took to get high forever, all the time, for the rest of my life. I was twelve years old and I'd found my calling. Stay high, stay drunk, at all costs.

⚜

I went out to visit Richard a few days later. I jumped on the BART train and watched through the window as the scenery flicked by like an old-time nickel arcade changing from Oakland's grime to Lafayette's shine. I felt like a different person.

When I got out there, I suggested to Richard we sneak off to go smoke cigarettes. He'd tried those and hated them but agreed to do it. We sat out on a hill and I fired up a stogie, took a hit, and passed it to him.

"You're inhaling it now, like my dad does," Richard said, his voice a mix of impressed and concerned.

"Ha, yeah, I learned how." I stared at my old friend, took a deep breath, and told him, "I smoked weed, too."

He stared at me, confused. "Wait, what?"

"Yeah, I smoked weed, dude, it was awesome. It's not like they say it is, you know? It felt awesome. Like jerking off but you're just cumming the whole time. It's crazy."

Richard took it in in silence, put the cigarette out, stood up, and said, "Promise me you won't do that ever again."

I laughed. "C'mon, man, what are you talking about?"

He seemed near tears as he yelled, "Fucking promise me!"

I got a taste of how serious it was. I stared at my friend for a second, trying to figure out what to say. What could I say?

"I can't do that, man, sorry. These guys are my only friends out there. It's different for you, you've got this awesome thing going on out here, you're playing baseball and shit, making tons of friends, I don't have any of that. Besides, all that shit they've been telling us about drugs is a lie anyway. The D.A.R.E. shit? It's bullshit. They just don't want us to know the secret."

"What fucking secret?"

"Why don't you let me bring some by sometime and I'll show you."

A look of anger passed over Richard's face, he was quiet a long time, and then he whispered, "I can't be your friend if you do drugs. You have to choose. That shit or me."

I never saw Richard again.

Chapter 5

"N.Y. State of Mind"
—Nas

Just after my mind had been blown open by my newfound experiences, my brother and I flew back to New York for a visit with my father. Back to Sea Gate. Back in time. My mind had been thrust into the future by weed and alcohol even as my body flew back to the Stone Age. There was no place I would have less liked to be at that moment.

This isn't to say I was unaffected by the allure of Jewish life. Growing up, I was sliced exactly down the middle of my psyche. As a boy, I said I wanted to be either a baseball player or a famous rabbi when I grew up. Neither career held any actual interest for me but just satisfied a deficit I imagined I had. Baseball for my manhood, Torah for my soul. I didn't have much of either.

My Bar Mitzvah was a tragedy. It was a kind of farcical movie shoot. Extras were hired to play the parts of my friends and loved ones, and I was given the starring role of "Fat Uncomfortable

Kid." I've never had less fun. I've had the pleasure (?) of meeting rich Jews who had pleasant experiences with Judaism and Bar Mitzvahs. They had elaborate parties to celebrate their ascent into manhood with themes like "Indiana Jones" and "The Yankees." Everyone dressed up and cheered as a Harrison Ford look-alike cracked his whip into a piñata, spilling a waterfall of chocolate coins onto the floor. I've always felt chocolate money to be an odd choice of a treat for a people so concerned with their reputation as shylocks and money-grubbers. What are gentiles supposed to think when they see us training our children to actually eat money?

The theme of my Bar Mitzvah was the Holocaust. An old rabbi mumbled in Yiddish and I hurriedly said the blessing over the Torah reading, terrified that I would fuck it up, bile shooting into my stomach, my guts turning to liquid, my asshole quivering and clenching to prevent me from unleashing a chocolate waterfall of my own.

After the horror show that was the liturgical part of my Bar Mitzvah came the "party." You know how parties are supposed to be fun? Now imagine the opposite of that. I sat, fat and awkward, in the chair of honor and received the guests. I knew none of them. A local Chassidic celebrity, Mordechai Ben David, crooned Yiddish songs to my father's delight. He had sprung Mordechai Ben David's performance on me as a big surprise, and he looked at me with joy in his eyes when the concert began. My father, being deaf, was spared the shocking realization of just how awful even the best of all Chassidic pop songs are.

My father signed to me, "Mordechai Ben David! See? He insisted that he be able to come perform here."

It wasn't until years later that I realized my father must have begged him to come and sing.

I just smiled and wished that my dad had hookups on a Snoop Dogg performance instead. My entire experience of Judaism was largely based on fear and terror, which was perhaps appropriate, as we are commanded to fear God always. I did. I mostly feared other Jews who acted as God's thuggish earthling enforcers. Every second I sat in the synagogue, or *shul* to use the Yiddish, I was paralyzed by the fear that I would be called up again to do any sort of liturgical rite. Being asked to wrap the Torah or to open the Ark or anything of the sort was said to be a great honor, but for me it was the stuff nightmares are made of. I would try, with every shred of my being, to make myself invisible. My entire consciousness, every second that I sat in shul, was focused on being transparent.

My brother, on the other hand, went the exact other way with Judaism. He saw it as a pool of my father's approval into which he could jump and be baptized (sorry) a true and actual Jew. He shucked and jived and looked almost like he knew what he was doing. My brother would sit at home in California and teach himself Hebrew for hours on end lest he be caught sitting in shul with an English prayer book, the ugly English lettering exposed for all to see, a sign that might as well have been flashing neon reading, THIS GUY HAS NO CLUE WHAT'S GOING ON! I felt like a fraud from the start. I was filled with shame.

Shame drove my father's family. Everyone was ignorant for different reasons—he and his new family because of their deafness; me and my brother because of our California-ness. My father's response was to keep it all a great secret.

When we would go out to a place where my father suspected there might be members of the Chassidic community, he would coach us on interrogation techniques. The Chassidic community is a particularly intrusive one and the big Jewish noses correspond exactly to big Jewish nosiness. It's not unusual for a complete stranger to lob a few quick questions at you in order to assess where you are at religiously and educationally. This allows your interrogator to feel: (A) Smug if you are operating below his children. (B) Embarrassed if you are learning at a higher level than his children. (C) Interested in arranging a marriage if you are operating at an equal level to his children. It's a very disconcerting process.

"If anyone asks you what yeshiva you go to," my father would sign to us on our way to Borough Park for kosher pizza, "you just tell them it's called Beth Jacob."

Beth Jacob was the name of an Orthodox temple in Oakland and seemed plausible enough for my father to suggest as a name for a theoretical yeshiva. *Yeshiva* is the yiddish name for the seminary school that all young Jews go to. It's the kind of place where kids spend ten hours a day studying Talmud and religious philosophy and an hour a day fulfilling the state's legal requirements for "secular studies." Every young Chassidic boy goes to yeshiva, and the thought of my father's children going to public school with a filthy sea of non-Jews was unthinkable.

So he made up a lie for us to tell.

My brother, ever willing to dance the Jewish Uncle Tom shuffle, thought better of the name.

"Wait, don't say Beth Jacob," he signed. "We should say it in Yiddish, 'Bais Yakov'; yeah, that's better."

"That's great!" My father clapped David on the back "You are a genius!"

My brother nodded eagerly but I shuddered in fear. I knew I would fuck this up somehow. I envisioned some awful rabbi's wife approaching me and asking, in the special grammar of the American Orthodox Jew, "So, *nu*, at what yeshiva do you learn?"

I knew I'd just sweat and piss my pants and scream, "I love black people!"

As it happened, reality was even more humiliating than my paranoid fantasies.

We went out to pizza and somehow, against all odds, the exact horror show we'd prepared for took place almost immediately. A nosy Jewish couple approached us, having met my father back in Sea Gate. They nasally whined some small talk before zeroing in for the kill.

They turned to me, their Jewish X-ray eyes searing into my secret soul. A single droplet of sweat beaded down my brow.

"So," she asked, setting my skin on fire, "where do you two go to yeshiva?"

It happened. Worst Nightmare. Deep Shame.

My mouth opened but no sound came. I mouthed "Bais Yakov" but only to myself.

My brother pushed me aside and said confidently, "We go to Bais Yakov!"

My savior. I felt relief flood me. I nodded vigorously. My father smiled and nodded, too.

But something was wrong.

The lady looked confused. Her eyes scrunched up in disbelief. "Bais Yakov, the *girls' school*?"

Panicked, I looked at my brother. He didn't know what to do. Apparently there was a famous girls' yeshiva in New York called Bais Yaakov. We hadn't been briefed on this logistic possibility.

I turned to my father for answers but he was signing to his wife, pretending he hadn't seen what just happened.

I turned back to the lady and whimpered. Then I peeled off my skin and handed it to them.

Actually they just wandered off, whispering to one another and shaking their heads.

I shuddered.

We all ate our pizza in silent shame.

❧

When my father first moved to Sea Gate, I knew that perhaps I was a bit out of my religious league, and so one day, about a year before I started getting high, I decided to ask the rabbi for help with my religious crisis. It seemed perfectly logical at the time.

Rabbi Meisels was a good man and a genuinely loving proponent of Judaism, and when he heard I had a question about it, he happily piled me into his car, an American-made station wagon with wood paneling on the sides (much like *every* Chassidic Jewish family owned in Sea Gate at the time), put on his oversized plastic glasses, which faded from black at the top of the frame to clear plastic at the bottom (much like *every* Chassidic Jewish man wore in Sea Gate at the time), and off we went for a drive. We exited the gates of Sea Gate and drove off into the real world. We pulled into Borough Park, an extremely religious neighborhood of Brooklyn but, compared to Sea Gate, a secular state. People here had televisions they wouldn't even bother hiding when company came over. That's how shocking and scandalous things were in Borough Park. Who knows, if my father had chosen to live in Borough Park, I might've been able to latch on to Chassidic Judaism in some way and this book would be about the wonders of Chanukah instead. Borough Park was religious, but at least it was alive. The streets were littered with religious bookstores and kosher pizza parlors, burger joints called "Kosher Delight," and if you looked hard enough, you could actually catch people smiling. Sea Gate was a trail of tears.

I turned to the rabbi and, my heart pounding, spit it out.

"Look," I said, trying not to pass out as I revealed my religious weakness, "I have a hard time imagining myself in, like, the long run...um, you know, being a Jew. Or, sorry, not a Jew but like being religious."

The rabbi stared at me like I was speaking Yiddish. Wait—no, like I was speaking Chinese.

I was falling all over myself as I tried to explain. "See, like, let's take being Shomer Shabbos. I just wonder sometimes, am I going to be? You know what I mean? Like, am I going to be religious when I grow up? What should I do? I mean, I guess I'm just asking if I should be religious."

Rabbi Meisels looked at me, confused. He stared for a few seconds and then looked ahead at the road and drove, in silence, for about five minutes. I squirmed in my seat, sure that he was going to drop me off at the gates of Hell. He finally spoke, "I don't really know how to answer your question."

I don't begrudge Rabbi Meisels for being unable to help me with the most rudimentary of all religious questions, "Should I be religious?" The truth is, he was operating at such a high level of religiosity, questions like that *never* came up. If someone in the community *ever* said, "I'm not sure I believe this crap," they would immediately be cast out and branded a heretic. It was only because I was essentially considered religiously brain dead that I was even allowed to get away with asking without social penalty.

You may see the fact that a rabbi couldn't answer the question "Is Judaism a good religion to adhere to?" as a shocking irony, but consider the fact that the vast majority of questions he received from his congregation were more similar to, "If a candle is burning prior to Shabbos and I blow it out one second before Shabbos begins, but it somehow sparks back to life the second Shabbos comes in and my house will literally burn to the ground if I don't blow it out, what should I do?"

Had I asked this question, Rabbi Meisels would have had a complex and thoughtful response to give. But unfortunately, my question was so outside of his worldview that he had no answer.

"What do you mean, you aren't sure you are going to keep Shabbos?" I'm sure he thought. "Why, that's a sin punishable by stoning death according to Mosaic law. Do you want to be stoned to death?"

That's the world I was living in. Finally, as we pulled back into Sea Gate, he spoke again. "I don't know how to help you with that. Maybe you should go ask the rabbi at Chabad." Chabad again. The great fixer of problems in the Chassidic world.

Chabad had become sort of a clearinghouse for those kinds of problem situations. After the Holocaust, most Chassidic branches had retreated to an inward-looking social policy. Realizing the rest of the world to be filled with godlessness, they turned their focus from interactions *with* the world to an outright rejection *of* the world in the hopes of preserving the last fragments of holiness *in* the world. In other words, they stopped talking to regular people. Chabad was the only sect of Chassidism that still cared to interact with the real world or to help less-religious Jews in any way, which made them the go-to group for people like me. No one in the Chassidic world really cared for Chabad, their fanatic worship of the charismatic Rabbi Menachem Mendel Schneerson smacking everyone's sensitive spots as heretical. A mention of Chabad would often result in a sort of Yiddish-based eye rolling, but no one ever outright called them heretics, as they had become an indispensable liaison between the secular Jewish world (aka money) and the insular castle in the sky that most Chassidic sects had become. Even years later, when Schneerson finally died, leaving his implicit promise to reveal himself as the Messiah unfulfilled, and most of his adherents declared that he would be resurrected and return to earth (sound like anyone you know?), most rabbis just kept silent and hoped Chabad would get their shit together.

Not fully aware of all this backstory but skeeved out by the residue it left on all of its adherents and their interactions, I decided that Chabad couldn't help me. One too many rabbis, one too few answers. I ran into the house that afternoon, red-faced with the shame that someone in Sea Gate knew my deep secret, that perhaps I wasn't cut out to be a rabbi after all.

"How was your meeting with Rabbi Meisels?" my father asked eagerly.

He loved the idea of me spending the day with the rabbi hashing out Talmudic treatises, talking about the Torah.

The truth is, despite all my father's bravado, all of his antideaf protestations stemmed from a deep insecurity about his own deafness. He knew that he was missing much of the dialogue. He knew that people smiled at him in synagogue because they didn't know how to talk to him like a regular man. He became, to them, a cartoon character, the deaf guy. My father took himself so seriously because no one else did. For all his strict adherence to Chassidic Judaism, my father didn't read Hebrew, didn't know Yiddish. He knew form and function but never got an opportunity to engage in the ultimate expression of Orthodox Judaism, the chance to study Jewish law. He was kept mostly ignorant and he knew it and it shamed him. So, when he had two hearing sons, he saw the opportunity for us to have what he and his other kids never would, the chance to be in on the dialogue. My perfect brother did just that, he learned how to be the scholar that Orthodox Judaism prizes above all. I just never could. I knew that and I was ashamed of it. It was just another thing that was wrong with me. I was only twelve and shame was starting to coil in me like a spring, creaking and gaining pressure, cranking down, winding me up, making me ready to pop.

So, when my father asked me how my meeting went with the rabbi, I just looked up and signed, "Great... It was great. I think I got the answers I was looking for."

In a way, this was true. I eventually realized that the Burning Bush God I'd been looking for in the Torah had actually been growing on a bush in Northern California this whole time, waiting for me to burn.

❧

Having been exposed to the joys of getting high and then having had them stripped away from me with a summer trip back to the old country, needless to say I was a bit miserable in New York. I needed something, so I had to content myself with gulping deeply when Shabbos wine was passed to me and indulging in late-night phone sex.

I'd found the joys of phone sex just before I'd left California in the summer of 1991. My mother had long since had a 900 number block placed on the phone line in some kind of preemptive psychic protection move. Luckily, the phone companies had arranged a neat work-around of those 900 blocks that I can't imagine wasn't a direct response to the plummeting profits that allowing parents to cut their children off phone sex had caused. If you can't call 900 numbers, perhaps you can call an underdeveloped country? Small, far-off nations had long-distance arrangements to charge something like five dollars a minute for the connection. After the phone company took a ten-dollar connection fee, these beleaguered nations could start scraping money off the penises of American hornballs.

I called islands like Antigua and the Philippines and jerked my horny little dick to the sounds of their moans and dirty talk. I ejaculated to both Trinidad *and* Tobago. I brought rivers of cum to drought-addled islands. I e-*JAH*-culated onto Rastafarian marijuana fields.

I can imagine those ladies now, six kids in a small tin shack, stirring a goat curry stew with a baby on their hip as they cradled the phone on their shoulder, boredly moaning to me about how much they wanted my big cock. I didn't yet have a big cock, but I was hardly going to tell them that.

I called every night. My father would ask me to bring him a cup of water and then ask me to rub his feet—a nonsexual but nonetheless extremely weird request. I felt more like a royal subject than anything else.

I'd wait until I heard snores to make sure everyone was asleep, and I would sneak down to the living room to call my tropical foreign queen.

Once, I called a number and got an older Filipino voice on the line. It sounded off. Like a grandmother's voice.

" 'Allo?" The huskiness of the voice threw me off, but my dick was hard and not to be deterred.

"I'm rock hard and ready for you," I whispered, trying to sound of legal age to be making a call like this. Nothing like the squeaky pubescent creak of a thirteen-year-old voice to ruin a good tropical jerk session.

"Oh. Sarrdy. Sarrdy. No. I not do that kind of call."

"You don't what?" This was bullshit, I didn't pay the $9.95 connection fee to be rejected by a woman saying sarrdy. I checked the number to make sure I hadn't misdialed. I hadn't. For some reason I decided to push the issue.

"C'mon, give it to me…" I panted, my voice cracking, revealing my youthful exuberance.

The reluctant phone whore spoke. "Oh, okay, you want puck me?"

I did. I really did. I'd never wanted to puck someone so bad.

Somehow, that grizzled old voice on the other end of the phone had melted a bit.

"Yes, that's what I want; I want you to give it to me."

And then, just like that, I had another tug session with an island lady.

To this day, I'm not sure if I convinced a random Filipino grandmother whom I'd misdialed to start a career in phone sex that day or if I pulled someone out of retirement for one last moan. All I know is that when the phone bill came, even that triumphant call wasn't worth it.

My father called me into the kitchen and was holding a phone bill up like a subpoena. I was busted. I slunk into my chair and waited for the fire-and-brimstone lecture to begin. I realized I hadn't thought this through.

"The phone bill is fifteen hundred dollars this month," my dad sneered at me, his nostrils flaring, his rage just sorta bubbling beneath the surface. My dad had this way of getting so mad that you wished he would just hit you and get it over with. He was a master rager, and I took notes on his form. This might come in handy someday.

I slouched farther in my seat. "Yeah, sorry about that."

My dad leaned into me and signed, "Phone sex?"

I shrugged. What could I do or say? My dad and the weight of the entire Jewish people were bearing down on me. I was fucked.

When I was eight days old, at my circumcision ceremony, Zeidi, then one hundred years old, held me in his gnarled hands and declared to my father and the Lord, "This boy will be a great rabbi, I can see into his soul."

Thirteen years later I was explaining to my father how I'd racked up fifteen hundred dollars in bills while pumping my dick in his living room. Maybe Zeidi had been looking into someone else's soul. Or maybe his soul-looking eyes had glaucoma. I'm not sure.

Conveniently, I had received approximately fifteen hundred dollars in Bar Mitzvah money from the complete strangers that my father had invited from the local Jewish community. I'd never had so much money in my life as that day after my Bar Mitzvah. But the day after the day after my Bar Mitzvah, it was liquidated on my penis.

I spent every penny of my Bar Mitzvah money on phone sex. I just imagined God, looking down at me, shaking his metaphorical head and asking me, "Phone sex? You spent your Bar Mitzvah money on phone sex? The holy rite I have commanded you to follow, you took and spent on calling 'Hot Island Bitches'?"

Ashamed, I can hardly look God in his third, flaming eye. "Well, sorta. I mean, yes."

God frowns. "This does not please me."

"I'm the one who lost all that money," I'd plead. "Anyway, isn't this a passage into manhood? What better way to become a man than that?"

Beaten, God would mutter, "Well...I usually don't cede to arguments as I am a being of omnipotent perfection, but that's a really good point."

At least I tried to convince my dad that that's how the conversation would go. My dad did not seem amused.

The rest of my trip to New York was spent awkwardly interacting with my family, longing for drugs or accented voices, and watching my stepmother lock the phone away at night. I tiptoed around the house but knew what they were all thinking: "Who *is* this pervert?" I couldn't wait to get home to Oakland.

Chapter 6

"In My Neighborhood"
—Spice 1

I arrived back in Oakland with a sigh of relief and headed straight back to my stomping grounds. The guys were from all over North Oakland, but we hung out and terrorized a neighborhood called Rockridge. College Avenue. For years, it struggled to establish itself as the stuffy yuppie stronghold it has now finally become. If you go there today, you will see throngs of white people, doing white people things, such as inspecting rare cheeses and riding in packs of thousand-dollar bicycles with penis silhouette–enhancing spandex outfits. Vomit.

At the time, though, it was still in flux, and we did our best to ruin the yuppie dream. Rockridge sat where the rich Oakland Hills, the North Oakland killing fields, and the psychedelic wasteland of Telegraph Avenue buttressed up against each other—where worlds collided.

We were the local shitheads. You know those kids who get

on the bus and you think to yourself, "Oh great, *these* fucking kids!"? That was us. Rockridge rats—shitty, loud, shoplifting, graffitiing thirteen-year-old menaces.

Officer Joe, the local beat cop in the neighborhood, hated us. At least six-foot-thirteen, with all of his body weight resting in his barrel chest, inside of which, I assume, were gears and clockwork cogs keeping a robotic pig's heart pumping, he was a giant.

Officer Joe, ignoring the conventions of probable cause, or perhaps assuming our very existence *was* probable cause, would search us on sight—every time, every day. Joe lined us up against the wall and a waterfall of contraband would spill out onto the streets. Sakura 64 permanent markers, pot-pipes screwed together from stolen plumbing supplies, knives, and pepper spray rolled down College Avenue, lowering property values with each rotation.

Officer Joe would then throw us up against the wall and cuff us, spin someone into a chokehold, and then drive us around in his car for an hour or so just to scare us. A piece of shit, that's how I'd describe him. (Author's note: My editor feels that the description of Officer Joe is a juvenile one. That I sound immature in calling him these names in my current narrator's voice. After much soul-searching and questioning, I have found that any other description of him is impossible. Really, he was a dick. In other news, I have just given money to a Sudanese charity in what can only be described as a mature act and *anything* but juvenile.)

One day, the higher-ups at the Oakland Police Department assigned Officer Joe a police bicycle. This was in the early days of bike cops, and you can't imagine how long and loud we laughed when Officer Joe rolled up with his bike and his little cop shorts.

"You have *really* pretty legs, Officer Joe," I spat out, barely able to keep a straight face.

Joe, not amused.

He trailed behind us that day for about an hour. Everywhere we walked, he followed at a distance of about fifteen feet, his bike giving him agility his beat car never had. Maybe this bike thing wasn't so funny after all.

We walked; he rolled. We turned left; he turned left. Finally Donny spun around and asked him, "Why the hell are you following us?"

"It's a free country." He smiled, obviously enjoying this game a bit too much.

"It *is* a free country!" I yelled back, one of my more brilliant ideas popping into my head. "Run!"

We all scattered in different directions, running at full speed playing cat and mouse through the streets. We darted here and there yelling at one another in code about where we would eventually meet once we shook this guy. We agreed on the monastery.

The monastery was an apple grove in the middle of Oakland, surrounded by an abbey, where Jesuit monks walked around in contemplation of the Lord and where we got fucked up and hurled apples at passing traffic. It was a space open for the public to enjoy, but by the time we got through with it, they built a six-foot fence around it and locked the gates forever. For a while, though, it was our spot.

We found each other there, breathing heavily and giddy with defiance. Someone had procured whiskey, and we cracked it and passed it around as we planned our next move.

Luckily, our next move walked right up to us. A group of guys from the grade below made the mistake of thinking they could find safe passage in these, the apple trees of the Lord. As they approached, DJ, our biggest, loudest, scariest friend, jumped up and screamed, "Break yo' self! Empty yo' mothafuckin' pockets!"

Translated loosely from the original gangster, this means, "Hello! We are robbing you! Give us your money!" Usually this kind of belligerence would be enough to get us ten bucks, but unfortunately, this group of fellas had an upstart. A short, chubby kid with a bald head boldly stepped forward and fearlessly confronted DJ with the bravery/stupidity of a hero:

"Fuck you!"

I felt DJ's excitement level rise at this kind of gauntlet toss. He cocked his head to make sure he wasn't imagining things. That, in fact, this little shit had said what we thought he said.

DJ grunted, "The fuck you just say to me?"

No hesitation, the little shit in question repeated, "I said fuck you!"

Then things started to move in slow motion. DJ's face lit up and I imagine his dick moved a little bit in anticipation of the violence he was about to inflict. The little bald dude didn't seem worried in the least and even smirked a bit.

DJ cocked back and fired on him, a one-two, face-chin combo, broken nose—a DJ special. Wiped the smirk right off his face. Even in the dark, I could see the blood start to leak down his face. As the kid grabbed his nose in pain, all of his friends started to yell at once, like a Greek chorus, bringing us bad news: "Dude, what are you doing?!? That's a girl!! It's a girl!!"

You just don't hit a girl.

That's the rules. Don't tag houses, trees, or cars (unless they are white box trucks); don't backwash into the forty-ouncer; and don't hit chicks. The rules. There is no chapter in the rules on what to do about chicks that don't look like chicks, though. Well, there is now.

DJ stammered, waves of adrenaline and shame flooding his system at once, turning him into an even less articulate version of himself, a very inarticulate boy.

"What?! Oh shit. I'm so sorry; I thought you were a dude! You just look so much like a guy, I'm sorry!"

I'm not sure what's worse: DJ socking that chick in the face, his apology where he explained he never would have hit her if she didn't look so much like a guy, or the fact that, years later, I ended up fucking that guy. I wish I was kidding.

We always looked for places like the monastery. With cops like Officer Joe on our backs, we had to have places to go. We crawled through Oakland looking for secret hiding places where we could be cool for a while. In the back of Chabot Elementary School, we found a freeway underpass behind cyclone fencing. We threw a rug over the barbed wire and climbed in. We set up a little living quarters complete with stolen barbecues and lawn furniture. For a while *that* was our spot. We moved on.

We staked claims on garage roofs with branches pulled down into canopies of subterfuge. We tromped around the neighborhood exploring places like Huckleberry Finn trippin' down the Old Miss.

We climbed up things and opened up manhole covers. We found abandoned houses and hollow bushes and made them our territory. We found alleys and garage roofs and sewers. Yes, sewers.

The sewer. Frohawk's place. Nate was his real name, but everybody called him Frohawk. A tall black guy with this grubby Mohawk. Get it? We'd found Frohawk one day when we were on a desperate search for someone to buy us booze. He was nineteen so he couldn't buy it for us, but he had some warm gin back at his place. His place turned out to be a bit farther away than we'd expected.

He lived in the sewers underneath Oakland. Literally. He was a hobo of some kind. A literal gutter punk, the kind who sits on the sidewalk and harasses you for change. That was Frohawk. He'd been homeless for years and found a place beneath the city where he could sleep undisturbed.

Walk about a half mile down a drainage tunnel off College Avenue with a lit candle and a bottle of hairspray to torch any spiders or rats you might see and you'd get to an antechamber, and that's where Frohawk nested. Nate had decorated the place with a stolen mattress and couch cushions. Everywhere you looked, there were empty bottles and candle stubs and Teenage Mutant Ninja Turtles, huddled together for warmth in the corner. There were rats and black widows and piles of cholera dust and skeletons and gold doubloons from shipwrecks and ghosts and gnomes and sewage water; there were dwarfs mining for precious metals and pet alligators grown to enormous size and then there was us, with another awesome place to get high.

Nate actually lived there. That was his house. After a while, Nate introduced us to Little Mikey Rip-It-Up's place. The ultimate spot. The land of milk and honey to a thirteen-year-old drug addict.

Little Mikey Rip-It-Up was a thirty-five-year-old man who lived in the attic of the First Church of Christ on College Avenue in Rockridge. Mikey had been given the job of fixing things and cleaning up around the church in exchange for free room and board. It never occurred to us that it was odd that a man lived above a church. Actually it was sort of cute. A little man living a little life in a little triangle of attic space carved out for him by the Lord himself.

Mikey looked a bit like an Eskimo elder with a face scrunched up from years of facing tundric ice winds. And much like an Eskimo, he was the type of guy you'd never know was there unless you smelled him. I'm kidding about Eskimos, but not about Mikey. He didn't smell great. Perhaps that was in part due to the fact that I never officially located a shower in his little parsonage in the attic of that church.

Imagine! A thirty-five-year-old friend. Lucky. Mikey was awesome. He bought us cigarettes and booze and pornography and we hiked back to his place and smoked and drank and jerked off and made Top Ramen and punched the walls in. "Punch the fuckin' walls in!" we'd scream.

Okay, relax. I know how it sounds, but it wasn't like that. Mikey was one of us. It wasn't an Old Man Don situation.

Now, Old Man Don owned an antique shop in town with an open-door policy: if you were young and broke, Don showed you *his* antique and you made some money the old-fashioned way. And no, I'm not into antiques.

No, Mikey was one of us, nothing creepy. Yeah, he was thirty-five, but he was cool.

More important, though, he offered us a better option than participating in the thirteen-year-old/bum-barter economy. Usually, if you're thirteen and need to get drunk, you have only a few options: find a crooked store; ask a crooked man; or take your crooked ass into the booze aisle and steal some shit. The crooked stores were the hardest to find. Fines and piety kept most of the local liquor stores out of reach.

The next thing to do was find a bum. Bums like smoking crack.

Yes, all of them. Crack, however, costs money that they don't have, because the bum industry is one of the worst-paying on the market. That's where we came in. For a five-dollar tip, we were able to get drunk, and the bums were able to smoke rocks. It was a good system; everybody got paid, so to speak. That is, until we met Little Mikey Rip-It-Up and threw the entire bum/kid economy to the wolves.

We were not the first to find Mikey. His place was constantly inundated with people eager to partake of the warmth of the church's secret shelter. A steady cast of characters came in and out of Mikey's place. Mikey and his flophouse attracted every strange hobo and street urchin in town. In his small way, Little Mikey Rip-It-Up was the ambassador of College Avenue, an ambassador representing only the cream of the crap.

At Mikey's, we met guys like Leotis, an older black guy who lived mysteriously, like a Jack London character, in a tent in Tilden Park. I suppose technically that made him just a homeless person, but to us, he was an urban buccaneer. He even looked a bit like a buccaneer, with his trademark thin red ascot wrapped around his neck, cutting through his black skin like a wound. Surprisingly, he always wore a crisp white dress shirt that sparkled whiteness in defiance of the woodsy home from which it emerged.

Leotis had an aura that made him seem like the wisest man who had ever lived. In retrospect, the wisest man who ever lived can probably afford walls.

"The thing y'all don't know about…is life itself," Leotis explained as we listened with rapt enthusiasm. "I been hustling for forty years."

"Please," I thought, "teach me how to hustle." I could, at that time, only dream of a life spent living in municipal parks in a ten-dollar tent.

A street philosopher, Leotis loved to pontificate. I imagine in the Middle Ages, he would have rambled into town in a great silken wagon, addled with trinkets and baubles, and the town would gather around, to hear him dazzle with charisma.

"The thing thou dost not knoweth about, is life itself!"

"Huzzah!" the people would scream back. "Huzzah for Lord Leotis!"

But flash-forward two thousand years to 1992, and Leotis was simply a creep who lived in a park.

Leotis always hustled but he never hustled alone. His main partner in crime was Shane.

Shane was about twenty-five when we met him, his cheeks already puffy and swollen from years of alcohol abuse. He always had the perfect amount of stubble, too. Not perfect as in: Hollywood-chic, but perfect as in: Yes, in fact I do drink beer with cigarette butts in it—what of it?

Shane was funny and liked us and would tell us about how to get by and make some quick cash if you needed it.

He taught us about Carlo Rossi. "Carlo Rossi is the best wine a man can buy," he told us. Hard to argue with. Only the best comes in 2.5-gallon bottles. Rossi was the finest wine we ever drank. We started with Cisco, and then came Boone's Farm, and on the nights of celebration, we cracked Rossi.

Shane liked Rossi but I liked Cisco. Leotis, a Cisco drinker, taught me the "bang for the buck principle." In the world of cheap drink, there are levels. Here's Leotis's Talmudic treatise on the wisdom of cheap drinks:

Malt liquor is standard alcoholic drinking fare, but there are levels. First, there's Mickey's—known as "white boy drink," reserved for chicks and people who are still employed. In the middle of the spectrum is Olde English, a drink for Shakespearean alcoholics. And then there's the bang-for-the-buck favorite, St. Ides. Ahh, St. Ides, the patron saint of cirrhosis. The only thing better than St. Ides is Crazy Horse, a true rarity, but if you ever see it on the shelf, you *have* to go for it. You know a drink is strong when, without any self-consciousness or irony, it is named after a leader of a culture that's been decimated by alcoholism.

Wino wines had similar strata. Boone's for girls, Rossi for groups, and Cisco for real men. Cisco was my favorite. A lethal sort of synthetic bum wine, it was made out of a combination of distilled Now and Laters, Ajax, and broken dreams. People called it Liquid Crack. I called it dinner.

Shane's favorite was always Rossi. He and Corey came home one day with two jugs of the stuff and a look of delight—and a girl! Melissa.

Melissa was, for a time, Shane's girlfriend. The only one of us who had one. She was an alcoholic, too, but much like alco*hol*, there's also a spectrum of alcoho*lics*. Melissa wasn't quite young and dumb like us, but also not as old and crushed as Shane and Leotis. She was pretty, although a few more years of drinking the way she was would take care of that. Mostly, though, she was sweet and quiet and racked with a kind of combination love/shame for Shane. Her father had been an alcoholic and had beaten her, and probably worse, all of her life. And—like many kids with alcoholic parents—in the ultimate irony, she started drinking to make that pain go away.

As we passed around the jugs of wine, Shane showed us how to cradle them in the crook of our elbows in order to raise the jugs to our lips without struggling with the weight of the thing.

"It's like my arms were made to hold bottles of wine!" Shane mumbled, barely comprehensible.

"You sound like such a fucking drunk, Shane," Melissa shot at him, clearly a bit embarrassed that Shane seemed to love this jug of piss wine more than her.

Shane, red-faced and humiliated, shot back, "You shut the fuck up!" She did.

I heard Melissa eventually ended up getting the courage she was looking for at the bottom of the wine jug and left Shane.

I still see Shane now and again, wandering the streets, babbling to himself, piss stains crusted on his pants, his mind a joke. He hasn't recognized me in years.

Leotis disappeared into the forest a long time ago to go join the Narinan resistance or to hustle up a life or something. But before everything changed, we had our little hustler training ground.

No matter where we started our day, we all always ended up at Mikey Rip-It-Up's.

Mikey Rip-It-Up loved to rip it up. He'd crack bottles of booze and drink till we told him to stop. He'd take any dare. He'd lick a car battery or punch himself in the face ten times if we asked. He just didn't give a fuck. I remember his teeth, too. They didn't give a fuck either. Yellow, grimy—like God knit him a little canary sweater for each tooth. A teeny Christmas present of yuck. Man, when you're thirteen and you have a thirty-five-year-old to hang around with, you are king. He was thirty-five, but cool. And he'd never kissed a girl! Just like most of us.

When I found that out, my mind was blown.

"Wait a minute, dude, you've never kissed a girl?" I asked him, terrified at the possibility of going another twenty years without getting some.

Mikey giggled and shook his head. "No, I've never kissed a girl, nope. I would, though. I'd kiss a girl. I'd fuck a girl, too."

"Yikes. Good to know. But wait, how can you be thirty-five and not have kissed anyone?" I was almost angry at this point.

"Shut the fuck up, dude, you're always talking." DJ punched me in the shoulder to accentuate his point.

"He's got a point, though," Jamie said, defending me. "I first French-kissed a girl when I was six." Jamie looked off into the distance after this lie, a self-satisfied grin on his face, ignoring the eye rolling going on all around him.

I looked back at Mikey Rip-It-Up. "So, seriously, you never kissed a girl?" I just couldn't let it go. It was disturbing.

Mikey, however, was disturbingly unfazed by the question that should've sent him into existential angst, or at least horny frustration. He simply mumbled to himself and we all changed the subject.

There was something a bit unsettling about Mikey's admission that he'd never been with a girl. But since none of us ever had been either, it fell mostly within the realm of our circle of normalcy. Then again, our circle of normalcy included four of the seven layers of Hell, so that's best taken with a grain of salt.

We spent every day at Mikey's place and treated it like our home. We were loud and hardly subtle about what we were doing. A parade of clear-eyed, sad-faced teenage boys tromped into Mikey's place every afternoon and every night; we emerged bleary-eyed, stumbling men. We treated the place like shit. We tagged on Mikey's walls and told the other janitors to fuck off. We climbed onto the roof and threw pinecones at passing cars. Basically, despite the fact that we loved Mikey Rip-It-Up, all we ever did to his place was rip it up.

Eventually the church took notice. Apparently the Presbyterian Church is weirdly uptight about thirteen-year-old boys getting high in the attic with their thirty-five-year-old custodian. They asked Mikey to leave the church, his house, and his position, and they called our parents and let them know what had been going on.

Donny's mom got a call from the church's personnel manager complaining about us.

"Hello, Ms. Moon, I'm calling to let you know that your son and a group of boys have been hanging about in our church, smoking marijuana, causing destruction to our property, and taking advantage of our handyman."

Donny's mom, unconvinced, asked the obvious question, "Taking *advantage* of your handyman? Those boys are thirteen."

The church lady dropped a bomb. "Well, Ms. Moon, Michael, our *former* handyman, is mentally retarded."

So that explained it! We literally did not know that, all this time, we had been hanging out with a sort of ne'er-do-well, drunken Forrest Gump (minus the inspirational story/good nature/running skills/happy ending). Now we knew.

See, Mikey Rip-It-Up was so especially cool to us, a group of thirteen-year-old boys, because he had the mind of a thirteen-year-old boy. He really *was* just like us. Sad.

Eventually, though, our minds had begun to build more sophisticated spiderwebs of thought and conniving and Mikey just stayed the same way. Mikey was gonna be thirteen for the rest of his life, and we, sad to say, were going to get older. The consequences of our age were going to chip away at us until some of us were dead, and some of us were in jail, and some of us got the fuck out of Oakland. But Mikey Rip-It-Up was going to stay the same. Too bad for him, our consequences ruined his little life. Mikey didn't go back to his parents and ask for help after he got in trouble. He may have seemed like one of us, but he really wasn't. We ravaged his life and left him severed from the charity that had been keeping him afloat. After we moved on, he sank.

Mikey hit the road and, as far as I know, is still roaming the streets of the old neighborhood, playing with little boys, hoping they won't grow up.

Chapter 7

"Mind Blowin' "
—*The D.O.C.*

Our days and nights were spent wandering through Oakland, looking for ridiculous fun things to do. Life as a thirteen-year-old outlaw is very difficult. Having blacklist fun is a constant challenge when you are that young. Much of the activity must be done under the cover of darkness. Some criminal activity was easy, as no one would suspect a boy with such a cherubic baby face was such a badass. That's how we all got away with going bombing.

Going bombing is what we called stuffing a backpack full of Krylon brand spray paint and going to cover the neighborhood with graffiti. The harder you crushed an area, the more solidly that place was yours. We owned Rockridge and much of North Oakland. Every block, every blank space and bus bench, was blanketed with our tags. Picking a tag was an important and definitive thing. It was like going on a Native American vision quest and coming back with a spirit animal. Except without any redeeming spiritual lessons. Or emotional journey. Actually maybe it wasn't like a vision quest at all. But once a tag was chosen, it became your identity, and your nom de plume represented you on every bus in the East Bay.

We *always* sat at the back of the bus. We did it for Rosa Parks. No, we did it to get away with tagging. Every time we jumped on the bus, someone would pass around a Magnum marker with a fat tip or a streaker, a grease paint pen that was nearly impossible to clean off a window once it dried. If we didn't have one of those tools, we went more lo-tech—shoe polish bottles with big round sponges soaked in black polish that would drip down from the letters we drew on the windows of the bus, weeping for the lack of artistic skill we employed. Or we would scratch our tags into the windows with sandpaper-tipped drill bits we called scribes. Anything we could do to get our names up. Did I mention that I was absolutely terrible at graffiti? I was. It was a source of deep shame, but I ignored it daily and tagged the hell out of Oakland anyway. Graffiti exists in two realms: quality and quantity.

Being a brilliant artist would get you respect and admiration, but if you only drew beautiful pieces in your sketchbook, you might as well have not existed. I tried every day to figure out how to draw old-school, New York subway–style murals, but I only ever managed to draw something that looked like very edgy piles of vomit. So I decided to go with option two. Bomb the village. Literally. I wrote my name everywhere I could. Every second I was out on the town was one where I scribbled my tag on whatever surface I could. I took a great pride in walking through my neighborhood and seeing my defacing tags staring back at me.

The P.A.G. had morphed into a graffiti crew called UCF, or Unconvicted Felons. Why people were so obsessed with out-

CITY OF PIEDMONT
Police Department

403 Highland Ave.
Piedmont, CA 94611
(510) 420-3010
Fax (510) 420-3002

Chief of Police

March 28, 1994

Mrs. Worthen
4407 Piedmont Ave.
Oakland, CA 94610

Dear Mrs. Worthen;

On 03/22/94 at 4:30pm, your son, Mark Kasher, was issued a Minor
Offender Program (M.O.P.) citation case #94-0221. The citation
was issued for a violation of 594PC, of the California Penal
Code, for vandalism. The victim, John Hellman 72 Wildwood Ave.,
wishes to drop charges against your son.

At the request of the victim, the Piedmont Police Department has
dropped the 594PC vandalism charge. Please disregard the
citation that you have received for your son.

If you have any questions about this case #94-0221, please call
me at 420-3015.

Sincerely

Detective ████████████
Piedmont Police Department

ADDRESS ALL CORRESPONDENCE TO THE OFFICE OF THE CHIEF OF POLICE

law acronyms back then is beyond me. Most graffiti crews had
one. There was 640, a crew named after the penal code for vandalism; AS, or Altered States; the LORDS crew; and our rivals, BSK.
Well, really, it wasn't much of a rivalry. BSK was a crew from the
neighborhood next to ours and truly a much more powerful entity

than we ever could have hoped to be. With deep connections to Mexican gangs in East Oakland, they were a legitimately fearsome group of kids. If only we had known that before we started talking shit. Someone in UCF had somehow crossed out one of their tags that showed up in our neighborhood. To us it was a display of our neighborhood dominance. To BSK, it was a declaration of war. We were totally ready for war until they arrived, an entire bus full of scary-looking kids from grades above us.

The mob gathered in front of Claremont with bats and bottles, ready to rumble. We took one look at the army in front of the school and snuck out the back way, immediately disbanding the UCF. We reconstituted ourselves into a new, war-free crew called SS, or Simply Savage.

I then suggested that we not have an acronym that shared its name with the Nazi secret police and we changed again to IA, or Illegal Art. We were perhaps not the most loyal to our crew's name, but we were certainly dedicated to the idea of graffiti. One day, we even climbed into a subway tunnel and risked our lives for it.

Tunnels are amazing. The act of man boring a tunnel through a mountain is a feat of human ingenuity that's pretty incredible to think about. It's so powerfully penetrative, it's almost sexual. (In fact, whenever I see a woman these days, I think, "Man, I'd love to fortify her walls and use a boring machine to grind out a passageway that would allow transit to and from her ovaries.")

There is and was something dangerous and exciting about the dark mystery of the subway tunnel, and it didn't help that we had one staring at us from the mountain that separated Oakland from the Contra Costa County suburbs. We often stared at the opening of that tunnel from the other side of the fence and wondered what mysteries lay within.

One day we found out. DJ heard a rumor of a small room about a mile down the main tunnel that the BART train tore through.

"A fucking room! A little fucking room!" DJ drooled, his tongue working slower than his head once again.

I wasn't sure why we should be impressed. "I mean, aren't we in a room right now? What's the big deal?"

"The big deal is your fat belly, you little bitch." DJ always became somewhat more articulate when he was finding a way to call me fat.

Of course, this was a bit unfair. Fat teens don't really have "fat bellies." It takes years of harrumphing, beer-swilling and Salisbury steak, "gotta get away from my wife" nights to grow a big fat man tummy. What I had was a soft boyish gel body. Pink puff tits and hairless "never had love" handles. The Lakota Sioux called me, "Swims with a T-shirt." I wasn't actually fat, I was undefined. The problem with DJ was that he didn't appreciate nuance.

"You are a fat bitch!"

"Don't I know it!" I shot back, settling into a familiar game. "I actually met your mom at the fat bitch support group I go to."

DJ, out of options, punched me in the chest.

"It'll be dope!" DJ continued, hardly noticing me rocking in the corner weeping. "We can shoot over the fence and we just have to walk single file down into that room and see what's in there. Plus, it's all virgin walls in there, and we could tag the whole fucking place up. Who's in?"

I didn't want to say what I was thinking, which was that I was scared, so instead I just grunted in a manner I imagined sounded both tough and noncommittal.

Donny, the plan maker, the brains behind our brainless operation, appeared lost in thought. I stared at him, trying to psychically will him to nix the plan, and it looked like he was just about to when he cocked his head to the side and said, "I've got weed. We could smoke in there."

Preparations began immediately.

We tromped up to the entrance of the BART tunnel silently, as if trudging toward a battlefield we knew could be filled with Vietcong.

Villagers ran up to us as we passed by, a single-file sentinel.

"You no go der!" they screamed, blessing us with incense. "Tunnel real bad, many enemy! American never return!"

But we soldiered on.

We arrived at the barbed-wire cyclone fencing and took in the signage placed there to warn kids like us against things like this. There were signs everywhere:

STOP! EXTREME DANGER IN TUNNEL!

NO, SERIOUSLY, THIS IS A BAD IDEA.

FUCK IT THEN, I GUESS YOU ARE GONNA DIE.

Ignoring the signs, we jumped past the razor wire and through truncheons of secondary security walls and finally we stood at the mouth of the tunnel, an expanse of blackness swallowing itself into the mountain.

This was not a good idea.

DJ, perhaps too dumb to be afraid, broke the silence, turning to me and saying, "Fats, you at the end of the line. You'll slow us down."

Fats complied.

We began our little march into the tunnel on an emergency

platform barely a foot wide, feeling the wall for reassurance, putting one foot in front of the other.

I tried to keep in step with everyone else from the back of the line, but I could feel the emptiness of the tunnel drilling into my head from behind. I would have pissed myself if not for the electric third rail threatening execution.

We got about a quarter of a mile in, far enough that we couldn't see the light from where we had entered, when something odd happened.

The air behind us got warm and then sucked away, like a vacuum hose had been clipped onto the other end of the tunnel.

We stopped in our fucking tracks.

The ground beneath us started rumbling and from the darkness two bright eyes blinked hello. We heard the loud, screaming, distorted beep of the train conductor blowing his horn.

Someone screamed what, at this point, was only too obvious: "TRAIN!!!!"

Even as I heard that, all sound disappeared and then the train was there, shooting past us at what seemed like the speed of light. *Woosh Woosh Woosh Woosh,* the train flew by our faces, inches away. Had I been a little more Jewish in the nose, I might've lost it.

Despite shaking with fear, I felt a kind of calm. I peered into the windows of the train going by, and I could see the shocked faces of people on their commute home, their minds clearly not ready to have pubescent teenage eyes peering back at them from the darkness.

I became sort of hypnotized by these people, sitting there, commuting home, living their lives while flying by, when the screeching of the brakes jolted me out of my calm.

The train had come to a complete stop in the middle of the tunnel and from the front car I saw the conductor leaning out of his window, his brain trying to compute the information he was receiving, a group of teenage boys standing in a death trap.

In the moment of pause, Donny got his head straight, and from the front of the line he screamed, *"Run!"* We ran.

Now here, an unfortunate thing happened. When everybody flipped around to run out of the tunnel back from whence we came, guess who was now first in line? That's right, Fat Ass.

I ran as fast as my fat ass could take me, but it was hardly fair. I was shaking with adrenaline and there was a back draft from the train still blowing against me. This was a "worst-case scenario."

From behind me in the faceless dark I could hear dearest DJ screaming, *"Run, you fat bitch, run!"* I ran against the wind, against the shame, against my body. I ran like that.

It was like some kind of twisted, bizzaro scene from *Stand by Me*, except the only lesson at the end was that weed trumps life.

As the light from the tunnel opened up into the world, I turned back to see Donny had actually jumped down onto the tracks and was searching for something.

"Donny, what the *fuck* are you doing?" I asked frantically.

"I dropped the weed!" he yelled back, as if that made perfect sense.

"Are you kidding me? You have to get out of there."

Donny looked up at me like I had just said the stupidest thing in the world. "Dude, it's weed."

No argument from me.

I leaned down and helped Donny out of the tracks but only after he had a baggy clinched in his hand. Trembling, we climbed over the fence and a few minutes later were crouched in a wooden play structure together and silently smoking. As the weed and the fear and the adrenaline mixed together, we couldn't help but wonder what that little room looked like. I still wish we'd made it.

❧

The best part of joining these guys wasn't just making friends, but joining a world. I had a secret life no one knew about. At first, my mother was happy to let me go and to stay out as late as I wanted just because she was so happy that I'd made friends. Of course, my friends and I were not learning how to tie knots for the Boy Scouts and help old ladies across the street. We were learning how to kick some ass.

I had my first drunken fight. Everybody should have one. I firmly believe that everyone should get punched in the face at least once in their life. It builds character. Getting your ass kicked teaches you that your body isn't a glass menagerie figurine that could shatter at any trauma. You gotta get lumped up sometimes. Then heal and know you are all right.

I got whopped as a kid. Big leather belts on my bare ass. Fuck it. My dad used to drag me around by my ears and twist them when I talked shit, which I realize now was a true cruelty, not because of some physical abuse issue, but because I'm already Jewish with floppy-ass Dumbo ears, and for my dad to pull on them was, well, it was anti-Semitic. Fuckin' Jew.

But back to my point. Getting punched in the face is good for you. Unless you get punched in the face too many times or too hard, and then it stops being good for you and mashes your brain into soup. But getting your ass kicked is generally a learning experience. And this night, I was the professor. Don't get me wrong. This isn't some "I'm the man" bravado. I've been in many fights and I've lost most of them. But this night I was the victor and it felt amazing.

To my credit, the motherfucker was talking shit. It was late at night, and a bunch of us were drinking on the upper field at the elementary school that Donny lived near. Donny was there and DJ and this kid Brian, whom you could never quite trust not to get violent. Some people just communicate in violence. Brian liked to strike. He wasn't a gangster, he didn't have guns. He just liked to strike.

The first time I tried nitrous oxide, I was with Brian. Donny knew Brian from back in the day. They had gone to camp together at Camp Winnarainbow, the hippie camp owned by that famous hippie clown Wavy Gravy.

Brian was a long-haired Hessian type. We all went down to Safeway late one night and stuffed cans full of whipped cream into our pants and walked out smiling in anticipation of the dessert party we were about to have. To me, it's cute to think of thirteen-year-olds using something as innocent as whipped cream to get high with. It seems the perfect thirteen-year-old party drug. Get high and have hot cocoa after.

Later, up in Donny's room, they told me what to do. "Crack it and suck it into your lungs," Brian explained, the excitement flickering in his eyes. "Take as much as you can and hold it in." I did as instructed. I peeled off the plastic ring from the spigot and pulled it toward me. The trick with whipped cream cans is not to shake them. You shake, you get a mouth full of cream. I cracked the thing and breathed in big. The rush of gas filled my chest and I held on to it. In about two seconds, my brain began to rattle and shake and the hippie crack started to do its duty. Nitrous oxide makes a sound. The *wah wah wah wah* sound you hear in your brain when nitrous hits is what we used to call the sound your brain cells make when they die. The death knell of your poor little brain wondering what it ever did to hurt you. So I sucked in big and listened to the symphony of death going on in my brain that first time I puffed nitrous, and just then, just as my mind started to go mush and the ecstasy of the gas took over... *bam!* Brian, in his loveliness, punched me, as hard as he could, in the chest. When I think back on that night, I still have no clue what he was doing or why he decided that that was the right time for me to be assaulted. I do remember that I didn't feel a thing and I laughed for twenty minutes about it.

So Brian was there on the upper field, polishing his brass knuckles or eating gunpowder or whatever someone like that does. And Donny was there and DJ and a bunch of other kids. And Gary.

Gary was a bitch. At least we called him that. I'm sure right now he's a lawyer or a postal worker or a bank teller. I bet he's a family man with love in his heart for his two daughters, Castanella and Deflores. He's a saint, too. Deflores was born with an extra eyebrow, but it never stopped Gary from loving her. I bet he prays at night and donates to charity. I bet he never jerks off and thinks of all races equally. I'm sure Gary is amazing. But to me, he'll always just be a little bitch.

And like a bitch, he talked some shit that night. I don't know what. But I know it was too much for me to bear and I attacked him. I jumped on top of Gary and started pummeling him for the injustice I can't even remember now. I punched him and punched him. I punched him so many times, my sweatshirt worked its way over my head and I was tied up in it. So I took it off and kept punching him. Then all of a sudden from my left, good 'ol Brian ran up and kicked Gary in the head with his steel-toed Hessian boots so hard I thought he killed him. It scared the shit out of me, but I guess Brian's violence had its advantages, too. Let him punch you in the chest, and he'll kick your enemies in the head. Seemed like a fair trade to me.

Gary made it, by the way. He didn't die. Later that night we drank together. I put my arm around him and told him, with a sensitivity far beyond my thirteen years, "It's okay, bro, no hard feelings, just don't act like such a bitch."

The kind of wisdom that I imparted to Gary was coming to me as a result of my exposure to this new drug-fueled consciousness. I walked around convinced that I had some private information that had been kept from the rest of the squares in the world. When I'd walk by a grizzled old hippie or a Rastafarian-looking man, I'd grin and nod my head as if to say, "Hello! Pot smoker here, too. I get it!" Lots of confused looks ensued, but I paid them no mind.

⚜

My mother finally saved enough money to get us our own place, and we moved next door to a bar called the King's X, a local hangout for the worst people possible. We had a metal bat that lived at our front door, and I couldn't possibly tell you the number of times I had to run outside with that fucking thing and bang it on the ground to scare off some awful mess pissing on my front door or some disgusting trolls fucking in the weeds next to the house. People loved to pull up to the King's X and rev their engines for forty-five minutes and play the latest Dr. Dre track at the highest volume possible without ripping through the space-time continuum. The bass would shake the house, rattling the windows and keeping me up at night. How lucky my mother was to be deaf. How awful our landlords were to rent her this place and not mention the decibel level her two hearing sons would have to deal with. We got used to it.

My little rickety house was stationed about a mile from the Rockridge BART station, the home base for me and my friends. One mile. So far. I was fat and lazy and hated to walk. I slumped myself over to the 59A bus stop and waited for the bus to come. I loved to hitchhike. I honestly don't know why, but every time I'd sit there, I'd throw my thumb up and start asking people if they were going my way. You think I could get a ride?

Most people stared straight ahead as if they were deaf, at which point I would sign to them, "Can I get a ride?" and laugh to myself. Only to myself. This little life of mine.

There are moments in a life that make you think maybe there's a thread of meaning through this bumbling little experience. Seconds and inches that peel open the epidermis of the universe to reveal the intricate nervous system of interconnectivity that lies within. Things that make you say, "There might be something to this God thing after all." Little God moments.

My God moment puttered up to me in a 1970 Datsun 510. It was a rusty thing with primer-gray-splotted rough blue paint. A little wagon that looked like it was going to self-destruct into a thousand pieces at any second. It pulled up and stopped right in front of my bus stop.

Inside was a hippie angel. I mean this guy looked like a fucking R. Crumb character. A Frank Zappa of a man with dirty curly hair cascading down his shoulders, gray streaks flecking his bushiness, showing his age. Next to him was a man ripped from a Jimi Hendrix concert photo, a withered old hippie wanderer whose leather headband might not have been removed for years. A thousand years, a million. *Namaste.*

Zappa turned his head to me and smiled. A big, white greedy smile. All love. I did my hand like, "Roll down the window."

The Man-Buddha complied.

"Hey," I said.

"Hey, brother!"

We were brothers.

"You guys heading to Rockridge BART?" I knew the answer.

"We are now!"

Zappa popped the door open and slid his seat forward. "Jump in."

I leapt.

Some people just won't understand these things.

I could sense the electric current in the air. Feel the power.

I sat down on the lamb's-wool seat cover. No introductions were made. None were needed. We'd known each other forever, life-times.

Led Zeppelin was blaring from the 8-track stereo.

Of course it was.

Was I in the past?

"Hey, brother, you smoke?" The Hendrix Experience handed me a fat beautiful joint. Filled with adult weed.

"Do I!" I sucked in, hard. I coughed out, harder.

"Easy there, brother!" Zappa laughed.

Adult weed!

Somehow, no matter how good the weed was back then, some trick of nature or special club allowed the adults to get the best weed in the world. Parents' stashes were filled with otherworldly shit. Crystal-crusted Indica and Maui Wowie, the best shit.

Only one thing was more powerful than adult weed. Adult *hippie* weed. Oh Lord, give me strength!

I smoked that joint and passed it back to Zappa, who put his hand up in supplication like Jesus.

"No way, keep smoking, you only have it for a mile, we smoke all day." He laughed like Santa. He laughed like the Buddha. He laughed like the universe.

I sat there, laughing, smoking. My mouth turned into a desert. The desiccating hand of cottonmouth swabbed my tongue, and just at that moment, when I could take no more, Hendrix turned back to me and smiled.

"Hey, you want a beer?"

"I'd love one. Nothing sounds better."

He handed me a Red Hook Extra Special Bitter. My favorite nice beer. I never drank nice beer. But today I drank like an alcoholic king.

The malt washed away my dryness. Hops washed away my sins.

We pulled up to BART, my mind blown, my joint cashed, my beer drunk. What a ten minutes.

I oozed out of the car and said my good-byes. Zappa pulled out a pack of smokes.

"Oh my God. Are those Newports?"

Newports. My cigarette. My favorite. Not a common smoke of the hippie. More a staple of the ... well, you know.

This couldn't be.

A FUCKING NEWPORT?!?

"Yeah, brother, you want one?"

"I'd love one." I trembled as a tear welled up in my eye.

"Here you go!"

Zappa handed me a smoke and I stared at it, waiting to wake up in Kansas.

I looked up.

The Datsun was gone.

The greatest moment in my life had passed. I lit the Newport and offered it to the Great Spirit.

I smoked in enlightenment.

If only every day were like this.

Of course, it wasn't. That moment was the best life could ever be for me. The pinnacle. The peak of my experience in the new drugged world I'd entered. I'd look back on that car ride over the years and wish I could go back. But, of course, right after the peak begins the descent.

❧

Back at Claremont, I walked the halls with a newfound confidence. The Jonos and Naomis of the world no longer seemed so attractive. The black kids no longer seemed so intimidating. Especially so for the real gangsters of the bunch. By and large, they got high, too, so at least in my mind, we shared some kind of understanding and kinship.

I, much like all teenagers who start getting high, *loved* the iconography of weed. I drew pot leaves everywhere. The fact that this was incriminating never occurred to me, as I imagined that no one but me and "my people" even knew what a pot leaf looked like. I figured those square bears would just think I was really into Canada. I remember I drew a huge one on my folder for Portable Three, and when I pulled it out, a girl from class leaned over, stole a glance, and whispered to her friend, "Damn, this white boy crazy."

My heart swelled with pride and I beamed. "He sure is..." I thought. "He sure is."

To be thought of as crazy was just fine with me. At least that pulled me out of the anonymous few white faces at Claremont. I was known. I was different.

Donny came up to me at lunch with Jamie and DJ. "Meet us out by the BART parking lot after school, we have to show you something."

Jamie leaned in and licked his lips. "It's a really good something!"

After school, I met the guys and they spoke in hushed tones. We quickly retreated into a bush that we had hollowed out in the back of the BART parking lot. Joey was in there waiting for us. Joey only came around these days when semi-serious things were happening. He was too old and too connected at this point to waste his time with kid shit. This must've been important.

In the bush, we were essentially hidden and could do the kinds of top-secret archcriminal stuff that is normally done in bushes.

Donny smiled and pulled out a handful of paper. "This is—"

"Paper!" I blurted out.

DJ the brute gave me a menacing look.

I blanched. "Right, sorry, go ahead, Donny."

"It's white blotter acid." Donny seemed intoxicated just holding the stuff. "And it's the beginning of our empire."

I was confused. "We have an empire?"

Donny started ripping out hits of acid, one at a time.

He handed one to me.

"The empire"—Donny pointed at his forehead—"starts in here. Put it on your tongue."

I did as I was told.

I'd heard about acid. My mother told me about her experiences as a young woman in the sixties, how she ate acid and the world melted. It was meant to be a cautionary tale, but all I thought during that conversation was, "I'm gonna try that someday."

Today was the day, I guessed. Tuesday afternoon at three thirty was as good a time as any for a thirteen-year-old to drop acid.

Jamie took his into his mouth and told us, "I once did acid with my grandpa, he had a pure LSD crystal in his office, and he handed it to me one day after I shot a deer. He licked it and told me to lick it. I was high for a week."

As one, we all rolled our eyes.

Donny, always a little bit more spiritual than the rest of us, gave me a little pep talk.

"You're gonna go places in your mind you never even knew were places, so don't fight it, just go with it." I swallowed my dose and began waiting for it to hit me.

We hung out for a bit just talking and smoking and I didn't feel much of anything. Donny told me to just relax and wait.

All of a sudden I felt a little tickle in my stomach, like a nausea, but not terribly unpleasant. I told Jamie.

"That's it, man, it's coming. That's the strychnine."

Strychnine is rat poison. It is said to be put into LSD to make it stronger—the poison was seen as some kind of hard-core badge of honor.

Jamie leaned into me. "Rat poison, that's what it is. It makes the shit even more powerful, but if you take too much, it could paralyze you."

Donny told Jamie to shut the fuck up.

"Don't listen to that shit. This is pure white blotter. As clean as it gets. No strychnine, no nothin'. Quit talkin' like that, man, you'll freak him out."

Jamie wouldn't be stopped. "Also try real hard not to think of the impending nature of death or losing your mind. That's a sure-fire way to never make it back from your trip."

"What do you mean, not make it back?"

"After I licked that crystal my grandfather gave me, I spent two months in a forest, convinced I was a bear, living on nothing but berries and moss. I only made it back because my dad organized a search party and rescued me." Jamie had a far-off look in his eyes and started grunting like a bear.

"Now I know you're lying. Your dad doesn't love you enough to look for you," Donny shot at Jamie, annoyed. He looked at me. "Let's bounce. We gotta go handle some business."

Me! Donny was taking me to handle business!

Donny and the guys were constantly doing just that, *handling business*, a kind of generic term for "doing something that you don't need to know about."

We left Jamie behind with his cautionary tales and hopped on the bus to Berkeley with Frohawk, the sewer dweller. Joey walked with us to the bus stop, and just before we took off, he handed Donny a fat wad of cash.

"Don't fuck up," he said to Donny and then looked at me. "And keep an eye on this kid, man, he's just about to jump into the deep end." Joey winked at me again and walked off. We climbed onto the bus, and my mind started to warp into its trip.

The world followed behind me in slow motion. The outer reaches of my vision wove themselves into a detailed three-dimensional maze, and the patterns in the makeup of the city revealed themselves to me. I stared at a square inch of the bus seat's fabric, the intricacies of its stitching calling out to me as it moved and pulsated like a handful of worms. We got off the bus right in front of UC Berkeley. This was about the time my mind exploded.

It occurred to me that none of the information being disseminated in the classes held in the buildings behind me mattered in comparison to the knowledge that was being leaked into my mind, *from* my mind, by the ruptured pipeline in my brain. A system that had, apparently, been designed to keep this kind of flush of understanding from me, lest I be driven mad by the things I saw.

I vaguely realized that I was alone and that, somehow, Donny and Frohawk had gone away; I just couldn't figure out why I should care. I did care about my mother, of that I was pretty sure. And she would be home in about five hours, so I knew I had better go to her. I walked home from the UC Berkeley campus, a four-mile walk, mostly because I couldn't remember what a bus was. I got home and realized that I'd lost my house keys on my way home and so I sat on my front step, staring at the inside of my eyelids, my head in my hands, for hours. By the time my mother made it home, I'd collected myself to enough of a degree that cohesive thoughts were possible again, so I just spent the rest of the evening telling my mother how much I loved her and the various ramifications of the deeper meaning of love. For most parents this kind of an odd interaction would be a red flag, but for my mom, it was exactly what she had been waiting for, and it made her psychoanalyzed heart swell with pride. "He finally gets it!" she thought. And that was true, I finally did.

When I finally came down, my body ached but my mind felt sharper than it ever had. The next day at school, I finally hooked back up with Donny.

"There you are, what the fuck happened to you yesterday?" I

said. I was furious at having been left alone, although I couldn't say for certain how and why that had happened.

Donny just laughed and told me, "We left you on the steps and went to go handle some business. When we got back, you were gone. So what happened to *you*?"

I sighed. "I don't really know."

After that day, I started eating acid constantly. I'd drop acid in the morning before gym class and float the day away. Morning classes were spent staring at my fingernails and the white roots of my nails doing loop-the-loops, swimming by like fish in a tiny aquarium. At lunch, the boys and I looked for one another, as our faces were the only ones that looked normal. We ate acid the way we smoked pot. All the time. There were no powwows of psychedelic healing. We dropped acid because there was nothing else to do. We never did anything cool on acid. I remember watching *The Doors* movie, and when Jim Morrison and the band went to the desert to eat peyote, I thought, "You can go places when you get high?" We would drop acid and hang around the subway station or go to class or go write graffiti. Urban psychedelia.

We ripped off slices of white blotter and made our world enjoyable. White blotter. Little white pages blowing my mind apart. The bad part about mind-expanding drugs when you are thirteen years old is that there really isn't much to expand upon.

"Did you ever notice *canibus* is spelled cani-BUS?" I asked Donny one night, lying in his bed, the Cream *Disraeli Gears* cassette autoreversing to the beginning of the album for the twentieth time.

"Fucking, we should start a cani-BUS where people could ride the bus like regular but they could smoke weed, too. The CANI-BUS!"

Donny was blown away by my entrepreneurial genius. "Whoa. Wait, isn't it spelled *cannabis*?"

I changed the subject.

We started to become legends with the acid. Joey and Donny had been impressed with the strain of acid they had given me and returned to the source of it to buy many sheets more. I and the rest of the guys were about to turn the empire of our minds into a much more real world drug empire. We set up shop at Claremont and word spread quickly. People knew who we were and admired/feared us. The black drug dealers wanted nothing to do with "that white boy acid." Because we weren't seen as being in direct competition with them, they allowed us to peddle our wares in peace. Kids from other schools would cut class and come and buy blotter. Dysfunctional children from far-off lands such as Berkeley and San Francisco would load up their donkeys and make the long trek to the promised land of Oakland, where wise men were offering enlightenment for three dollars a hit. The money flowed, and we lived like boy-kings. That is, until Justin Sabbaro came along and fucked everything up with his weak-ass heart.

Part THREE:
Fun with
Problems

Chapter 8

"Things Done Changed"
—Biggie Smalls

This fat seventh grader walked up to us one day interested in stepping into a brave new world.

"Hello, I would like to purchase some LSD, please."

"Name?"

A nervous look around. A fat sweaty-brow wipe. Nothing too out of the ordinary. This was a sketchy world we were introducing kids to.

"Justin Sabarro."

"Age?"

"Twelve."

"Perfect. LSD is an amazing mind-expanding drug that costs three dollars, won't find more bang for your buck anywhere. Transports you to another world, drippy walls, profound ideas, all that shit. Here you are and enjoy!"

Little Justin popped a dose into his mouth in ignorant bliss.

Oops, one thing I forgot to tell him, "Oh, and don't take LSD if you have a weak mind, dead parents, or a history of heart problems."

He looked up, clutched his chest. "Heart problems?"

Well, I wish I'd warned him like that. I didn't. Justin Sabarro ate the acid, and fucked everything up.

Up until that point, my mother was desperately seeking information about just how bad she could sense I was becoming. At home, things were a chaotic mess, mostly due to me. If she had been able to piece together what I was doing at school, she would have rung the alarm bell much earlier, but thankfully, I, for the most part, was able to keep her from that information.

Partially this was because, due to apathy and financial restrictions, I was used as the conduit to relay information to my deaf mother.

At first, Oakland Public Schools didn't want to hire interpreters, and so I was allowed the rare and inane privilege of sitting in on and interpreting my own parent-teacher conferences. This was to become a pattern, and no matter how far down the ladder I seemed to crawl, it didn't seem far enough to warrant the school system's breaking the bank on an interpreter. It took years until they woke up to what I was doing and sprang for what should have been an obvious thing. I got really good at it, too. Not at interpreting, mind you, but at subtly changing the message I was hearing and giving it over to my mother in such a way that she was never quite getting the real story.

"Mrs. Kasher, your son has been truant an unacceptable amount of days this semester." The vice principal's voice rose to a yell in the hopes that my mother would hear at least part of it.

I would look right at my mother and sign, "Mrs. Kasher, while your son has *not yet* been truant what I'd call an unacceptable amount of days this semester, we *are* concerned that he not make a pattern of it."

I'd always give *some* of the real information, lest my mom just grin back at the vice principal and give a thumbs-up. She needed to look concerned enough not to arouse the curiosity of the teachers, and they needed to look satisfied enough with her answers not to make her smack me. It needed to *look* like what they'd said so that her lip-reading eyes wouldn't suspect anything. A very delicate balance. I was a master. Often my mother and I would walk out of a meeting discussing how weird the faculty at Claremont was, how very paranoid.

Then came Justin Sabarro and I couldn't ease the blow. His arteries blew open the doors of denial that I had been welding shut with misinformation. How could I deliver this message? "A boy here has a very big heart. Very loving! So loving that love literally explodes all over... Oh, forget it, his heart exploded." I was fucked.

Justin was a fat kid in the seventh grade. At the time, the white kids in the lower grades looked up to us like we were gods. We were eighth graders and we were bad. We were like a rumbling pack of greasers, except we all thought we were black, so leather motorcycle jackets were strictly out of the question.

At this point, school attendance was mostly optional, and Donny and I and the boys had become more of a burden than anything else to the faculty at Claremont. The black gangsters and crack dealers, the Mexican gangbangers, and the white fuckups. We had arrived. Officer Joe made regular stops at the school to fuck with us.

Mostly this was just to scare us and to keep the administration at Claremont feeling like something was being done about us. He would saunter onto campus, walk right up to us in the yard, and stick his snout into our business.

"Hey, you assholes thinking about cutting class again?"

I hated this guy. "I was thinking about it, you know any good spots?"

"I'll be watching for you," he'd say, sneering at us.

"Is that Dirty Harry or Charles Bronson you're pretending to be right now? It's very convincing!" I never did know when to shut up.

Things changed dramatically when Justin fucked everything up. The stakes got raised all of a sudden, and it wasn't something we were ready for.

Donny pulled me aside in the hall one day. "I'm fucked, man. That kid Justin had a fucking heart attack."

It seemed hard to believe. This tiny piece of paper had somehow short-circuited a kid's fragile little coronary system. This drug that had introduced me to the power of my mind had introduced him to the weakness of his heart. Anyway, there was little need to figure out how to believe it—Donny was standing in front of me, looking like he was working on a heart attack of his own. He was scared.

I'd never seen Donny without a kind of layer of protective gangsterism. Donny had always been the kind of person who walked through the world at ease. He seemed older than us all just because he was cool. People flocked to him for that reason and they worshiped him without knowing it. It was mostly because he was never afraid and always knew what the fuck to do.

"I don't know what the fuck to do." He looked scared.

Not good. He's asking me? He's my guide to things like this. "Um. I don't know either, dude."

We were all kind of stuck on stupid. Luckily Justin made our next step pretty easy to figure out.

Nikki, a girl Donny had been going out with on and off for months, went to visit Justin, to make sure he was okay.

"He tried to rape me!" she reported back to us after the visit.

How about that Justin, huh? Weak of heart, strong of dick. We paid Justin a visit that day. Heart attack or not, he got beat down by Donny while Jamie stood back, yelling about the Crips he would call if anything like this happened again. After that, Justin disappeared from Claremont and from Oakland altogether.

The Justin thing changed everything, however. Everyone's eyes were instantly on us. We changed overnight from invisible white boys to "those guys." Mrs. Hojo, the principal at Claremont, pulled us in, one by one, to ask about our connection to Sir Justin the Weakhearted.

I went in close to the end of the interrogation session after DJ had drooled all over her desk and Jamie had regaled her with tales of his childhood in Guatemala shucking coca plants for his uncle Pablo. Jamie and I locked eyes as he walked out and I walked in. The look said it all: "Keep your fucking mouth shut." Easy. I'd been lying to therapists all my life. Principals were a piece of cake.

"Hello, Mr. Kasher." She peered at me from behind a stereotypically principalish pair of horn-rimmed eyeglasses.

"Hello, Mr. Hojo ... Sorry, *Mrs.* Hojo ... Sorry, I'm nervous."

"It's okay. Take a deep breath and tell me what you know about Justin Sabarro."

My pudgy cheeks went rosy, I looked five years younger. "Is that the man who had a heart attack?"

Mrs. Hojo did not look amused. "The *boy*, yes. Did you sell him the LSD?"

"LSD? Is that like what the hippies took at Woodstock?"

She knew she was being worked. A look of anger flashed across her face. I'd won.

"You can go now. I'll be calling your mother about this."

I smiled. "She's deaf, but would you like me to relay a message?"

"I'll call your grandmother then; just get out of my office."

I winked at Donny as he took my place in the interrogation room. Maybe this thing was gonna blow over after all.

A few weeks later I was ambushed.

The UCSF Center on Deafness was my mother's home base. A center focused on my mother's two great loves: deaf equality and psychological diagnoses. Joy. I'd been in analysis at that point for eight years and I was only thirteen.

I got sent to analyst after analyst until at one point I was in therapy eight times a week. Individual therapy, behavioral counseling, group therapy, and my mother's favorite: family therapy.

Our family therapist, Dr. Patty Susan, was a typical deaf fetishist. A hearing therapist fresh out of school with a dual degree in deaf studies and psychotherapy. People like this *worship* the deaf. These are the people who stop you in the streets to exclaim how beautiful sign language is, unaware that you just signed, "The roast beef gave me twelve hours of explosive diarrhea."

Every week's session was essentially an hour of Dr. Susan pointing out what a martyr my poor deaf mother was and what an asshole I was. To be fair, she was right. I *was* an asshole. The deeper into my little world I got, the more concrete my mother's everlasting fear of something being wrong with me was made manifest. I was now the problem child my mother had always suspected I'd become. Strangely, the worse I became, the more deeply into her own neurosis my mother dove.

My mother has always been a frantic, emotional waterfall of a woman. She wielded emotions like weaponry. Love was her shield; guilt was her sword. The more I rebelled, the more completely she tried to swallow me whole. She lived on my chest. When I became old enough that I could no longer wear the literal leash she tied around me when I was a baby, she began to work on weaving an emotional leash. That one I couldn't chew through. It was forged out of strong stuff. She had a kind of psychic link to me that I just couldn't shake. If I snuck out at night, my mother would wake up the next morning with my absence palpable in her brain, vibrating like Spidey sense. Somehow she always knew when I wasn't there. To be fair, I left a lot. Having a deaf mother makes sneaking out of the house a rather simple affair. Actually it wasn't really sneaking as much as just leaving in the middle of the night. I could tramp and stomp and break-dance if I so desired. I left almost every night. Unfortunately, often I would sneak over to a friend's house and drink a bit too much and pass out. When I'd pass out, drunk on DJ or Donny's couch, I could count on, at seven in the morning, being shocked awake by desperate banging on the front door. I'd shoot awake and sigh as the realization that my crazy mother had tracked me down sank in. I'd stumble to the car with her and try to ignore the trouble I was in. My mother would reach over and pat my leg, pretending to be reassuring me that everything would be all right but, in fact, patting me down for cigarettes or drugs. If she felt the hard square of a pack of smokes, she would, one hand still on the steering wheel, clinch her hand down, hard, on the pack in my pocket, trying to snap my smokes in two. I'd pull away and scream in rage, and the car would careen across lanes of traffic as we wrestled and struggled.

My mother's insanity just compounded the deep mistrust and

resentment I had for all the other adults surrounding me. I was a ball of hate. Of course, you could have split that ball in half and seen the white-hot magma core of fear. That's what was really driving me. I didn't really hate them, I really hated myself. I felt worthless, broken, and terrified. Then again, I couldn't have told you that. All I knew was that I was angry. The complex language of suffering and fear bewildered me when I heard it coming from inside me. I couldn't express it, I couldn't translate it. To me it just sounded like snarls and screams, so that's what I spoke in. Maybe I wasn't an asshole after all. Maybe I just couldn't figure out how to stop acting like one.

One day, I arrived with my mother to my weekly family therapy session hardly armed for battle. I'd forgotten to wear socks that morning. Maybe if I'd remembered, I never would've been put away. I was ill prepared for the escape to the streets. Damn those socks! I walked into Dr. Susan's office and knew immediately that something was off. Maybe I could just smell the coffee breath of the cop sitting in the office. This wasn't going to be a normal therapy session.

"So," Dr. Susan started in on me, not making any mention of the huge black cop in the room, "your mother told me you and your friends sold LSD to a boy who had a heart attack. How did that make you feel?"

"Heartbroken?" I said, the paragon of compassion. "How should it make me feel? I don't know, it wasn't me who had a heart attack."

Her eyebrow twitched and I could feel her set her clinical phasers to kill mode and gear up.

"And have you taken LSD?"

This was the time for evasive maneuvers, but the best I could come up with was, "Me? No. No...I just sell it. Er...sold it. I used to sell it."

Unconvinced, the good doctor said, "And do you take other drugs?"

"No."

"So if I took a urine sample from you right now, it would be totally clean?"

The cop laughed as she said this, and I imagined shooting his scalp off and seeing a brain made of stuck-together donut holes fall to the floor.

I thought quickly. "Okay...I've been in a car maybe...you know what hot boxing is? People smoking out the car? I might've gotten exposed that way."

Doc thought quicker. "So if we tested for LSD, then, that would be negative?"

"Look," I said, scrambling through my scrambled brain for something to throw the dogs off the scent, "I've been in a car maybe...you know what forced dosing is? Where hippies tie you up with hemp rope and rub whetted LSD crystals on your lymph nodes and genitals as a retaliatory action for deals gone wrong? I might've gotten exposed that way."

The cop laughed again.

Dr. Susan shifted her ass in the seat, hunkering down for the assassin shot. "Well, we can't even check for LSD, but thanks for the story. Do you drink?"

I could feel the walls closing in on me. This was definitely going somewhere...

"I mean, I have, you know, Passover, Bar Mitzvah, other Jewish stuff."

As she spoke, Dr. Susan scribbled furiously on her clipboard.

"Your mom told me you've been stealing from her, getting violent, cutting class, picking on retarded people?"

I was shocked. "But *I'm* retarded!"

"She said you've been tagging on the walls inside your house?" Every question she asked, she gained a kind of giddy confidence, like she was finally living out one of her grad school role-playing fantasies.

"There's no way she can prove that was me," I shot back, starting to realize the futility of the entire conversation.

Dr. Susan smirked. "She saw you doing it."

Desperate, I shot back, "She's deaf! You can't trust what she sees!"

The deathblow.

"Here are your choices. I'm going to recommend that you be institutionalized for a few weeks. To have a safe space where you can be evaluated and find some proper medication."

She passed me a pad of legal paper and a pen. "Here. I know it's hard for you to say, so why don't you write your answer. You write yes and you drive there. Or write no and be put in restraints and taken there in an ambulance."

There was only one thing to write:

"FUCK YOU!"

I handed the paper back to her.

She smiled. "I guess that's a yes then?"

I was then transported to the Ross Hospital teenage psychiatric lockdown hospital. The ride there was sick and panicky. I could feel doors slamming shut around my life a thousand per second.

There's a scene in the movie *Labyrinth* where Jennifer Connelly takes a wrong turn, walks through the wrong door, and finds herself tumbling down an endless black hole. Covering the walls are hands, thousand of bodiless hands that slap and brush by her as she falls. These hands could help her, could stop her, but they just tickle her with the suggestion of rescue. I felt just like that. I was still free, but I was on my way to a place where I knew I wouldn't be. My mother, the one who was supposed to be my protector, was right there. She was the person who was supposed to put a stop to things like this. When my mind screamed for me to go to her, I was then smacked with the realization "Oh, that's right, she's the one sending you here."

The doors clanged shut behind me. I was in the labyrinth.

One of the coolest things about being locked up in a mental hospital when you are thirteen is . . . wait, I'm thinking.

I looked out on the foot-thick door that closed after my mother when she left me in shock. How the FUCK did I end up here?

I sat, staring at that door for about an hour from the intake lounge, expecting it to fly open and a flustered young intake worker to run in with a stack of papers, screaming, "Mr. Kasher, Mr. Kasher! I'm so sorry, we have made a grave mistake! You don't belong here. What a crazy lady your mother is, huh?"

We'd share a cigarette and a cappuccino and laugh at the insanity of women and the injustices of the world. Then I'd be released and I'd go get high.

I kept staring, but my intake worker never came. I slept that night on a thin hospital corner bed in a room devoid of sharp things, shoelaces to hang myself with, or anything remotely comforting.

I woke up the next morning and opened my eyes to the realization and the rotten flood of memory of the fuckup chicken coop I was sleeping in. I blinked my eyes awake.

FUCK.

I'm in a fucking mental hospital.

I am in a mental fucking hospital.

I am in a fucking mental fucking hospital.

A fucking MENTAL HOSPITAL.

MENTAL HOSPITAL.

Fucking Fuck.

There was no time to wallow in my anger, though, as the regimen of life in the crazy house is quite strict. Rounds began at 7 a.m. with an orderly opening your door with a policeman's knock and a firm, "Kasher, out of bed for showers!"

I stepped out into the hallway in my foam "safe slippers" and smelled the fetid, chemical custard stink that wafts in every hospital and institution. I can never wash that stench memory out of my nose. To this day, every time I go to the doctor's for an appointment, my nose sends me back to that hallway, staring down at my feet, wondering how it all happened.

I shuffled to the showers and was handed a measly towel and a hotel bar of soap. "Five minutes," the orderly barked.

You know the feeling of tranquility and cleansing a nice long shower gives you? Yeah, that's not available during the five-minute mental hospital shower. Even in there you feel institutionalized. I scrubbed myself and dreaded the rest of the day.

First up was some kind of group ball game led by the most chipper counselor you could ever hope to vomit directly in the face of.

"This is FEELING BALL!" Her gross shimmering teeth gleamed bright white in juxtaposition to the blackness emanating from my heart. "Emphasis on feeling! When I bounce the ball to you, you tell me how you are *feeling* about your new journey into mental health!"

The chipper little thing bounced the ball toward me with a huge smile. "Your turn!"

"What?" I couldn't believe I was doing this.

"A feeling!" She grinned and I wanted to rip her face off with my mind.

"I *feel* like you are bad at your job." I bounced the ball to someone else as my therapist's electric grin went dim.

The girl standing next to me whispered, "I'd suck your dick."

I was flattered until I realized she was looking through me to her hallucination a thousand yards away. I'd never had a blow job at that point, though, so I got real excited about the prospect of convincing this girl I was the lizard king and getting a royal suckoff. But since there was a total lockdown after hours, I could do little with that invitation except jerk off to the memory of it well into adulthood.

Crazy Dick Suck Girl got bounced the ball. She looked at the happy little ball bouncer and growled, "I feel like kicking your fucking teeth out." Ahh, apparently I wasn't the only one.

Dick Suck snarled at the chipper little counselor and threw the ball directly at her head, knocking her down.

Alarms blared.

Orderlies ran in, not to exonerate me like in my fantasy, but to strap my new friend into four-point restraints and drag her into the quiet room. She kicked and foamed like a feral raccoon. Maybe I'd pass on that blow job after all. Welcome to the nut house. Enjoy your stay.

That night I went to bed again, one day down, with no clue when this would end.

The next few days were spent in and out of groups, engaging in a pathetic attempt at in-house schooling and hours upon hours of psychological testing.

They gave me thousand-question personality tests and talk therapy sessions, role-playing, pills, and Rorschach inkblot tests, on which there were inky shapes of figures with fat bulges in their crotch and big busty chests, but if you said you saw she-males, you had "gender identity issues." (No fair!)

I got diagnosed. Drug addicted, oppositional defiant disorder. Conduct disorder. Clinically depressed. Narcissistic, attention-deficit/hyperactivity disorder, and "on his way to becoming a first-class sociopath." First-class. I guess if you're going to be evil, best to do it in style.

There were meals and groups and games and meds and movies and levels and points and, of course, a padded cell. It's not so bad in there. Cool and soft and a place to wonder how you landed yourself in a place like this. There were babbling teens with thick gauze wrapped around their wrists and abuse victims who couldn't make it back and secret drug addicts and Jesus fucking Christ. Jesus Christ? Yeah, even he was in there. Or at least some guy said that's who he was.

I could feel, from deep underneath my belly, this fire of anger bubbling and smoking and trying to get out. I had been getting high so much at this point that it had been awhile since I'd felt that. But with a two-week break courtesy of my 5150 and that terrible Dr. Susan, the topical anesthetic I'd been dabbing at my life was starting to wear off. I couldn't believe what they had done to me, where they'd sent me. I hated those fucking adults so much, I could hardly stand it. This therapeutic environment hardly seemed therapeutic.

I was so angry I couldn't believe it. And I imagine I'd have been angrier still had I known then what I know now due to the advantage of my 20/20 hindsight goggles—that all of my therapists were right. I wasn't angry, I was scared. The anger just served as a line of defense from the terror that it protected. Sure, I hated those adults but mostly because they represented something I wasn't. In control. Stable. Powerful. I was none of those things. I stayed angry because what was right beneath that was too painful. I was scared. A scared little kid.

Every day would end with a line of questioning from some doctor or another.

"Are you ready to talk about your drug use or behavioral problems?"

"I'd really love to talk to you about that, but unfortunately, I don't have either of those problems. I really thank you for your concern, though."

"Do you think your sarcasm is helping you get out of here sooner?"

I could feel his annoyance start to spill into his voice and crack his therapeutic veneer.

"I don't know, do you think the anger in your voice is helping you get through to me?" I grinned real big.

"You little prick." He'd lost it.

There was something I found so phenomenally satisfying about the process of cracking a therapist's professional armor. I'd look for a small chink, poke my little vitriolic prick into it, and start pumping it until they lost their shit and I ejaculated victory all over them. When they lost it, I'd won. I felt so powerless, so at the mercy of these square-ass adults so much of the time, that grabbing their power from them felt orgasmic.

Unable to get me to conform to any sort of talk therapy, they began prescribing me medications, one at a time, willy-nilly, attempting to see if they could toss enough chemicals into my bloodstream to make me better. All they ever did was make me feel crazier. Zoloft, Ritalin, and Desipramine saturated my blood, scraped my bones, serrated my brain, and whirlpooled my focus. I swear to God, every second that I was force-fed psychotropics, I could feel them, almost physically, in my body, changing my chemistry, fucking my brain. I stayed on meds for years.

I went to bed at 10 p.m. on New Year's Eve that year. Celebrating from in bed, behind thick Plexiglas windows and walls, and hospital corners, determined never to have to come here again. Every second in that place was a screaming reminder: YOU ARE NOT NORMAL.

At the same time, I found a comfort in that place. There was one normal kid there named Nate. He was an older kid, at least sixteen, and I thought he was as cool as anyone I'd ever met. He and I would hang out in group making fun of the real crazies and talking about all the pot we were going to smoke when we got out. I wanted to impress him with tales of how much I got high, and it never occurred to me that anyone was listening. Not too bright, but I was pretty medicated at the time. He wasn't just cool, he was tortured by his life like me. We used to knock hello to each other from across the walls of our kitty-cornered rooms at night. I'd knock "shave and a haircut," and he'd answer back, "two bits." I guess we did that just to let each other know that someone else was there who understood. One night I knocked and no one answered. Nate was gone. He'd been released. That night, I cried myself to sleep, hyperventilating, terrified, and I really didn't know why.

I remember I cried when I got out, too. How quickly you get

institutionalized. A two-week stay and I was ready to move in. Ready to be a thirty-year vet with my ass hanging out of a hospital gown doing the Thorazine shuffle, yelling about how the pudding on Tuesdays has arsenic in it because the Libyans are trying to kill me. Fuck that. I got out and went back to the real insane asylum— Oakland Public Schools.

⊱❦⊰

"Yeah, that's him. That kid was locked up in a mental hospital."

I could feel the other eighth graders' eyes burning into me back at Claremont. Somehow, while I was away, this school that had been my world shifted on me. People were freaked out by me.

"You think he's dangerous?"

You see, kids at Claremont were used to hearing about someone going to jail. That was par for the course in Oakland. But a mental hospital, that was something different. No one knew quite what it meant. Even though I'd already been at Claremont for years, when I returned from Ross Hospital, I returned, at least in their eyes, as something frightening.

"I heard he ate a kid here last semester."

"I heard he thinks his dad is a walrus."

"I heard he's Jewish. Like for real."

Of course, my real friends weren't scared of me. Donny and the gang agreed with my assessment that my lockdown was mostly due to my mother's insane overreactions. But kids at Claremont seemed genuinely freaked. I heard their whispers in the halls. It was embarrassing, but I have to admit, part of me loved it. The idea of them being scared of me, when I was so scared of everything, was delicious. There was one kid who wasn't scared, though, Peter Cooke. A seventh grader with a big mouth.

He saw me in the halls and just had to say something. "This fool is straight crazy! You ate somebody? You Hannibal Lecter or some shit?"

"Are you talking about me eating your mother's pussy? 'Cuz I kind of think she liked that," I shot back, punchy from a day of glares and sideways comments.

Peter swung back, this time below the belt. "At least my mom can fuckin' hear me!"

So I slapped him across the face as hard as I could. I had hoped that my dangerous cannibalistic reputation would put a stop to everything once I initiated contact. Almost no one wants to be eaten alive with their peers watching. Peter hadn't gotten the memo, however, and he squared off on me, ready to scrap.

Here's how the fight went. I'd swing on Peter, he would dodge my fist, and then he would punch me in the face. Then, I would swing again and he would dodge and again he would...punch me in the face. This went on and on and on until the fight was broken up. Apparently Peter actually knew how to "fight." The next day I had two black eyes and a week-long suspension.

By the end of the week, though, I still had the traces of the black eyes. I looked like a little wounded raccoon. It had been a rough few weeks.

"I'm not going back to school looking like this," I told my mom flatly.

"The hell you aren't. I can't stay home and watch you."

"I don't need you to watch me. Just let me stay home."

My mother laughed so long and so loud that I began to be offended.

"Well, what the hell am I supposed to do then?"

My mother smiled at me with what was either compassion or sadistic delight—I couldn't determine which. "Maybe I can help."

And then, like a true gangster bad boy, I let my mommy put makeup on my wounds. I looked like a geisha who had been beaten up and then started listening to hip hop. Finally I was satisfied with the job in a suspension of disbelief that I can only account to a drug haze.

"No one will know, right?" I asked my mom, my tranny trainer.

She cringed.

I took my painted-lady face back to school with my pride low and my tail tucked firmly between my legs. When I returned, the whispers were louder, and they weren't so much whispers anymore. My myth had been shattered.

I took a deep breath and entered the halls of Claremont for what I didn't know would be the last time ever.

A kid walked right up to me and snickered. "Ha ha, you got your ass beat!"

I smiled. "Yeah, I did, thanks for saying something. I had almost forgotten, so I appreciate the reminder."

This was gonna suck.

All day, kids filled me in on even more of the details, as if I could ever forget any part of that humiliation.

I knew I was going to be getting fucked with when I returned, and so far, all of this I could take. I thought I might just make it until a kid named Cornuts, perhaps the only kid in Claremont with a bigger mouth than mine, walked up to me and took his turn fucking with me. "Ha ha, you got your ass beat by a seventh gra—!"

He stopped short, staring at me like he saw something very

wrong. He leaned in close to me, his pupils contracting in a kind of confused semi-recognition.

Horror.

Terror filled my blood as my mind tried to will him from understanding what he was looking at. Time slowed to a psychedelic crawl. Cornuts's head cocked to the side to allow the impossible information he was receiving to register to his whole brain. His eyes lit up. He got it. He knew.

No...No...NOOOOOOOOOOOOOOOOOOOOOO!!!

He spoke. "Is that makeup?"

Cornuts turned to the gathering crowd, and screamed, "THIS NIGGA'S WEARING MAKEUP!!!!!"

That was it.

I never went back to Claremont again. I was a junior high school dropout. I was thirteen years old and I'd just gotten out of a mental institution and had dropped out of the eighth grade. It wouldn't have mattered anyway if I hadn't dropped out. My report card from Claremont that quarter arrived in the mail the next week. Truancy and sleeping in class meant I was going to flunk out if I hadn't dropped out. Staying at Claremont was *not* an option. Another year there would have been some kind of fucked-up dystopian horror version of *Groundhog Day*, except Punxsutawney Phil seeing his shadow would instead have been Cornuts screaming, in slow motion:

"THIIIS NIIIGA'S WEAAARRRING MAAAKEUUUP!!"

My mother and grandmother were devastated. I absolutely refused to go back to Claremont. I absolutely refused.

This refusal was a kind of emotional atomic bomb in my family.

My brother had been a straight-A student since anyone could

201 CLAREMONT MIDDLE SCHOOL
OAKLAND UNIFIED SCHOOL DIST.
5750 COLLEGE AVENUE
OAKLAND CA 94618

STUDENT NAME	STUDENT NUMBER		GRADE	FROM	TO	COUNSELOR
MARK KASHER	0157		08	12/07/92	01/29/93	LAWRENCE C

PER	COURSE	TEACHER	ACADEMIC/MARKS 1GTR 2ND 3RD	CREDIT ABSENT EARNED	CREDIT EARNED	ATTENDANCE ABS ABS TARD	TEACHER COMMENT
1	8 GEN SCIENCE	PREDOVIC M P	C F F	D 10			
1	PE 8	FALLEY D M	F D F	F 15 2			
2	8 GEN SCIENCE	DINELL M	C C NC D+	F 19 1		REDUCE ABSENCES	
3	8 WORKSHOP RSP	BAKER L	F F NC F	B 21 5.0		NC = UNEX ABSENCES 20% OR MORE	
5	8 GEN MATH	BAYNE L	F F NC F	F 25			
6	AMERICAN HIST	ALGER C L	F- F- F- F	F 19			
7	8 ENGLISH	CAMPBELL W J	F D+ D+ F	F 23 1		IMPROVE ATTITUDE/BEHAVIOR	
							IMPROVE/DO HOMEWORK

BEATRICE WORTHEN
RE: MARK KASHER
4407 PIEDMONT AVE
OAKLAND CA 94611

ACADEMIC, CITIZENSHIP GRADES

A EXCELLENT	4.0	P PASSING	
B ABOVE AVERAGE	3.0	NC NO CREDIT	
C AVERAGE	2.0	I INCOMPLETE	
D BELOW AVERAGE	1.0	NM NO MARK	
F FAILING	0.0	W WITHDREW	

GPA
0.17

TUTOR MARKING PERIOD 1ST SEM

remember. He had gotten through Claremont an unscathed exemplary student and been offered a full scholarship to the best private college-prep high school in Oakland, where he had gone on to continue to get straight A's and, I assume, participate in fancy-lad sodomy parties where they wiped the cum off each other's chests with their paisley ascots.

My mother had been struggling her way through school for years, determined to become a teacher for the deaf. She chased her master's degree like it would define her and cancel out the bad decisions she'd made in the past.

My grandfather, Dick the Dick, had been an English professor at a local community college. Lecturing on such topics as "Spousal Abuse: How to Do It!"

My grandmother was a teacher in the Oakland Public School System. No doubt setting up the curriculum that would allow me to fail years later.

Her mother was a teacher in Arizona at the turn of the century.

Her mother's mother was a teacher in Utah in the 1800s, teaching Mormons to be creepily friendly (yeah, that was her idea!).

Her mother's mother's mother was responsible for teaching Abraham Lincoln as a youth. (Not true!)

Her mother's mother's mother's mother was Jesus's after-school tutor, pop-quizzing him on things like "How to avoid the pull of Satan in the desert" and "Why the Jews seem cool now, but you should never trust them."

Her mother's mother's . . . oh whatever, you get the picture. My family valued education.

So my refusal to return to school and, more disturbingly, my refusal to care at all about the repercussions devastated them. They had no idea what to do.

Luckily for everyone, good ol' Dr. Patty Susan called my mother with a suggestion. Guess what? It was a shitty one!

"Apparently, the doctors at Ross Hospital overheard him constantly bragging to his friend Nate about how often he drinks and gets high with his friends Donny and DJ and Jamie. I'm sending you some pamphlets about an outpatient rehabilitation center for adolescents in your area called New Bridge."

Only slightly lower on the "you are going nowhere" list than mentally ill junior high school dropout is mentally ill junior high school dropout in rehab. I was thirteen going on fourteen when I entered my first drug rehab. The New Bridge Foundation. A rehab for kids!

New Bridge was run by ex-cons and former junkies who, not surprisingly, had an odd bedside manner. My first day at New Bridge, I was welcomed by a scary man named Clarence and his soliloquy about "just what the fuck we are doing here."

So . . . just what the fuck are we doing here? This is the New Bridge Foundation. We are a New Bridge back to life. Won't you please walk across with us? In New Bridge there are some rules. This is a UA cup. You will piss in it in front of me twice a week. This is the part of my job I enjoy the most. I'm a fucking ex-con. I shot hundreds of thousands of dollars of dope and borax and HIV and hepatitis into my arms. I have veins of steel and blood of mercury. I have killed men with my bare hands and purchased men in prison for matchsticks. Don't fuck with me or I will treat you like a pretty cell mate.

We will also learn arts and crafts here. We will learn how to make stained glass and then we will talk about our feelings. Do not cross your arms as this is the universal sign for being closed off and defensive. If you are closed off and defensive I will punch you in the stomach as hard as I can.

I'm not sure it went exactly like that, but that's the best I can recall. The stained glass thing was real, though. For some odd reason, we would spend hours processing feelings and being yelled at and then retire to a basement to solder glass. I'm not sure what the therapeutic value of that was, but I do remember I soldered a glass effigy of a spray can and was quite pleased with myself.

Every rehab has a familiar trope: "You need to get rid of your using friends. You need new playmates and new playgrounds and playthings."

The idea, of course, is that until a person leaves his drug-based social unit behind, he has little hope of staying sober.

It's logical and sensible. Unfortunately it's also the most unrealistic request to make of a teenager who is getting high and fucking up because he hates literally everyone but his friends.

My buddies were the only thing I had. Getting high with Donny and Joey and DJ and Jamie and Corey and all of those fuckups was the only thing in my life I enjoyed. And these fucking adult ex-cons were trying to scare me straight and telling me to get rid of them? And do what? Make fucking stained glass? Yeah, right. More to the point, I was, at this time, completely unconvinced I had a problem with drugs. What I had was a problem with adults having a problem with my drugs. To me, drugs were the solution to my problems. I used to feel alone, ashamed, and broken, remember? Drugs and my friends made those feelings go away. Anyway, I could quit whenever I wanted to, I just didn't happen to want to.

One of the good things about New Bridge was that they convinced my mother and grandmother to deprioritize getting me back into school, as they felt my "recovery" ought to come first. One of the bad things about New Bridge was that my "recovery" also got in the way of my "drug use." Twice a week, on random days, I had to piss in a little cup next to Clarence's greedy eyes. This forced me to figure out some creative ways to leave the world behind.

Leotis, the semi-homeless buccaneer, had been to rehab a thousand times and told me what to expect from my time there. "Those fucking piss tests make it pretty much impossible to smoke weed for any considerable period of time without getting caught. You got be careful."

This was true. Pot, more than any other drug, stores itself in your system and builds up over time, the more you smoke. You might beat the test once or twice, but eventually you are going to get caught. That didn't stop people from trying. No one, and I mean actually *no* one, at New Bridge was there attempting to be sober. We were *all* just trying to figure out how to beat piss tests.

Kids ate niacin and tried to flush their systems, we drank teas and cranberry juices and tried to wash the THC from our bloodstream with water. Once I drank a quart of vinegar, seared my insides, and vomited up acidic poison. But I passed my drug test!

The second time I got a pass-guaranteed tea, drank it, and failed. I eventually had to resort to just drinking and eating acid, snorting speed, sucking down nitrous, and eating mushrooms. Life in rehab is so tough.

I hated New Bridge, but I loved it, too. I met kids like me who were so absolutely unacceptable to everyone that they were shipped off to be fixed. Every day I'd take the bus up to New Bridge and they would try to force me to talk about my feelings. I didn't care about that; I was used to being analyzed. But right beneath that callousness, I sensed that something was shifting here. I hadn't left that mental hospital behind. I hadn't left

Claremont. I hadn't left that chaos behind, it was still all over me. The suspicion of something being deeply wrong with me that had defined my childhood was being made manifest here in these groups. What kind of thirteen-year-old goes to rehab? I couldn't have articulated this shame, so instead I did what I always did when I was overwhelmed—I acted like an asshole.

I would cross my arms and mock everyone. I talked so much shit the other kids told me to shut the fuck up. You know you are an asshole when other drug-addicted kids in rehab are telling you to chill out. But they liked me, too. I was saying what they were thinking.

FUCK THIS PLACE.

"Fuck this place!" I'd yell across the room during family group. My mother's sign language interpreter struggled to keep up with the pace of my vitriol. Health insurance was a little more able to afford interpreters than Oakland Public Schools. The interpreter didn't seem to be too grateful for the opportunity to interpret for a real-life teenage dickhead, though. I was pissed.

A new counselor, fresh from university, had started work that night at New Bridge and seemed intent on fucking with me.

"Hi, everyone, I'm Tim Hammock and I'll be heading up the adolescent groups here from now on. I'm very excited about the new job and very excited about some of the changes I plan to implement here in the near future. We have some kids I really think want to change, some kids who want help. And we have some kids who are essentially just here to be road bumps on the highway to someone else's recovery."

Tim looked right at me. I blew him a kiss.

I had been caught going to a party with a kid at New Bridge

named Mateo, who was old enough to drive, and another, much stupider boy in rehab named Thor.

Thor was named after the Norse god who wielded a mighty hammer, but our Thor seemed a lot more like he had been beaten in the head with an actual hammer.

The previous weekend, after we all had been drinking, Mateo and I dropped Thor off. Later that night, he took his dad's car without permission and, when stopped at a red light, saw a police cruiser drive by. Even though they were driving right past him, not giving him a second look, Thor's little fish brain was sure they were going to bust him. He floored it through the red light as fast as he could go. The cops probably high-fived at what an easy bust they'd made as they flipped their car around and threw the siren on.

Thor led them on a high-speed chase that ended with him driving the car directly into someone's living room, crashing into their house, jumping out of the car, and continuing the chase on foot. Thor not smart.

Tim buckled down in his seat and leaned forward. "Thor has made some bad choices in the last week and he knows it. But after talking to him, I'm convinced he wants to change, and to prove it to us all, Thor has agreed to empty his contracts here, on group level."

Emptying your contracts is essentially rehab doublespeak for snitching on all of your friends. As a way of avoiding the lengthy jail stint he was sure to be facing, Tim had convinced him to dish all of the dirt he knew about the other people in the rehab. This not only served as some kind of sick proof of sincerity, but also shook the group up and pulled all the secrets and dirt to the surface.

There was a lot of dirt. Gerald was gay, Claire kissed the space where Mateo's dick and balls met in the bathroom during group, Pablo was flirting with the ex-whore receptionist, I went to that ecstasy party, and we were *all* getting high.

Thor's confessional done and everyone's secrets on the table, I yelled, "Fuck this place!" searing Tim with my glare. "And fuck you for using Thor's stupid ass to bust us."

Thor looked up from his stupid stupor. "Did you just call me stupid?"

My eyes darted to Thor's hulking girth. Yikes. "Of course I didn't. I wouldn't do that."

Thor smiled and nodded, satisfied at this.

My mother, who was at every group, every counseling session, following closely as the interpreter translated my raging stream of obscenities, had become a kind of model rehab parent, by which I mean constantly involved and totally oblivious to the fact that her own dysfunctions were at least part of the problem. She was constantly humiliated by me. The tables had turned. I grew up humiliated by how she said things; now she was humiliated by the things I said.

"This place is a fucking joke! You bust us for stuff you know we are going to do anyway." I looked right at Tim. "Do you just enjoy being a dick because you are an adult?"

Tim bristled at this and shot back, "Do you enjoy wasting everybody's time here? Standing in the way of the kids who want to get better here?"

"Nobody wants to get better here! You dumb ass, can't you see that? We are all fucking trapped here like little rats. We all want to go get high. Most of us already are!"

Oops. Too much information.

"Like who?" Tim asked, hungry.

"Well, like your mother and I smoked some rocks together before I bent her over the soldering equipment." Maybe I'd gone too far.

Tim's face flashed in anger, and I thought maybe he was going to hit me.

I loved pissing adults off.

My mom jumped in at this point, speaking through her interpreter, who was flustered by now, fucking up every fifth word. "Why don't you *hug* some respect?" he'd ask.

"Have. *Have* some respect." I was simultaneously mocking him, correcting him, interpreting for my mother, and participating in the group dialogue all at once. Everybody liked to talk about what a dick I was, but no one talked about the communication savant I was becoming.

My mom shot back, "Don't blame Tim for catching you do something *mistake*."

I sighed. "Doing something wrong. Not mistake. Wrong. Seriously, guy, you are making her sound like Frankenstein."

"Right, sorry." The flustered little interpreter hardly looked grateful for the public correcting I was helping him with.

"It's time for you to take responsibility for your own *acting*."

"Actions! IT'S FUCKING ACTIONS. Jesus. You"—I turned to the interpreter—"go back to interpreting school. Mom, leave me the fuck alone. The rest of you, go fuck yourselves."

I was asked to leave New Bridge. Tim winked me a good-bye. What a prick.

Chapter 9

"Sorta Like a Psycho"
—RBL Posse

With my first stint at "recovery" over and the monkey of Claremont off my back, I thought I was headed into an amazing summer. Unfortunately my mother wasn't as excited about things as I was.

I came home the next night and she was sitting at the table crying. When I walked in, she looked up at me and started sobbing. "What did I do to make you like this?" she signed.

Oh Jesus. This kind of conversation was starting to happen more and more, and I just couldn't deal with it.

"I try so hard to help you change. I just keep believing that you'll somehow change yourself and become better. But I'm just starting to think you are going to be like this forever. I wonder, did I make you like this? I wonder sometimes what you would be like if I wasn't deaf."

My mom looked up at me with this helplessness on her face that I'll never forget. I remember it because I remember thinking, "She doesn't get how helpless she really is. Nothing she can *ever* do or say is going to change me. I'm not changeable." I went to her and sat down on the chair next to her. Took her hand. Tried to care. Tried to be human again. I looked at the books she had piled up around her on the kitchen table, *The Difficult Child*, *Tough Love*, *Parenting a Child with ADD*, dozens more books whose titles pointed to the theme of my household: I was broken and it was the only topic of conversation.

I hated my mom's crying. I loved her. But never, not for one second, did it occur to me to change for her. I only thought how crazy she was for crying over me. Maybe first-class sociopath wasn't so far off the mark after all.

We sat there for a while, silently, she trying to forgive herself, me trying to blame myself. Eventually I got up and left her to her tears. I couldn't deal with that shit. I told myself I didn't care, but the only thing I wanted to do in that moment was go get fucked up and obliterate myself, obliterate the memory of my mother's tears.

I did just that.

I wanted out of those memories. Maybe that's a kissing cousin of caring. I got high and forgot. I got high and silently fortified another paper-thin membrane wall around my feelings. Next time, next time I'd feel even less. That's all I ever wanted. I didn't want to feel good. I just wanted not to feel at all. With shit like this happening around you, who would want to feel it? I wanted out, and lucky me, at the bottom of every forty-ounce bottle of malt liquor was a trapdoor into oblivion. I leapt in and checked out.

The next day, my mom informed me of my summer plans.

"Things are going to change. I can't keep accepting you trying to control me and the family. Larry is going crazy, too."

"Fuck Larry."

My mother's eyes narrowed. "I've been trying, but having you in the house kills the mood."

I mimed vomiting all over the kitchen.

Poor Larry.

Larry was my mother's long-term boyfriend. The poor bastard. He had not signed on for me and, unlike most stepparents, actually tried his damnedest to just mind his own business. I hardly made that possible.

Larry was a Ph.D. student of entomology at UC Berkeley. Nerdy, meek, and funny, he was a damn sight better than my mother's ex-boyfriend, Ward, who used to enjoy nothing more than throwing us around the room to exert his authority.

Larry just sat back and read such nerd anthems as *The Lord of the Rings*, *The Hitchhikers Guide to the Galaxy*, and the classic, *The Principles of Pesticide Alternatives in the Controlling of Northern California Aphid Populations*. My mother, after much searching, had found her beta male. He was content to sit back and wait to be bequeathed a little deaf pussy. And I couldn't even let him do that.

Cool or not, he was still an adult, and thus, I hated him even if he was pretty nice. One day I pissed him off so bad by waking him up repeatedly with my screaming matches with my mom that he actually screamed, "FUCK YOU!" Larry grew some nuts! I was impressed.

At any rate, my insanity had pushed their relationship to the breaking point, and it definitely would have been snapped in two had I simply been allowed to loll about the house all day, no school, no rehab.

My mother had other plans.

"This is a contract. I am going to tell you the school options you have and then you are going to sign it and agree to go back to school this summer. If you don't, I'm sending you away."

—NO SPITTING.

— MARK WILL WRITE IN WEEKEND PLANS ON CALENDAR. HE WILL CALL TO FILL IN DETAILS. HE WILL CALL THRU RELAY SERVICE.

— MARK WILL CALL ½ HR. BEFORE CURFEW.

— CAN'T TAKE OTHER PEOPLE'S POSSESSIONS W/OUT PERMISSION (NO ONE IN FAMILY).

— MARK WILL BRING HOME REPORT TO MOTHER AFTER SCHOOL HAS BEEN IN SESSION ONE MONTH.

— MARK WILL LEAVE ROOM W/ FRIENDS TO SPEAK W/OUT SIGNING. IF HE'S TALKING W/ BEA PRESENT, HE'LL SIGN.

— MARK AND BEA WILL NOT CHANGE CONTRACT UNILATERALLY.

— IF BEA FINDS ANY CIGARETTE PARAPHANELIA (OR CIGARETTES), SHE WILL DEDUCT $2.75 FROM MARK'S ALLOWANCE

Please list any other agreements not already covered in this contract.

— Will not ride in cars driven by people who are high.

— PICK-UP THINGS AROUND HOME EVERY DAY — WILL TRY TO.

— BEA WILL GET MARK RADIO ALARM. MARK WILL BE WOKEN UP ONCE BY BEA.

— FAMILY WILL GET SHOWER.

— MARK WILL FEED DOG. IF DOESN'T FEED, BEA WONT.

— BIG CLEANING ON SUNDAY.

— IF BREAKS THINGS, PAYS FOR OR FIXES.

— WILL NOT HARASS DRIVER. IF DOES, STAYS HOME.

— NO WRITING ON WALLS; CAN WRITE ON PAPER OR MIRROR.

— MARK AND BEA WILL GET OFF PHONE W/IN 5 MINUTES WHEN OTHER NEEDS TO USE IT.

— MARK WILL NOT SAY "FUCK YOU" TO BEA AND/OR LARRY.

———————

Oakland Public Schools, at least at the time, had a couple of different routes they would send you on if you started fucking up. There were the continuation schools, which were like regular schools if someone had had a hard life and been sent to prison; and then there were the special ed schools, which were like regular schools if they had had a schizoid break and lost their minds.

Oakland Public Schools had had just about enough to do with me by the time I'd dropped out. Between the endless fighting, the constant class cutting, the incessant pot smoking, and the general malaise of horrific behavioral problems, I had been deemed more of a nuisance than anything else. I became a problem rather than a student, and a crack opened up beneath me large enough to fall into. I dropped out of junior high after Peter Cooke beat my ass, and that was, unbeknownst to me, another trapdoor that opened up behind me and dropped me down into a deeper level of insanity. I was lost in the system.

My mother and grandmother, probably due to the clinical, therapeutic lens through which they viewed the world, chose to send me down the path of the crazy, rather than the path of the criminal. But the truth is, at that age the difference is really marginal. Then again, maybe it is at any age.

I was informed that I had flunked eighth grade and that if I didn't want to go back for another year of junior high, I needed to spend some time in a school that would help me close some of the academic credit gaps I had accrued. I agreed to what was to be one of the great bait-and-switch jobs of all time.

The next day, the short yellow bus came to pick me up and take me to school.

The short yellow bus is the lowest form of transportation possible for the adolescent. It's the retard bus, the transport for kids who can't walk, talk, or think. I saw that thing pull up in front of my house and I turned red. I looked at my mother like, "You have to be kidding me."

She just signed, "Go," and pointed to the bus. My self-esteem plummeted 50 points the second I climbed aboard and was greeted with thick-browed paste eaters waving a happy, "Hello, mister!" Fucking kill me now.

If this information got out to my friends, I would be a virgin for the rest of my life. The fucking short yellow bus! Do you have any idea how hard it is to get girls while taking the short yellow bus? It's hard. You have to unbuckle their helmet. You have to convince the girl your penis is made of candy. You have to bribe the bus driver to look away. I'm kidding!

I had, without quite understanding what I was getting myself into, agreed to go to a school with a rather telling name: The Seneca Center for the Severely Emotionally Disturbed Youngster.

The second I arrived, I smelled something wrong. Thick security doors shot open and slid shut behind me, autolocking. Fortified entrances to schools, never a good sign.

I looked around. This was not a place that was set up like any school I'd ever been to. At each of the entry and exit points of the one main classroom were adults standing sentinel, their eyes scanning back and forth at the students, looking for something, anything, to happen. You got the feeling as soon as you stepped in that anything *could* happen. You can feel when you are in a room of people who cannot control themselves. You can taste the tinny chemical dump of the insane when you share the air with them. The teacher droned on as if this weren't a cuckoo's nest situation and she was just teaching a regular class, not these mad kids. Meanwhile, the kids were muttering to themselves and pulling their hair out. Students looked up at me with evil grimaces I interpreted to mean, not "I'll whoop your ass, white boy," which I was used to, but rather, "I will eat your ass after disemboweling you, white boy," which was new to me.

People rocked back and forth or laughed at jokes that weren't told. These kids were the people that made their fellow gang members uncomfortable with their level of violence.

I scanned the room looking for friendly faces. There were few. One kid, a guy named Ray, smiled at me. A gorilla of a boy, simply enormous, he was as good an ally as I could hope to have here. I smiled back.

When you become involved with clinical settings such as this, you grow adept at scanning a room and tasting its energy to see what role you are going to play in each situation. Some places, New Bridge, for example, I'd quickly become the loudmouth clown and get people to like me by making them laugh. Some places, I'd become quiet and try to be invisible. Seneca Center for the Severely Emotionally Disturbed Youngster was such a place. "Keep your fucking head down," I told myself.

I took a seat. Within seconds, perhaps to impress the new kid, a boy named Jonathan, who had been sharpening his pencil with fervor, lunged at another student and tried to jab the pencil into his neck. He barely had begun to swing when security swarmed upon him and pulled him, foaming and kicking, mad with rage, into the built-in padded cell at the back of the classroom. Four huge men, hardly even having an emotional response to the seizure of anger they were holding, tossed that kid into the "quiet room," hard. Jonathan screamed fucking murder for the rest of the period. The funny thing about the quiet room is that by the time you end up in one, you are anything but quiet. Just another bullshit clinical term. It wasn't a quiet room, it was a padded fucking cell. A padded cell right here in class! How convenient. Where the *fuck* was I?

I'll tell you, there is nothing quite so distracting to a lecture on the *Niña*, the *Pinta*, and the *Santa Maria* as the low, deep thudding of a severely emotionally disturbed youngster's head repeatedly slamming against an inadequately padded cell door. I think that child *was* left behind.

After the attempted murder, a Mexican kid sitting next to me leaned in and hissed, "What you claimin', fool?" He was essentially asking me what gang I was affiliated with. I puffed myself up and answered, "I'm from Oakland, man, we don't gangbang!" The Mexican kid stared at me with dangerous eyes for a beat and then nodded his acceptance and turned away. I tried to look tough as I evacuated my bowels.

The bell rang for recess. Everyone, like a military operation— no, more like a prison routine—lined up in twos. I looked at the line; everyone was paired off, relationships having been already established.

Finally, the bell rang for recess. Kids opened their palms to show that they weren't carrying anything as we were released, two by two, out onto the yard to essentially just get some air and walk laps around the yard. It was as if they were training us to be the prisoners they were sure we were to become.

Everyone had a yard buddy, except that huge guy Ray. He smiled and signaled that I should come stand with him.

Uh-oh.

So, let me get this straight, here at the Stab You in the Neck Academy, the place that is saturated with the worst of the worst baby Hannibal Lecters, is one boy twice the size of everyone else with no friends and a huge toothy grin beckoning me to stand with him?

I'd never been raped and murdered, and it seemed totally unpleasant. I knew for sure that I was going to be killed like one of Lenny's pets in *Of Mice and Men*, and I was trying to think of an excuse to scream like "My appendix!" or "My anal virginity!" when one of the Gestapo guards screamed at me, "Kasher, line up!"

Yes, massa!

I took a deep gulp and accepted my fate. Good-bye, cruel world!

I feebly scooted over to Ray and smiled. He smiled back. He didn't speak. I didn't either. I whimpered.

I could feel his big grin as he turned to me and smiled. Fore-play?

He handed me a small notebook.

I looked down and read, expecting a "We can do this gentle or we can do it rough" message.

The note read "My name Ray. I'm Deaf."

Relief flooded my pores, I breathed again. I tossed my head back and laughed. Ray's face scrunched up in anger, thinking I was laughing at him. He had cocked his fist back to end my life when I signed, "No no, don't hit me! Ha ha, I'm just happy there is a deaf kid here!"

Ray smiled big and shook my shoulder.

"You deaf?" he signed to me, his eyes recognizing the fluency of my signing.

"No, my mother, father deaf."

He smiled again.

"Mother, father deaf" is how people like me establish ourselves with deaf people, the simple grammar a kind of entrée into deaf society. It's a membership card into a very elite club. Regular hearing people can work all their lives in the deaf world, they can establish themselves as true allies to the deaf community, they can be loved by all, but they will always be "hearing" and "other."

But a kid with deaf parents, signing "mother, father deaf," is instantly accepted as family. We aren't hearing. We are the rare exception to the rule, hearing people trusted as insiders in a society that is inherently mistrustful of the hearing. Can you blame them? Envision how you would speak to a deaf person should you meet one in the street. Imagine your slow talking, buffoonish gesturing condescension . . . Now, would you want to talk to you?

Anyway, this was a good thing. The biggest guy in this insane cesspool who was alone because no one knew how to talk to him was now my nuthouse school buddy. This was good news. Ray had been put in Seneca for a somewhat similar reason to me—no one could figure out what to do with him. He, like many deaf kids, was the only deaf student in a small school district, and being the only bruised fruit, he was left to wither on the vine. It wasn't until he started smashing the other fruits that he got someone's attention. He smashed enough to be diagnosed as "severely emotionally disturbed" and fell through a trapdoor of his own. Everyone around me was like that, trapped. Stuck in the greasy cogs of the system. Trapped in the first of what was absolutely certain to be an endless stream of institutions.

Some of these kids were absolutely hopeless, no doubt, their heads fried by drugs or beatings or just biology playing a trick on them, flooding their brains with crazy-guy chemicals. But most were like me, kids who took a soft left turn at some point and didn't even notice they were headed into no-man's-land until they had gone so far that when they looked back, they realized they had no idea how to get back. They were trapped. They were lost. I lived among lost boys. I was lost, too.

At Seneca, if we ever spoke out of turn, even one word, we had to stand, with our nose touching the wall, for five minutes. Standing there, with my nose touching the coolness of the concrete pylon in front of me, I thought, "If you weren't severely emotionally disturbed when you got here, you sure would be by the time the bell rang to go home."

When it was time to go home, I said good-bye to Ray and got back on the fucking yellow bus. I slumped into my seat as a severely disabled wheelchair-bound passenger screamed in impotent agony at her broken body, her broken brain. Here was my new school life, prison bookended by horrors. All I had wanted was to feel okay. I felt anything but.

I convinced my driver to drop me off a half block from my house, lest the neighborhood boys see me getting out of the short bus. I went home and smoked a joint and reassessed. I needed to get the FUCK out of that school, and the way I would do that was to be an absolute angel every second of every day. I'd never make a peep, I'd never say anything smart-assed. Be invisible.

I never made a sound. I stayed in Ray's pocket. Months passed. My severe emotional disturbance was arrested for the time being. Every day at Seneca I had the realization that if there was a Hell, this was where the young people who lived there went to school.

I managed to straighten up enough to scramble and fill out a fevered application to a school called Maybeck High. It was known as a hippie school and a place that "creative thinkers" attended. I only hoped that "creative thinkers" meant "slightly severely emotionally disturbed." Somehow, I pulled all of my intellectual resources into this application and managed to make something impressive.

It was a private school and not something my family could afford, but I had a feeling that it was also the only place that would be willing to look at my inability to have graduated from junior high as a result of my being understimulated intellectually, rather than having been busy selling acid.

I wrote an application that included a personal statement, a funny hard-luck story about my life that pulled at your heart-strings, not unlike the book you are currently reading.

It worked. Somehow, not only did they let me in, but they worked out a deal with my mother where she could pay a paltry amount, I could work in their office twice a week, and we would be able to afford to keep me in that school. When I got the acceptance letter, I triumphantly showed it to my mother and grandmother as if it legitimized me finally as an intelligent human being rather than a psychological equation to be solved. My mother and grandmother beamed with pride. I felt like I'd been given a chance to start over, a clean slate.

DJ, Donny, and I shared a joint in celebration that night.

"Here's to me *never* going back to that fucking Seneca Center."

I was feeling an unfamiliar feeling. Optimism?

"I just have to make it in this school, man. I can't fuck this up." I meant it.

Donny looked at me. "You'll have to wait to get high till the weekends then."

I looked at him like he'd just spoken to me in Cantonese.

"I'm serious, man. It's something I figured out at Kaiser," he said.

Donny had also been sent away to a rehab recently, the Kaiser Chemical Dependency Program.

"They said you could get high on the weekends? What the hell, your rehab sounds *awesome*!"

"No, fool, they didn't tell me that, it was something I figured out," he continued. "The first things they tell you in rehab are the first two things you ain't gonna do. Get rid of your homies and stop getting ripped up altogether? No one is gonna do that, but you gotta see through the message, though, man. At the rate we get high, there's, like, no room for anything else. So, if you want to make it in school, just wait until Friday to get high and you should be all right."

It made a certain kind of sense. Odd, though, that I was getting this advice from Donny, the biggest weed smoker I knew.

"But don't you get high every day?"

"Yeah, and have you noticed my school career going well?" Donny said flatly. It was a good point; he was in almost as much trouble as me and had recently been kicked out of a private Catholic school called St. Mary's.

I decided to take Donny's suggestion seriously. If I wanted to pull myself out of this little nosedive I was in, I had created my chance. It didn't make sense to me that I would be an educational failure. I knew that on some level I had a keen mind. The rest of my family was intelligent. I was the fucked-up one. The cause of all the problems. The "identified patient." I would show everyone. I'd start this school and turn over a new leaf. Hardly a sober one but a sensible one at least. No getting high for me from Monday to Friday. I wanted this more than I remembered wanting anything.

My first day, as if to confirm that I was in the right place, I saw that my math teacher had a hand deformity that left him with only his thumbs. So the moment I walked in, all I saw was his two big thumbs up. Waaaay up! I chose to take this as a positive omen.

I loved it at Maybeck. I was being challenged for the first time since I could remember. There were pretty girls paying attention to me. There was a social scene that I could invite Donny and DJ into that made me valuable to them. It was a really nice four months.

At around the one-month mark, I sat in the park after school and a kid named Jonah busted out a joint.

"Let's smoke," he said.

"Nah, I can't. I can't smoke during the week or I'm fucked. I'll never do my homework if I smoke now."

"Oh, c'mon, smoke now, you'll get your head straight by six and *then* do your homework. That's what I'm doing."

Oh yeah! It made so much sense now. Smoke and *then* do the work! At six. Do the work at six. Work at six.

Six. Six. Six. Six.

666.

I grabbed the joint.

Oblivion.

Of course at six, I was sitting in a bush with Donny smoking and drinking Maybeck away.

Three months later, I was failing out of school and got officially thrown out after getting into a physical fight with our flamboyantly gay drama teacher. (Is there any other kind?)

I'd been fired from the school production of *Our Town* for missing rehearsal repeatedly and mocking our teacher's tremendously stereotypical "lithp."

I was teetering on academic probation and there seemed little hope of me making it to the end of the semester anyway. I was pulled from the production at the last minute and replaced with a clod from the grade above me. No charisma, no finesse, only enough manners to ingratiate himself with "Our Lady of the Stage."

On opening night, I barged into the theater, rooted my way backstage, determined to give the cast a good-luck hug. My flamboyant enemy met me instead.

"Who thaid you could be back here?"

"It's *said*. I'm just here to wish the cast good luck."

"Thorry, no thanks."

"It's *sorry*. You stuck the *th*, on *thanks*, though. C'mon, don't be a dick, lemme just say hi."

I moved to scoot past him and realized that, lisp or no, he was a fucking man. He threw me up against the wall, slamming my head against it, waking me up.

I started screaming every obscenity I knew at him. "You fat failure, get your FUCKING hands off of me. I'll fucking slit your throat."

He smiled. "It's pronounced *thlit* your throat." He threw me outside onto the sidewalk, hard.

"You couldn't think of a more original high school production than *Our Town?*" I feebly whimpered into the concrete.

I was kicked out the next day. I was baffled. I'd genuinely wanted to be at Maybeck. If you had offered me two doors, à la *Let's Make a Deal*, and told me flat out, "Behind door number one is success at Maybeck, the ability to make it through school, and feel good about yourself. Behind door number two is . . . you guessed it: a bag of weed and a forty-ounce bottle of malt liquor," I would have laughed at the absurdity of the choice.

No question I wanted Maybeck more than I wanted to get high. But, and I hardly realized it, I had already crossed over a little invisible line. Another Y in the road. I'd passed into the realm where desire had little or no effect on whether or not I drank and got high. I was heeding the beckoning of the reins-snapping monkey on my back, not engaging in a battle of will. I had lost control and I had no idea.

I wanted to make it through that school more than I wanted to get high, of course I did; but here I was, high as fuck and booted from that school. I didn't understand how I had managed to out-run my own mind.

I kept going back to Maybeck for a few weeks. My new, exciting social life was there and the people I got high with were there, too. I didn't want to let it go. Every day, I'd take the bus to Berkeley and show up at lunchtime with Donny in tow and we'd smoke with kids at The Grove, a eucalyptus forest by the UC Berkeley cam-pus. We'd show up and just nonchalantly say hi and then sit down to get to the business of getting high.

I kept showing up, unwilling to accept that I needed to move on from the fantasy of that school and accept what I was becoming: a fucking fourteen-year-old failure. I showed up one day alone, weeks after I'd been thrown out, and was rounding the bend into the grove when I heard my school friends talking about me. I crouched behind a bush and listened, shaking with shame, quak-ing with hurt.

"It's, like, kind of pathetic he just keeps showing up here, man. I mean, hello, you don't go to school here anymore."

That same fucking kid Jonah who convinced me to get high at six was now judging *me*?

A girl, Olivia, whom I'd had a crush on, laughed and agreed. "I mean, he never really did go to school here, did he? I mean, techni-cally, yeah, but really he was just here to get high. We better smoke quick before he gets here and starts mooching off of us again."

They laughed. I could've cried.

I didn't go back to Maybeck after that.

I took the bus back to Oakland, wondering what the hell I was going to do next. Wondering what the fuck was wrong with me, wondering if I'd ever be okay. Fuck it. I'd find a friend, a forty, and a way out of my brain.

Donny and I drank Crazy Horse that night and laughed about everything. Everything was laughable. Fuck everything. Fuck the world.

⚜

Jamie the liar had been missing for weeks. He popped up one day battered and bruised. He was speaking with a Mexican accent. This was new.

"I been in prison, Holmes. I been into some real gangster shit. I'm a Norteno now." Jamie pulled out a red rag and began waving it in front of us like a matador.

The Nortenos are a Mexican street gang in Northern California that have a lasting rivalry with their Southern counterparts, the Surenos. Jamie's claim to have gone to prison and joined the gang was, let's just say, difficult to believe.

Confounding our dubiousness was Jamie's new friend, Miguel. Miguel was a terrifying-looking Mexican kid dressed head to toe in Norteno reds. He was the real thing. Miguel was a gangbanger from West Berkeley, a notorious Norteno neighborhood. He stood a foot taller than any of us and was huge, 250 pounds at least. He was tough and scary-looking, but there was also something quite off about him. Miguel muttered to himself and laughed at the end of his own sentences, having hardly made a joke. It was disconcerting but really, we were happy to have him around; when's the next time we'd get to hang out with a real live Mexican gang-banger? Miguel looked a bit like a cartoon character of a sly weasel who was sent to prison and gained fifty pounds by lifting weights in the yard. When he looked at you, you couldn't be sure you weren't going to have to defend yourself from being eaten alive. Miguel was one of the more bizarre and off-balance people I had ever met, and Jamie loved to show him off like a prize buck he had shot while hunting.

"Have you met my carnal, Miguel?" he'd say. "My true Norteno hermano!"

We would all roll our eyes and then anxiously look to Miguel for some kind of reaction that would explain the social dynamic between the two of them. Had Jamie actually done something real? Or was this just some bizarre, long-form practical joke?

Unfortunately all Miguel ever did was chuckle and shake his head at Jamie, as if he were the most adorable thing ever. Miguel eventually stopped being an exotic social anomaly and just became one of the boys. A real gangbanger! We were proud.

I was prouder still of the day I fought Miguel. Normally, a six-foot-tall, 250-pound linebacker of a gangbanger would be enough to make me make up an excuse about how "fighting you isn't worth it," which is really just code for "having my face smashed in isn't worth it because I really like my face."

But for some reason, that day I stood my ground. Maybe it was because Miguel had been hanging out with us so much he seemed just like one of the boys. We were sitting in his living room taking bong rips, trying to cash entire bowls full of Mexican schwag weed in one hit. Miguel finished his bowl. Donny finished his. I sucked in big and took as much as I could but started coughing halfway through. Everyone laughed at me, which was nothing new, but then Miguel started in on a little chant, "Faggot Ass Lungs! Woo!" He repeated this, over and over again, for most of an hour, until I'd had enough.

"Faggot Ass Lungs! Woo!"

"Dude, shut the fuck up. I'm not as used to finishing whole bowls of things like you. You don't just finish bowls of weed, you look like you've polished off a few bowls of carnitas, too."

Miguel, not used to any of us talking back to him, looked puzzled and pissed. "Fool, I'll slap the shit out of you."

I snapped, "I don't give a fuck. Go ahead and do it!"

Wait, what was I saying? I *did* give a fuck. I gave a fuck very much.

"Wussup then, you little white bitch, let's step outside."

Miguel got up and started walking outside, ready to fuck me up.

Jamie, DJ, and Joey all looked at me like I was crazy. But I got up. Fuck it.

Once outside, I grabbed a brick from the front yard of Miguel's neighbor's lawn, presumably to crack Miguel in the face with. I don't know exactly how I planned to leap up and do that but it never mattered.

Miguel looked at me and shouted, "Why don't you drop that fuckin brick and fight me man-to-man, you little white faggot-ass-lunged bitch?"

It hardly seemed fair, as I looked more like a kid Miguel was babysitting than a man when I stood next to him, but nonetheless, I dropped the brick and rushed him, screaming.

"Fuuuuuuuuuuuuuuck yooooooooooooooooou!!!"

We clashed. Well...more like, I crashed into Miguel's belly. It was like the Ghostbusters going after that forty-foot Stay Puft Marshmallow Man or Westey when he fights Andre the Giant in *The Princess Bride*. I ran into his belly and nothing happened.

No movement, no effect.

"Fuck," I thought. "What have I gotten myself into?"

I looked over at Joey and Donny, but their eyes contained no answers for me.

"You fucked up now, you little bitch," Miguel whispered into my ear.

I thought, "Believe me, I know."

Miguel, in his mercy, perhaps bemused by my valor, never punched me. He just kind of laid his weight on me, collapsing me to the ground. I was trapped, helpless under the weight of his blubbery countenance. He started laughing. He was *always* laughing.

"You done, faggot lung?"

"I guess," I wheezed, my lungs popping like a novelty squeeze toy's head.

"Just say, I got faggot lungs, woo! And I'll let you up."

"Are you serious?" I began to fuse with the gravel beneath me, sinking into the earth.

"Hell yeah, bitch, serious as a heart attack, woo!"

Oh God. "Fine. I got faggot lungs," I relented.

"Say woo."

I was losing consciousness. "What?"

"Woo, motherfucker, say woo." Miguel was grinning like a Mexican Cheshire cat.

I wheezed, "Wooooooooooooooooooo."

Miguel rolled off me, and I felt a relief more pleasurable than a thousand orgasms.

As I lay there, waiting for my body to re-inflate like Wile E. Coyote after being flattened by a steamroller, I felt a pretty nice sense of pride, like I'd fought a grizzly bear. Sure, I'd lost, but at least I'd tried.

Miguel sat there next to me for a few minutes, smoking a cigarette. He patted me on the shoulder.

"You were pretty down back there, man. *Órale!*"

I grinned. *"Órale."*

"If you ever want to join the Nortenos, you let me know. We got a new white boy expansion program right now."

"Thanks, Miguel, but I'm more down with the Surenos." A look of anger flashed across Miguel's face. I urinated on myself and then whimpered, "I'm kidding." Miguel stared at me for a second with death in his eyes and then started laughing maniacally. He grabbed my shoulder and pulled me close to him. *"Órale!* You fuckin funny!"

That same weekend, Larry and my mother had gone out of town, presumably to get away from me. I was supposed to be staying at Donny's, but you know, empty house, no parents, what was I supposed to do?

I broke into my own home and invited everyone over. Party time. Joey Zalante brought mushrooms. We all sat around and broke the mushrooms up into pieces, which we then downed with handfuls of CornNuts to mask the taste. Classy. There is no better way to begin a psychedelic trip than with chile-picante-flavored CornNuts. That's how the ancient Mayans used to do it.

After the mushrooms came Donny's Ritalin, which we crushed up and snorted. Speed and mushrooms—to make the cartoons play faster.

Now that we were high, it seemed like a really good idea to steal the car. Larry and my mother had spent years slopping together a VW bug out of two non-working cars. It was an eyesore of unparalleled proportions. Multicolored, unpainted, and rusted through the floorboards, my mother and Larry had been foolish enough to leave it at home, thinking I'd be too embarrassed to be seen in it. Little did they know that the mushrooms I'd be eating would make it look like a Transformer. I loved Transformers.

We all piled into the bug and Joey climbed into the driver's seat. I didn't know how to drive. None of us had a license. We picked up forties to drink and a bag of weed and headed into Tilden Park, a kind of wilderness reserve in the hills of Oakland.

We drove through the hills, pounding our beer, trying to find a spot to smoke and look out at the city. At one point, we went too far and attempted to turn around by pulling onto a steep dirt hill on the side of the road and then rolling back down it in the other direction. At least that was the plan. What happened was, due to the instability of the dirt, the shoddiness of the car, and the weight of five idiotic stoners in the backseat, the bug began to tip over backward, ready to flip on its end. We all jumped out, like an insane Chinese fire drill, and coaxed the car, by hand, back onto the ground. We sat in the car panting in fear and decided not to keep driving but to smoke where we were, right at the side of the road.

Then, as if on cue, the exact moment we lit the pipe, light flooded the car. The cops. We were busted.

Fuck.

This was it. My mother told me that one more bust by the cops and I was going to be sent away to a group home or, even worse, to study Talmud in Sea Gate with my father. Armed with that information, I had promptly stolen her car. These were the kind of decisions I made.

I couldn't believe how stupid I was. It seemed like, in the face of the most obvious answer in the world, I always chose the dumbest thing to do. It was like I wasn't in control of my own brain. Well, there was no use in trying to figure that shit out now. There were more-pressing issues at hand.

I dropped the pipe out the passenger window and sat staring straight ahead, trying to will the smell of pot out of the car.

The cop, making the closest thing to a joke possible for a police officer, walked from his car, right over to the pipe, and handed it back to me with a grin, saying, "I think you dropped this." I tried to look like I'd never seen a pipe before.

"What is this thing?"

"You mean the pipe that I just saw you drop out of the window that's still warm from you smoking from it? Is that what you are asking about?"

I sighed. I was fucked.

"So..." the cop began, "what are you guys doing?"

I took a deep breath. "Okay, well, here's the thing. I just finished the final touches on this car—as you can see it's a bit of a project car!" I laughed hysterically as my speedy shroomy brain spun into action, pulling the next line of bullshit directly from out of the sky.

"Soooooo then I thought, well, jeez, just like a boat needs a maiden journey, so does a car! AM I RIGHT? So we piled in and took her for a spin, in fact we were just on our way home when you stopped us, which I appreciate because it's like... TIME TO GO HOME! Am I right?"

The speed was coursing through my veins, pumping me up. At that moment, though, Miguel, seated in the backseat, leaned forward and broke the awkward silence.

"He's lying to you, Officer!"

What. The. Fuck.

Every head in the car spun around in shock at Miguel.

"He just stole his parents' shit!"

Miguel had had some kind of psychic break. Or at least, it

seemed as though he had. Even the police officer looked a little surprised at what a weird snitch Miguel was being.

I looked at the cop. I exhaled, deep.

"Look," I started, defeated, "this *is* my parents' car. I lied to you because if I get busted again, I'm completely fucked. Sorry about the swearing, my mom lets me. She's deaf. Like totally..."

I was cuing up the string section, trying for pity. If lying wouldn't work, maybe heavy indulgence in the truth would.

"It's tough having deaf parents and sometimes I act out to get attention. They just told me that if I fuck up again, I'm going to be sent away to like a group home or something. I know I fucked up, and if you could just give me a chance and let me call my sister and have her come meet me and drive the car home, you would be essentially making sure my life doesn't get ruined. This is the moment. I could get sent off, fall into the cracks in the system, fall into crack, catch AIDS, and die. Or you could let me call my sister."

The cop stared at me for a second, his face showing something in the middle of pity and bemusement.

He smiled. "All right. Let's call your sister."

I tried not to look shocked. Amazing. He was going to let us go. All I had to do was call my sister. Only one problem. The only sister I had was ten years old and lived in Brooklyn.

"You follow me down the hill and we can call your sister from a pay phone when we get back into town."

To clarify, a real-life police officer allowed a drunk, high, unlicensed kid in a stolen car to drive down a windy mountain road at night. Sometimes there is only one set of footprints in the sand. That's when God carries you. And that night, he carried me with a gentleness that suggested, "I forgive you for the phone sex, I totally get it."

Donny turned to me and exhaled, the first one of us to do so in many minutes. "How is this happening?" he asked.

We arrived at the base of the hill panting, our hearts beating in fear, sure that somehow this would turn out to be a trick.

When we reached the bottom of the hill, I sighed. "Here goes nothing. Hey, thanks for the help back there, Miguel."

Miguel was too busy talking to himself to hear me, though.

I opened the car door and walked to the phone like a convicted killer walking to the gallows. I stared hard at that pay phone, willing my mind to work quick. I picked up the phone and dialed a neighborhood girl named Seena. We'd hardly ever spoken on the phone. Hopefully she wouldn't be too surprised to remember she was my sister.

I plunked a quarter into the phone like a gambler playing his last cent on a slot machine. "God," I thought, taking refuge in the prayer of the coward, "I know maybe two times in one night is too much to ask but...help me out here?"

The phone rang...

A click. A sleepy voice. An angel.

"Hello?"

"Sis! My sister! Oh, the girl with whom I share parents! It's me, your brother!"

Confused and a little pissed, Seena spat back, "Huh? Brother? Why the fuck are you calling me this late? Wait, why are you calling me at all?"

"Totally!" I said, masking relief as brotherly love. "Hey, look, I stole Mom's car. I know, I'm an idiot! Anyway, the cops are here and they said they'd let me go if you just come pick up the car and drive it home."

A pause. I could hear the gears turning in Seena's head.

"Oh, wait. Is there a cop right there with you? Are you pretending to be my brother to get out of trouble or something?"

DING.

I turned to the cop. I smiled big.

"Yes!" I yelled, hoping.

"You fucking asshole. You better get me high if I come out there."

"Of course!" Hearing her agree to rescue me was so amazing, I might as well have ejaculated a river of relief all over the sidewalk and paddled home in that. My sister was coming! My sweet, sweet, fake sister.

"I love you, sis!" I panted.

"Go fuck yourself," she snarled. You know how my sister can be!

I turned to the cop and shouted, "She's on her way!" From inside of the bug, I could hear my friends cheer like we'd won the lottery. This was a good night.

Seena showed up bleary-eyed and glaring at me just like a real sister would. I loved her more in that moment than I'd ever loved anyone.

"I'm so sorry about my brother, Officer," she said as she pulled up. "I was sleeping and didn't hear the boys take the car out."

The boys. She should have won an Oscar.

"No problem at all, glad you could help." The officer smiled.

"My boyfriend will drive my car home and I'll take the bug. Thanks again."

The officer stared at Seena's blond hair and anti-Semitic features with a grin.

"No problem. You know, you two look exactly alike." He smiled. Was that sarcasm? Jesus, who was this cop?

Just at that moment Dean Stockwell appeared and the cop quantum-leapt away (nerd joke!).

Or rather, we all drove away, waving the most amazing police officer since Robocop a disbelieving good-bye. We drove home in silence, awed by the miracle we had witnessed. All but Miguel, who suddenly came out of his mushroom stupor, leaned forward, and asked "Hey, what just happened?"

If he hadn't been huge and Mexican, I might've hit him. As it was, I just laughed.

When we arrived at my home, Seena turned to me and said, "There's no way you are going to get popped twice in one night, let's take this hooptie out and go have some fun."

Made sense to me. I ran upstairs, grabbed more booze, and we continued on with our evening, the majesties of the Lord forgotten the instant a suggestion for more fun was made.

Have you ever pushed a Bug on its last legs into the 100-miles-per-hour zone? It will make you remember past lives. Seena gunned the Bug down Highway 580 as we passed a forty around and laughed at our luck. As we sped down the straightaway, the poor little engine screamed, trying to keep up with our party. As the needle redlined, all of a sudden, out of nowhere, the car's radio, which hadn't worked for decades, squealed to life, blaring oldies into our insane night.

My brain was spinning as we pulled back to my place at four in the morning. I was shaking with speed and mushrooms, slurring with booze and pot; I was fucked.

It seemed, at that point, like a logical next step for me to snort some Zoloft. Keep in mind that Zoloft has no psychoactive proper-ties. But I figured, what the fuck, why not give it a whirl.

I shook out a couple of pills alone in the kitchen. I could hear the sounds of my buddies laughing and partying in the next room, but no, this rare delicacy I would keep for myself. I squinted at the pills, willing myself not to hear the thought that was creeping in the side of my head: "This is a really lousy idea." I chose instead to heed the other much less logical but much more compelling thought, "What the hell, why not? See what happens, it could be awesome. Fuck it." *Fuck it* is the great battle cry of the drug addict. It's the rebel yell we all scream as we charge into the dumb, the ridiculous, the danger-ous pool of bullshit that we inevitably drown in.

My hands were shaking as I crushed up these pills that had been jacking up my brain chemistry for the past year. Chunks of the protective easy-swallow coating stuck out from the white lines like coral rocks jutting out from a foamy surf, warning, "Bad idea! Pain Ahead!" I grabbed my surfboard and jumped in.

I leaned down and snorted half of a comically large line of Zoloft. I could feel the grit fly into my nose like sinking into quicksand in reverse. The back of my sinus cavity filled up in a split second and the inside of my face caught on fire. Pain shot through my head like the devil was giving me an old-school, ice-pick lobotomy. My head shot straight up as I slapped at my face, desperate to make it go away. I ran screaming to the bathroom, hoping there was some-thing there to make the pain stop. I ran to the sink and looked at my face. Scary. My right eye was literally bloodred. The right side of my face felt like there were a thousand little elves on it, aerat-ing a lawn with spiky little golf shoes. I felt like I was going to die. There was poisonous pain shooting into my brain. Oddly, the left side of my face was just fine and looked like my handsome old self. I should have gone and fought Batman with a face like that (nerd joke!). Getting to that threshold of acceptance that you must come to in moments of great pain, I accepted that, perhaps, I was going to have a stroke. I waited. My face still hurt, so that meant it wasn't paralyzed. Tears were streaming down my face that were opaque with medicine. I think my eye turned purple. I crawled to my bedroom window and spent the next hour sitting there, spitting out loogies filled with rocks of Zoloft onto the sidewalk below. If a depressed dog had walked along just then, he could have lapped it up and tasted happiness for the first time in dog years.

I slunk out of my perch, my poison face having backed off to enough of an extent that I could walk upright. I walked into my living room, where my friends were all sitting and drinking with each other.

As I walked into the living room, everyone screamed.

"A zombie!" Jamie yelled. "This happened to my uncle!"

Seena wept.

Miguel crossed himself. *"Dios Mío. Es El Diablo!"*

Donny and Joey approached me like I was a feral animal.

"Dude," Donny whispered. "You all right?"

Right! My eye.

"Oh, this? Ahh, this is nothing. I was just snorting a little Zoloft, you know? Seein' what would happen."

"Looks like you've been snorting a little cyanide, bro." Joey sounded genuinely concerned.

"I'm fine, I'm fine. I can see the future in my right eye, but other than that, I'm fine." I laughed and coughed up a full pill of Zoloft. "Anyway, let's go up to the roof."

One by one, we all, even Miguel's huge ass, climbed up to my roof. The bastard sun was making its threats on the night, revealing to us all that this dark night was going to crash to an end. Teenage vampires we were, sucking down whatever blood we could find in the bottom of a bottle. Donny and I stood there, looking over the city lights to the west, the purple-red middle finger of the sun to the east, passing a cigarette back and forth. Just me and my friend Donny smoking again. I felt okay. In charge. Alive. The magic luck of the drug addict had been sprinkled on me, and I'd had a night to remember. But drug-addict luck always runs out.

I woke up the next day groggy, hungover, and ready to die. Donny was up and said something about going to the store to get booze. I threw him the keys and rolled over back to sleep.

I woke up a few hours later to my grandmother's voice shrieking, "Wake up! Get up! Where is the car?"

Shit. The car. Where *was* the car?

Right! Donny. Fuck.

I was pretty fucked. I'd been given a thousand second chances the night before, but I'd fucked up and lost anyway.

But right then all I could do was vomit in my lap. I did so.

"Ugh, disgusting," my grandmother sneered. "Just like your grandfather." This was her version of the worst thing she could say to me. "Where is the car?"

"Well, I don't *know* in the classic sense of knowing. Well..."

I thought fast in what seemed like a pretty good lie in the moment.

"I..."

I remembered the radio from last night.

"I fixed the radio!"

"What?" my grandmother asked, confused.

"Yeah!" I yelled, gaining confidence. "I fixed the radio. I have a buddy who does that kind of repair work, and so I wheeled the bug down to his shop and fixed the radio to surprise Mom and Larry when they get back. Yep. That's where the car is now. The radio-fixing shop."

A pretty good, pretty high-grade lie. Jamie would have been proud.

"You *pushed* the car?" My grandmother looked dubious.

"Well, yeah! I didn't drive. I don't have a license. That's illegal! Duh."

"You *pushed* the car down the street to repair the *radio*?"

"Yes. Exactly." Why didn't she believe me? I was lying, but there was no way for her to know that.

"To repair the *radio* for your deaf mother."

I paused.

"You know, I totally didn't think of that! Ha ha!"

My grandmother looked less amused.

Just then I heard the car pull back into the driveway. Saved!

"Well, there's the mechanic now, delivering the car!"

We walked downstairs together, me covered in vomit, my grandmother covered in doubt. Joey crawled out of the driver's seat with a bottle of Jack Daniel's in his hands.

"Hey, thanks for fixing the radio, champ!"

"Yeah." Joey stared at me, confused. "Anytime . . . *champ*."

I sat down in the driver's seat and looked up at my grandmother with a confident smile. "Here we go."

I smiled, flipped on the radio.

Silence.

Somehow the radio had rebroken itself.

I felt God's hands snatch away from me. I crashed hard onto the sand. Apparently God, much like everyone else, was tired of my shit. Once again, I was fucked.

PART FOUR:

Just

Problems

Chapter 10

"Illegal Business"
—Mac Mall

"Get out of bed!" My mom snatched the covers off me for the fourth time that morning. "Get up, get up, get up!"

My mother and Larry were back from vacation, and after a debriefing from my grandmother, my mother stormed into my room determined to get to the bottom of the story. The problem was, I was crashed out after having stayed up for days.

My mother was constantly experimenting with creative ways of getting me out of bed. She would grab my feet and tickle-torture me, pour ice water on my head, snatch the covers off me with little reverence for the morning erection she might be uncovering.

"You can't just sleep forever. You have to get up!" my mom screamed at me as I lunged for the covers, falling out of the bed.

"Look at you," she signed, disgusted. "This isn't working. You are going to have to get back in school if you want to keep living here."

"Don't you remember? I need to focus on my recovery instead." I tried to look sincere.

"What recovery? You got kicked out of New Bridge months ago."

"Yeah, but I've been going to meetings and staying clean the last few months," I lied.

"You have?" My mom looked so hopeful, it was sad.

"Of course," I said, pulling the covers over my legs. "I learned a lot in New Bridge. I'm pretty hurt you didn't notice."

My mom's deepest hopes manipulated, she crumbled. "I'm really sorry. I had no idea you were taking sobriety so seriously."

"I'm super serious. Jeez." Just then I had an awesome idea, evil but awesome. "In fact, I'm on the ninth step right now."

My mom looked impressed. "That's great! What happens in the ninth step?"

"You don't know? How seriously are *you* taking my sobriety?" I stared deeply at her, accusing her of not caring enough about me, her deepest fear. "The ninth step is the most important step of all. It's where we make amends to people we have harmed through our drinking and drug use."

My mom looked so sincerely pleased that it was hard to do what I knew I had to do next.

"Yeah, it's a pretty big deal. And well, here's the thing ... I owe some people money. People I stole from and some people whose property I damaged. You know I don't have a job, so ..."

My mom looked at me, pride in her eyes, naïveté and codependency hemorrhaging from her every pore like an emotional Ebola virus, covering her reality sensors, making her insane with the desire to help. She smiled. "How much do you need?"

I grabbed the money and jumped on my bike, went to Terry Candle's house, and we sucked that amends money into our lungs.

I have been to many twelve-step meetings, but I've yet to meet another addict who spent his amends money on drugs. I'm still kinda proud.

I figured out ways to hustle money daily. Being a fifteen-year-old drug addict is a constant job of scraping and stealing enough money to get high. No one's allowance is big enough to cover the bill of addiction. I had no job, I had no stuff, I had only my ingenuity and a sociopathic bent.

My house became like a puzzle. How to break into places I didn't belong and then how to take things I didn't own. I squinted at locks for hours, trying to see them from different angles that I could break into. A kitchen knife became a screwdriver. A doorstop became a wedge to pry open a door. I pried freedom from my house against its will. I scaled the walls on the outside of my own house and ran out the backdoor with a handful of cash as the police banged on my front door, looking for a cat burglar that oddly resembled the kid who lived inside.

I started, little by little, taking stuff around the house and selling it for drugs.

I'd strip the house of stuff I thought wouldn't be missed. A little thing here or there.

I'd grab big atlases from the bookshelves and nice hardcover books like *The Power of Myth* and *A Guide to Western Civilization* and take them to the bookstore and sell them.

I'd grab stacks of CDs from Larry's CD collection and take them to Amoeba Records to sell. What a responsible business that place was. They saw a fifteen-year-old blurry-eyed kid with his pants sagging and Fila cap cocked to the side selling a handful of Wagner and Vivaldi CDs and never even raised an eyebrow.

I guess they just figured I was more into Vivaldi's later work.

No one asked questions, they just took the goods and gave me money. I took that money to the dope spot and they gave me the real goods. The only ones who lost out were my parents. I took money and credit cards, I took CDs and books, I sold my own clothing and my grandmother's collections. Her jewelry disappeared. When I needed cigarettes, I stole my mother's food stamps and walked to Safeway, snagged three packs, and brought them to the back of the store where the coffee grinder was. I'd drop the packs into a one-pound coffee bag and fill it with arabica beans, covering my plunder. I'd then walk to the front of the store confidently and plunk down the beans.

"Just the coffee then?" the clerk would ask me, suspicion dripping from her eyes.

"Yep! Just that!" I'd reply cheerfully.

"Cinnamon hazelnut coffee and nothing else? At one o'clock in the morning?" She knew something was wrong but couldn't place it.

"What can I say... I'm a hazel-NUT!" I smiled big.

I'd drop the food stamps and try to look like a hard-luck case.

When I needed booze, I'd walk directly to the hard liquor aisle and grab a bottle. It would be in my pants before I had a chance to hesitate and before anyone had a chance to notice me. I stole hundreds of bottles of booze. Seagram's Extra Dry Gin had a bumpy bottle that gripped my waistline and prevented the bottle from slipping out, so I mostly trafficked in that. I'd also grab Maker's Mark bourbon, which came with a hand-melted wax topper that I could pull out a bit and rest on my belt for grip, ensuring that it wouldn't slide down my pant leg and crash onto the floor, revealing my crime, wasting my medicine.

I got good at it. It became like an art. I'd make it in and out of the grocery store in less than five minutes. No one saw me coming.

As soon as the bottle's coolness was against my waist, I'd glide up to the front counter and ask an inane question that would give me an excuse to walk right out again.

"Excuse me?" I asked, pudgy and innocent. "Do you guys have birdcages?"

Now, I knew that no Safeway in Oakland, or indeed in history, had a birdcage for sale. But they didn't know I knew this.

"No, sweetie, we don't carry those." The poor clerk tried to soften the blow.

"Aw, man! I just found an injured pigeon and wanted a home for it. Well, wish me luck!"

"Good luck, sweetie." She'd stare after me as if I were a boy hero as I left, limping, frightened that the bottle would fall out.

"And he's got a limp, too," she'd likely think. "That poor, sweet crippled child."

"God bless us!" I'd turn back and yell. "God bless us every one!"

My friends were impressed with my thievery, but they manipulated it, too. They knew that I was desperate for their approval, and they used that to get themselves free booze.

"C'mon, man, get us some drink!" Joey would yell at me. "I'd do it myself, but you're just so good at it!"

"Aw, I'm all right," I'd mutter, pride painting my face red.

"All right? You're the best! No one does it like you!" Joey was really leaning into this role, pouring it on. I knew what he was doing, but I chose to ignore it.

"Yeah, all right, Joey, what do you want?"

"Bailey's Irish Cream." Joey smiled.

"Irish Cream? Ugh. Why waste your time?"

"Because, motherfucker, that's what I want. I'm getting it for a bitch. Don't fuckin' ask questions." Joey cocked his fist back like he was gonna sock me.

Embarrassed and too scared of Joey to tell him to go fuck himself, I just gulped, tightened my pants, and went into Safeway. This wasn't right, of course. Bailey's, besides being a drink for gay leprechauns, had a fat bulky bottle that just didn't work for my needs. The edges were too smooth, the sides were too oblong. I never stole Bailey's. I stopped and thought about it. Another mistake. I never stopped. A fifteen-year-old kid staring thoughtfully at stacks of bottles he wasn't even close to old enough to purchase was a suspicious sight. Fuck it. Ride or die. I grabbed the bottle and pushed it into my belt and rested it precariously on my waist and bolted for the door.

Waiting for me at the exit of the store was a huge black man wearing street clothes, holding a badge.

"Hey, pal, you take something that wasn't yours?" Just like that he grabbed me, flipped me around, and snatched the bottle from my waist.

My friends were all there, waiting for the booze, and as soon as the cop grabbed me, they turned and started walking away.

"Get off of me!" I yelled, struggling to get away.

"Look at your friends, huh? Look at them walk away. Real nice guys."

"Oh, go fuck yourself," I snarled, pissed. "What are they supposed to do? Rush us and try to spring me free?"

"Something other than just walk way, I guess," he said, a little sad, a little mad.

The cop walked me back into a little room and my grandma got another "Come pick up your kid" call. She showed up, wringing her hands, looking ashamed, rescuing me like she and my mother always did.

The guy just shook his head at me when he saw her. "I should have just sent your ass to jail."

I'd never been caught stealing before and it stung. But what stung more was that I couldn't get that security guy's words out of my ears. They rang over and over. "Look at them walk away... Look at them walk away."

My grandmother drove me home in silence but my head was loud with that ringing. Look at them walk away.

Another disappointment. Another failure. My mother's suspicions that something was terribly wrong with me had been, at this point, fully confirmed. Zeidi's prophecy that I would become a great holy man had been proven false. I was an utter failure. Everyone knew it. Everyone but me.

I was convinced that I was the victim of a persecution campaign. I mostly lamented the idiocy of the people around me. If they would just get off my back, if they would just stop trying to find things that I had done wrong, I would be free and okay.

I knew in some dull way, at the base of my brain, that I wasn't meant for this. I was smart, I knew that, and I looked at my brother and his successes as a sort of ripe fruit dangling from a branch just out of my reach. I could see it, understand how fresh and perfect it would taste, bursting onto my dried-out-bone leather tongue, but somehow, I was powerless to grab it.

"If you'd just stop fucking up, you could get high if you wanted. I get high but I never get into the shit you do." My brother had begun a familiar speech about getting high responsibly. Hardly a resonant message to a fourteen-year-old.

"That's easy for you to say," I said to him. "No one ever expects you to fuck up so no one ever looks."

"Yeah, maybe," he said, "but you fuck up so much no one could manage to *not* look. You're waving a flag in their faces like, 'Look! Over here! Bust me!' "

What a logical idiot my brother was. In so many ways, my brother was the only real partner in the world I had. He was the only person in the world who had been through the ridiculous insanity of my family and lived to tell the tale. And yet, he wasn't just living, he was thriving. It was like looking at the mirror and the reflection coming back smarter and better-looking than you. David seemed to have it together and he just wasn't the asshole I was. So how could I blame my family or my circumstances for any of my problems? He even offered to give up getting loaded for me.

"Look," he said, "would it help if I quit, too? We could quit together. I'll stop smoking weed and drinking and you can, too, and we can, like, do it together? Like, as brothers! What do you think?"

"I think my suspicions of your hidden homosexuality have been confirmed."

"All right, man, make jokes. It doesn't bother me. I'm not the one entering my second year as a high school freshman. I'm not the one they are installing locks on the windows for."

This was true. Dead-bolt locks were being drilled into the windows all through the house. A fire hazard for sure, but Tough Love didn't concern itself with such details. Maybe if I burned to death in a fire, I'd finally learn my lesson. As the flames licked at my feet and the soles of my shoes melted, I'd scream in anguish, "You guys were right! I'm the creator of chaos in the family! I'll chaaaaaaaaaaaaaaaaaange! What a world! What a world!"

After I got busted with the car gone and with the evidence of my lost weekend everywhere in the house and my grandmother shrieking about my shoplifting adventures, my mother again attempted to buckle down.

"Things are going to change around here," my mom said, kicking me awake and affecting the no-nonsense air of a deaf drill instructor.

Part of the problem with getting tough all of a sudden after years of being a codependent mess is the deep groove of pattern that you have carved yourself into. I knew my mother's ways and I could tell this newfound sternness was some new affectation. I could count on her to be crazy but never tough.

"Okay, so is this some new thing you are doing? This tough-guy act?" I laughed.

"This is the new way we are going to live. I'm installing locks on every door in the house, on every window, too. No more sneaking around stealing things, I'm putting my foot down."

Of course, the problem with my mom keeping me from going into her room as a means of stopping me from stealing was that she was quite an absentminded lady. Sure, she'd lock the windows and her bedroom, but she'd also leave her purse lying around, its gaping mouth wide open as if inviting me to take a bit, just enough to feel okay. My mother was broke and I knew it was wrong on some level, but I simply had no choice.

I took full advantage of her absentmindedness, knowing that she'd never quite remember exactly how much money she had in her purse on any given day. I took a twenty here, a twenty there, and then I'd bring her her purse and admonish her for leaving it lying around.

"You really need to be more careful with your purse. It's okay now that we are at home, but if you leave it around in public, you are gonna get ripped off."

She'd sign, "I know," and I'd jump on my bike and ride to Monk's house to buy a twenty sack.

Stealing from your deaf, welfare-assisted mother is like killing a man. Well, I imagine it is anyway. The first time you do it, you feel sick and wonder what's happened to you. Then, very quickly it changes from a shameful secret to just what you need to do. It's just a source of income. Then you move on to stealing from your grandmother.

I know what you're thinking. That's sick. And I know it. And I *knew* it then. But the moment you get desperate enough to steal from your mother's purse is the same moment that you simply don't have any choice in the matter. I've known grown men who have robbed their parents blind. No one's ever high-fived about it. Everyone who is like that wishes they weren't. You just have a little beastly monkey on you snapping the reins, saying, "Do it." Denying the monkey is not an option. At least you know your mother will still love you afterward. You have to feed the monkey.

Over the course of weeks I started to see the changes in the house, though. I couldn't open my window. I was on house arrest. I couldn't enter any rooms in the house save my bedroom and the bathroom and kitchen. Valuables were stockpiled in locked rooms, but somehow I managed to break in, steal them, and sell them to pawnshops.

I stole colossally. I stole damnably. I stole like an animal. Oh wait, animals don't steal. I stole like an asshole. Yeah, like an asshole. There were times I felt like a terrible person, but mostly, I just did what I had to do. I'd push my feelings about what I was doing to the side and replace them with the relief that comes from knowing your moment of discomfort is about to end. The moment I even had the money in my pocket was the moment that my relief began. It wasn't just the high itself, but the knowledge that the high was coming. That I held in my pocket the means through which to make myself okay. I had control. I, the most powerless person I knew, had power. In the recovery world a familiar admonishment is to "live in the moment." No one lives more in the moment than an active drug addict. I was always willing to accept a catastrophe that would be taking place in some abstract future for a fleeting moment of pleasure that could occur right now. The future had no meaning to me. I had no future anyway. Everyone told me that. Even my mother had adjusted her message from "Get your shit together and you can do whatever you want in life," to "Get your shit together or you'll never do anything in life," to "Get a life."

I could feel my life sinking in the quicksand, I just couldn't see with clear eyes the reason why. I was absolutely convinced that every time I was about to get pulled out of the pit, some adult would come by and push me back down. I was surrounded by teams of people who claimed to have been commissioned to help me, but all they seemed to do was send me places that made me feel more broken and ruined than the last. All they ever did was lock my windows and lock my life. All they ever did was remind me what a fucked-up piece of shit I was.

My friends, terrible though they were, never suggested that I was worse than them. Only that we were all bad together. And that's why we stuck close. Thick as thieves we were. Wait, we *were* thieves.

It wasn't just stores and parents that we stole from either. The core of my friends had been corroded. Somehow, as the years went by, the hustling got to the point of us betraying one another. And no one seemed to care. We all changed. Everybody was hungry. I guess we had graduated into being real drug addicts. I began stealing from my friends, and they started stealing from me, too. No one was safe. Especially not kids from Piedmont.

With the Oakland Public School System breathing down all of our necks and OPD constantly harassing us, DJ and his brother Corey managed to switch to a fancy public school in a city called Piedmont by using a fake address to switch districts. I was super-jealous. Oakland Public Schools had already marked me with so many huge red flags that my record looked like it was a Chinese Olympics opening ceremony. Anyone even considering a district transfer would take one look at my record and drop it instantly, badly burned by the secrets sizzling inside.

Piedmont was a town adjacent to Oakland but, in truth, a world away. Piedmont has an odd history of having created itself as a sort of citadel of white flight. With the black writing on the wall in Oakland, a group of rich white people, rather than being chased across the tunnel, created a sort of fortified imaginary suburb. There are no logical borders to the town of Piedmont; it is literally surrounded on all sides by Oakland. The only barriers are psychological and socioeconomic.

Corey and DJ entered that school with instant street stripes just by virtue of being from Oakland. They went from *White Boys* at Claremont to *Those Guys from Oakland* at Piedmont. Instant status.

They quickly found themselves courted by the guys for protection and the girls for attention.

DJ and Corey would, intermittently, bring new friends into our social circle with the express plan of softening them up to the point of being able to rob them. It was like a group of foxes bringing a new, fat chicken into the den and trying to convince them they were safe.

"Hey, thanks so much for coming, the other foxes and I are really glad you are here."

Chicken looks up, wanting so bad to be accepted, eyes darting back and forth. "Why are you licking your lips?"

Fox thinks quick. "Oh, that? That's nothing, I have problems with dry mouth."

Chicken wants to believe, does. "Oh, yeah, I know how that can be, I was just afraid you might be about to pounce on me and eat me."

Fox tries to look shocked. "What?!? Me? What would make you think a thing like that?"

"Well…you're a fox. And there are feathers everywhere. And you have buckets of KFC littered around the den. And there's your raging fox boner."

Fox looks down, his red face turning redder.

"How embarrassing," says Fox just before he pounces.

Rich kids would be brought to us one by one, smiling that they'd been let in on a slummy secret. They would hang out for a few days, just long enough to feel comfortable, and then someone would set a trap.

"You need to buy a gat?" Donny leaned into a new mark from Piedmont, who sat there looking stupid with an upturned hat brim trying to look hard like Eazy-E but actually just looking like a punk-ass bitch.

"What's a gat?" Pudge Face asked.

We all laughed. It was calculated. A laugh designed to say, "You don't know this? You should!"

"A gat is a gun, you idiot," I shot at the kid, feeling powerful, happy that it wasn't me that was being called names.

"Oh! I don't know, I mean, yeah, I need a gun for sure." The kid was clawing, begging for approval. What would he need a gun for? To defend his mansion from the invading Mongol hordes? What he needed was for us to think he was cool. We knew it and we used it.

Donny passed him a joint and said, "I knew you were down! I told everyone you looked too hard to be from Piedmont."

The kid beamed, pride shooting from his eyes. "Yeah, I hate that place."

You see, in the Bay Area, bastion of the social equality movement, wealth was something to be ashamed of. There were no Upper East Side rich kids avoiding slumming it with the kids from the Bronx or Harlem, like in New York.

Rich kids in the Bay hid their wealth, excused it, and tried to pretend it didn't exist. They tried to act poor, imagining poverty bestowed depth of character and extremity of experience. But what it actually provided was a disdain for bitch-ass rich kids.

"I'm getting a shipment from my man next week, and I can get you a twenty-two for like six hundred bucks." Donny might as well have been drooling.

"Sick! I'll have the money for sure." We all smiled at each other.

The poor kid.

The following Tuesday, Donny and DJ pulled up with Joey to meet that kid. A box containing a cast-iron dumbbell was sold for six hundred dollars to a flesh-and-blood dumbbell. The deed was done, everyone got paid. I had nothing to do with it.

A week later I was riding my bike home when a BMW screeched to a stop alongside me and six rugby player–looking kids jumped out and surrounded me.

"Where's our fucking money, bro!?!" a team captain type yelled at me, furious. I was amused.

"Oh, you got jacked? Yeah, well, that can happen, welcome to Oakland." I grinned.

They didn't think it was so funny.

All of a sudden, I felt a heavy blunt shock and I woke up on the ground, in the dirt, with kids kicking me. Aww fuck.

Not the fearless gangsters they wanted to be, they didn't beat me up much, just enough to send a message. I got up screaming.

"You sucker-ass bitches! I didn't take your fucking money, you stupid Piedmont bitches. Coward-ass hoes. I'd box any one of you one on one but you guys had to jump me? You fucked up now! There's gonna be a bullet in each of your fucking heads for putting your hands on me!"

A note on the bullets.

I didn't have a gun or bullets. But I was always threatening people with imaginary guns. Yelling things like, "I'll be right back with a posse!" Like a cowboy movie. "Wait right here, motherfuckers!"

Then I'd run off, presumably to go retrieve my many guns and return with them a-blazing, but really what I'd do is leave the scene altogether and hope they ran in fear.

Unfortunately my position in the dirt, bloody and screaming, didn't really strike fear in the hearts of these rich pricks.

But it did start a little mini war.

Joey freaked when he heard the news. We all thought we were beyond reproach. We had assumed that we could continue to rob kids from Piedmont with impunity and their fear of the Oakland in us should have kept them from retaliating. The realization that it wasn't true was taken as a personal insult to Joey and the others. Jamie freaked, too.

"They betrayed us!" he screamed, his voice quaking with such emotion that it made us all uncomfortable.

"Actually, we betrayed them. I'm pretty sure that's why they kicked my ass." I was bruised up, but my snarky commentary would not be stopped.

"There are rules! The code of the streets has been broken and someone must pay. I'm calling my uncle." Jamie looked close to tears.

We all rolled our eyes.

Joey called one of the kids who had jumped me and, with fire in his voice, explained how things worked around here.

"You ever fucking touch another kid from Oakland again and you'll wake up with your fucking house on fire, you got that shit, you fucking faggots?"

Joey yelled for a few more minutes and then handed the phone to me.

"Hey, man, I'm sorry we jumped you," a frightened voice bleated.

"Go fuck yourself." I slammed the phone down.

Mediation, Oakland style.

After that it was essentially open season on Piedmont kids. We would drive around the streets of Piedmont at night, looking for prey.

One night we were riding, about ten-deep, in a kid named Dave Hansen's Chevy Suburban. Dave was a bizarre cat with a Piedmont address, but we let him hang out because he drove a Suburban, a vehicle that could fit an entire army of fuckups. Dave, after hanging out with us for just a couple of months, started screaming, "North Oakland for life!" when he got too drunk.

We considered kicking his ass every time, but just as we made moves to, someone would point at that sweet people mover and our rage would leak out of us.

It was late and we were driving through the hills of Piedmont passing a plastic gallon jug of Popov Vodka around the truck. Popov Vodka is so cheap there are potato chunks and miniature Russian peasants floating in it. But it does the trick.

From the corner of my eye as we passed a dark hill, I saw three guys walking, unaware that they were about to have the worst night in their recent memories.

"Guys, shut up and turn left. It's time to hit a lick."

We pulled up to the left and all ten of us jumped out of the car and hid in a long hedge, seemingly built for hiding a group of wayward youth.

I could hear the kids laughing and enjoying their night. They sauntered by, getting closer. They passed the hedge, they walked too far. Bad timing, kids.

As if with one brain, we all jumped out of our hedge screaming, "Break yourself!" "North Oakland Motherfuckers!" "Get these Motherfuckers!"

We pounced on those kids like a fuckin' cat on some mice. Like a fuckin' fox on some chickens. Like us on them. Their eyes went wide like plates. One kid took a look at us and bolted, full speed away, up the hill. Smart.

The other kids? Not so lucky.

Dave Hansen rushed them, fists swinging. As he punched the kid, I noticed he made, like, some kind of karate chop noise as he hit him, as if we were playing kung fu. *Boom! Biff! Pow!* What a loser.

The two kids fell to the concrete hard. One of them scrambled to his feet and we kicked him down again. This time he looked up at us, tears falling from his eyes, shame all over him. He screamed, "What do you want from me?" Poor kid.

"Your fucking wallet!" I screamed, excited at this turn of the karmic wheel.

You punch me, I rob you. The fact that these kids had literally nothing to do with my little situation meant little to me. I had power again.

We jumped back into the car screaming, our hearts pumping with adrenaline. We counted our spoils. Ugh. Eight dollars. Not enough to give us each a dollar.

"Fuck those fucking white boys," Donny barked, pissed.

"Wait, aren't we white boys?" I tried to inject my patented levity into the situation.

"Shut the fuck up, dude." Donny didn't seem as keen on the redemptive aspects of the robbery as I.

Well, whatever, we still had enough for another gallon of Popov. We rode the Suburban to one of the only liquor stores we knew of that would sell to a group of underage banditos, a little spot on Park Avenue in East Oakland.

East Oakland was and is like a lawless refugee camp after dark. A scary, dangerous place to visit, buck wild and terrifying.

We stopped in and spent that last eight dollars between the ten of us and got some more potato soup firewater.

For some strange reason, we then walked out of the liquor store one by one in a kind of procession as some of us grazed the aisles for Twinkies to steal (still fat!) and some of us just hurried back to the car.

As I exited the store, I noticed immediately that something was off. Donny and Corey were talking to a tall black dude and then disappeared past the side of the store. The dude approached me next. Calmly, he raised his T-shirt to reveal a .32 stuffed in his pants. He leaned in and whispered to me, "Go around the corner and lay down on the ground."

No argument from me.

I rounded the corner to see all my friends, lying prone on the sidewalk with their hands behind their heads. I'd seen this so many times with Officer Joe that, for a second, I entertained the illogical idea that we were being busted by the police. The police that looked like forty-year-old thugs from East Oakland and carried their police-issued pistols in their underwear.

Right, that didn't make sense. We were getting jacked. We lay down on the sidewalk in a line behind a Cadillac Coupe de Ville that was double-parked in the street. It created a kind of privacy curtain between us and anybody that might have driven by and, seeing a bunch of white kids in East Oakland lying on the ground, called the police and ruined everything for these guys.

I looked at them from the corner of my eye. Old. They were old guys, too old for pathetic jack moves like this one. Forty-year-old guys who rob fifteen-year-old kids for their pocket money have made some serious bad investments on the criminal retirement plan. I almost felt bad for them.

"All y'all empty your fuckin' pockets." I'd heard this kind of thing before. Oh yeah, twenty minutes earlier when I was yelling it. It sounded so much more convincing from an actual black person.

We complied.

All of us in the line emptied our pockets.

The loot was pathetic. We didn't even have the eight dollars.

We gathered a pile of scraps for these, the real wolves, to devour. It was a sad sight. A half a pack of Hav-A-Tampa cigars, a pack of Newports, a dollar fifty in quarters, house keys, and a book of matches. Ten white boys must've looked like the fuckin' jackpot to these guys. I'm sure they saw us and thought we were a bunch of suburban rich kids, fresh from the other side of the tunnel, our pockets fat with our parents' money. Sadly we were just like them. Except twenty-five years younger. And slightly paler.

They collected the pile of slop with a grimace.

"Get the fuck up!" the gunslinger of the bunch yelled. We jumped up like Marines after a push-up drill.

We got the fuck up.

We stood there, scared but also a bit frustrated at the turn of the events.

Jamie leaned forward to our captors. "You know it's funny, we rob people, too! I mean less tough kids than us obviously. I'm pretty impressed that you caught us slipping actually."

"Shut. Up." the short one with the gun snarled.

"Yeah, no doubt, no doubt." Jamie tried to look cool as he nodded assent.

I took a step forward.

"Hey, um, guys? You have my house keys. They can't be useful to you, would you mind throwing them back to me?" The other guys looked at me like I was insane, but what the fuck, I needed my house keys. If I lost my keys, I just straight up couldn't get into my house. My mother's absentmindedness had allowed the flashing light system that was wired into our doorbell to fall into disrepair years ago. Without the lights flashing, my mom had no way to know anyone was at the door. I'd stand outside of my door for hours just hoping my mom would look out the window for me. So I asked for my keys back.

The tall dude with the loot in his hands stared at me for a second and then tossed me the keys. I smiled at him, grateful.

"Thanks."

People started asking for their shit back, and piece by piece we stole back the shit they'd stolen from us.

This was like a scene from a Laurel and Hardy robbery.

The tall guy, apparently sick of how pathetic we were and how pathetic we were making him feel, muttered, "Broke-ass mother-fuckers," and lunged at DJ, clipping him in the jaw, dropping him back to the sidewalk.

DJ screamed like a wounded child/wildebeest and collapsed. Inside I grinned a bit and thought, "Karma's a bitch."

The guys drove off and left us panting, hearts pounding on the sidewalk. Then Dave Hansen looked up and grinned. "Well, they didn't get everything." He pulled out the new bottle of vodka safely hidden in the deep pockets of his hoodie. We all smiled. Maybe this guy wasn't so bad after all.

I guess after all that, we ended that evening at a moral zero.

We robbed, got robbed, and one of us even got punched in retaliation for the karmic punches we'd sprayed into the world. We didn't realize it, but it was perfect. Or maybe we did realize it.

We piled back into the Suburban a bit lighter.

The engine spat to life and we were off, driving back to North Oakland, to home and safety. We rode in silence for a few minutes, breathing through what had just happened to us. I broke the silence.

"Hey, you guys wanna go rob somebody?"

The guys turned and looked at me. Donny cracked a smile.

DJ, holding his face, punched me in the arm and started laughing.

We all started laughing. The noise filled that truck. We laughed into the truck and we laughed into the air. We laughed like lost boys. Dave put on some Gangstarr, a track called "Soliloquy of Chaos." A fitting soundtrack to the evening's festivities. Someone produced half a joint, pulled from the ashtray of the Suburban. A smoke, a drink, and the whole debacle was puffed away. I curled in and fell asleep.

Chapter 11

"You're in Shambles"
—Del the Funkee Homosapien

Things were beginning to unravel. My friends, my cadre of support, my second family—they loved to beat my ass. They threw me around and used me as their whipping boy for the sins they couldn't look at in themselves.

"Damn, you're a fucking crazy dog," they'd say. "You talk to your mama like that? You're nuts, Pork Chop."

Pork Chop. Sweet boys. They'd call me *Pork Chop* and *Fat Ass* and other things and sock me in the chest and throw me around and slap me when they got pissed. I'd leave, lump in my throat, night after night, walking myself home alone in the dark, tears streaming down my face swearing to myself, "I'll never hang out with them again."

My little lost boy family was becoming as painful as my real family.

Donny stood silently. He never participated. He never stopped it either. He stood and stared. I tried to laugh it off. I tried not to cry in front of the guys. I tried to stay tough. I couldn't keep this up. I was falling apart.

The next day I'd go back, pretending I forgot what they did, and what I'd said to myself. I'd go back because I didn't have any other place to go.

I took all that shame and turned it into rage that exploded at home.

Anytime my mother ran screaming after me for coming home late or the cigarettes she found or the money I stole, I'd explode with rage, screaming in her face on a level I am simply not capable of anymore. A kind of primal snap. A little solar flare from the hellfire.

I'd go mad. I'd throw whatever was in my hands at her head, trying to kill her.

It got bad.

I'd overturn kitchen tables and break the doors. I'd throw off my own shoes and toss them through windows.

My body was racked with rage like the devil was squeezing my spine, pumping anger into me.

My mom would run into the fracas and try to make me stop. Try to make me right.

I'd throw her to the ground. I'd hit her. I'd kick her. I'd scratch her. My own mother. My grandmother, too. I'd become what she'd always told me men were. *An abuser, that's who I was.* An abuser. I'd abuse at home and be abused in the streets. I'd abuse the ones I loved and be abused by the people I called friends.

⚜

Jeremy Moritz was a kid from Piedmont that DJ and Corey brought around one day. Just like Dave Hansen he had a car and long money so we welcomed him in. Unlike Dave Hansen, however, Jeremy Moritz was completely insane. No, really. He was toxically, chemically, Manson-level insane. A disgusting, violent weasel of a twerp, everyone loved him but me. Maybe that's because he liked to hit me. I was so tired of being slugged and punched and fucked with, and Jeremy Moritz made everything worse.

Jeremy had a kind of skittish, ratlike energy. He came from money but had the demeanor of some kind of street crackhead. Am I painting the picture that I disliked him? Maybe that's because he almost killed me.

One summer day, me, Jeremy, and the rest of the guys sat in the cemetery smoking cigarettes and talking shit. Maybe it's odd but the cemetery was a constant source of sanctuary for us. The brothers at the monastery were increasingly hostile toward us, but at the cemetery, the ghosts of dead delinquents rolled out to greet us every time we arrived.

We'd spend our days in the cemetery getting high, sitting on the larger graves and looking at the city. At night, we'd sneak back in and spook ourselves by getting drunk among the ghosts and creaky noises of a hundred-year-old cemetery. We'd climb in mausoleums. We'd write graffiti on graves. We'd outrun the security guard we'd affectionately named *Elmer* after the big *Elmer's Security* logo we read on the door of his white pickup. We'd knock graves over. We'd fuck shit up.

That day was a mellow one. Donny busted out a huge bag of mushrooms. More mushrooms, more madness. We passed it around, chewing the gross stems and caps, trying to ignore the taste. Mushrooms taste so bad and bring you to such psychedelic heights, it's like tossing God's salad.

We passed the bag to Jeremy Moritz but he waved them off,

citing something about clashing with his psych meds. What a pussy. I was pumped full of meds at the time but I didn't let that stop me.

I constantly felt the sway of psychotropics charging through my bloodstream, zapping my psyche, making me different. From the first day I started on a regimen of meds at Ross Hospital, I could feel them in me every second I was awake. I hated those things.

The only bright spot was that anytime I saw "Caution, do not combine with alcohol or other drugs" on the side of the bottle of the new medication they were experimenting with on me, I got excited in anticipation of the chemistry experiment I was about to conduct on my brain.

Zoloft + weed = buzzy high with a tinge of tweakiness.

Desipramine + malt liquor = a drunk with 3-D visuals.

Ritilan + Nothing = Meth

You get the picture.

I hated being on psych meds, but at least this way I could make them fun. That's how I lived. But Jeremy Moritz was too scared.

"Don't be a pussy, fucking eat some," I told him, dangling the shrooms in his face.

Out of nowhere, he snapped, tackled me, and threw me into a bush of razor grass. I got sliced to pieces, blood scratches crisscrossing me all over, as if little Zorros had declared victory on me.

I pushed him off me and he started laughing like everything was just hilarious.

I swallowed hard, holding back tears of shame. Ugh. I felt like such a bitch.

My emotions were starting to flood out against my will. Years of medicating them with smoke and pills and malt liquor had stuffed them into places they didn't belong. They would fall out when I didn't need them, didn't want them.

Every time I got really angry, my bitch-ass tear ducts would betray me. I couldn't start fighting without tears bursting out, declaring me a little sissy.

It was all I could do at times like this to just stay perfectly still and hope I didn't shake any bitch water loose upon my face.

No one noticed anyway because just then Jeremy jumped off me and, I suppose to prove his manhood, took a little pinch of mushroom powder from the bottom of the bag we had all eaten from and sprinkled it on some hash he had packed into a pipe and smoked it. By the way, smoking mushrooms has absolutely no psychoactive effect (this information will be important later). He puffed those mushrooms like it was the toughest thing anyone had ever done and then stood up declaring, "My grandparents just died!"

All of our faces dropped, and DJ's brother Corey put a hand on Jeremy's shoulder to comfort him.

Jeremy shrugged Corey's hand off and cackled, "Let's go fuck their old house up!"

We looked around confused and then, deciding there was nothing better to do, jumped into Jeremy's minivan and drove out of the cemetery toward his grandparents' place in Concord. The mushrooms kicked in and my brain melted.

We drove out to the suburban wasteland of Concord, one of those places that isn't quite a podunk little town, but only because it has a mall. A terrible, terrible Orange Julius mall. But at least it was an actual mall.

In Oakland, the malls we had were on planes of existence far below the malls in Concord. We only had ghetto malls. If you've ever been to a ghetto mall, you know. It feels similar to what I imagine walking into a refugee camp in Somalia would feel like. There are people slaughtering live goats, there are tribal feuds, and it's possible to buy products by yak barter.

The ghetto mall usually has 80 to 90 percent of its storefronts closed due to violence or economic inactivity, and the stores that do remain are mostly odd places you have never heard of. There are ethnic hair supply clearinghouses with such creative names as "Ge-Cho-Hair-On," "We Be Doin' Hair and Shit," "Tyler Perry's House of Haircare," "nappy 2 happy," "The NAAAHCP or National Association of African American Hair Care Products," and "The Place Where Black People Can Buy Haircare Products." There are your Korean import fire hazard electronics stores. Only the finest brands are available at these stores, like electronics from "Bro-shiba" and "Smacintosh," and there's indigestion medication from Mrs. Butterworth and tennis shoes made by Alpo.

The food court would be one Vietnamese lady making egg rolls and a closed-down Popeye's Chicken. Oh, and there was always a Chess King. A place for pimps to buy pimp peacock feathers. It was a ghetto mall.

Far beyond the urban blight of Oakland, though, was the Pollyanna expanse of the Sun Valley Mall. A place that dreams were made of. A mall with real stores like Sears and Macy's to frolic in. A place where gentile children could pretend to visit their God, Santa Claus, at Christmastime. In Oakland, the Santa was just a fat homeless guy with a bag of garbage at his side. At least he was real.

We pulled up to the Sun Valley Mall and my brain was liquid. I didn't know it until I stepped out of the van but I'd never been higher on psychedelics in my life.

The ground was unsteady like a wave and undulated beneath my feet. The world felt like a fun house. Jeremy Moritz's nose grew five inches, and he looked like a gargoyle, standing sentinel on a building. His nose kept growing until it slid, flattening onto the ground, springing into a bridge across reality into a world of broken glass visions. I skipped across.

We stepped into the mall and I immediately knew it was a mistake for me to be there. The walls bent in half like they'd turned into a rip curl and my body followed in kind. I felt like I was walking in half, my body folded in two, my head perpendicular with the ground. I could feel the force of gravity pulling me into the earth. Like there were a thousand little Batman-esque grappling hooks latched to my head, pulling me down. I felt like I hadn't drank my V8. I was going to fall over at any second.

Donny saw me walking funny and put a hand on my shoulder. It was like a grounding. I straightened right up. The guys took me into a Sharper Image store and left me there, staring at one of those pin table art things for what might've been hours, might've been years. I slipped away.

I woke up in Jeremy's recently deceased grandparents' house. From the other room, I heard a crash and then DJ exploded through the thin walls like the Kool-Aid Man, drywall dust everywhere, Jeremy laughing in the corner with tears streaming down his insane cheeks, painting white dust streaks down his clown face.

I woke up in Jeremy's van again, on the freeway going ninety miles an hour. Everyone was painted white like geishas. We looked like we'd been partying In the Night Kitchen.

Just then, Jeremy threw his hands into the sky from behind the steering wheel and started screaming, "I'm too high! I forgot how to drive! I forgot how to drive!" Too high? On a puff of nothing?

Reality surged through my brain like an ice pick.

What the fuck! I looked over at Donny as the van started swerving across five lanes of traffic screeching as it moved. He had an insane smile on his face.

"You ready to die, bro?!!"

"Fuck it!" I screamed. This was as good a time as any. Donny and I threw our heads back in end-of-life laughter as our doom approached. I decided to blip out. My brain went gray. I remembered no more.

I woke up at home. I wasn't dead. Pleasing. Somehow, organically we decided not to fuck with Jeremy Moritz anymore. In a world of very scary things, that dude was too scary even for us.

✼

Donny's world was starting to spin out of control just like mine. One day, quite out of the blue, Donny's biological father got in touch with him. Since I'd known him, Donny had been raised by his mom and stepfather, Sheriff John. Well, John wasn't an actual sheriff but he sure liked to act like it. Donny, much like me, had been given increasingly limited access to the various areas of his house. In fact, his parents had taken it one step further. Upon John's suggestion, Donny had been disallowed the privilege of ever being in his own house when his parents weren't around. In the morning, they would kick him out on their way to work, and later that night when they returned, he was allowed back in. Privacy was not permitted. He couldn't close his bedroom door or open his window. This was the world in which we lived. Every time Donny's stepdad walked upstairs, we would woop like a police car and Sheriff John would sneer at us.

"You'll never catch me alive, copper!" Donny would yell as John walked by his room, peering in to see what we were doing.

"Does that mean you're planning on dropping dead?" Sheriff John was pretty good at comebacks.

Despite all of the antagonism and resentment between the two of them, John was the only father Donny had ever really known.

"My dad is a gangster. A straight G fool! He did time in prison!" Donny told me one night while we were frying balls on acid.

"Well, as glad as I am that you are bringing up prison during an acid trip, do you mind explaining what you mean?"

"I mean it. My biological father, not the sheriff, but my actual dad was straight Mexican Mafia, bro! It's complicated, but basically, my dad was a gangster." Donny seemed really proud as he said this, as if this man he'd never met was somehow genetically toughening Donny up. If he couldn't be a father to him, at least he infused Donny's DNA with enough street smarts to guide him.

"I don't know everything about it but I know he spent years in San Quentin. Hard time. Fuckin' cool, huh?"

The more Donny explained his father's criminal past, the more excited he got. That might seem odd to you. This kid bragging that his dad was a crook. Well, consider that this was really the only story that Donny knew about his dad. The only narrative that his mother had provided for him. It was the only image he had of his father.

Divorced parents tended to do that. They only thought about their own traumatic memories of their former partners and so, without thinking of how fucked up it would make us, explained our fathers to us through the lens of that memory. Donny's dad was a gangster, mine was an abuser, and the only people keeping us from that criminal abuse were our heroic mothers. At least that's the way the picture was painted.

Over the years, though, feeling half-fused by our childhoods, Donny and I would stare at those memory paintings looking for the information that could explain to us the kind of men we would become. Sadly, they were warped by resentment and so they looked like Hieronymus Bosch hellscapes. Good luck, boys! The journey to manhood became like walking through the forest in the dark. Hansel and Gretel trying to find their way home.

We grew up lost.

That's not to say that these tales were false. Donny's dad was a drunk and an absentee father and, I guess, a gangster, too. But he was still his father. And so when, fourteen years after Donny Moon was born, Papa Moon got out of prison, gave him a call, and said, "What's up? I'm ready to get back in touch after all these years," Donny got excited. Then he got high.

At that point, he hadn't gotten high in months because he was still technically at that Kaiser Rehab in Walnut Creek, though he was already teetering on the edge of being thrown out. He, much like everyone who gets sent to adolescent rehab, rather than cleaning up and getting his shit together, met a new group of exciting people to get high with, people with new tricks and new drugs. People like James Burnside.

James Burnside was a stocky, strange kid. Long sideburns and a demeanor that suggested a madman who used his brain as a test tube for experimental drugs. Oh, did I mention that James was an amateur chemist who made experimental drugs? That's probably why he seemed like that.

"This is Ozone, man," James whispered into the air between

Donny and me, not quite looking at either of us. "It's crushed-up morphine and acid and a few specialties that I threw in."

"So, like, when did you first become a mad scientist?" I asked. "And are fifteen-year-old chemists common in your tribe?"

"Who the fuck is this guy, man?" James looked at Donny like he was ready to kill me.

"Don't worry about him, man, he's just always cracking jokes." Donny looked at me like "Shut the fuck up."

"You a fuckin' cop?" James stared at me with ice in his eyes.

"Um, I'm fifteen." I hoped this would get me out of my predicament.

"Excuses are like assholes." James said this matter-of-factly like it made sense. Of course, it did not.

"Yeah," I said, "yeah, I get that. I'm not a cop, though."

"Good." He seemed satisfied. My life expectancy shot back up immediately.

James turned to Donny and said, "One of these pills is the equivalent of taking fifty-two hits of acid at once but, like, more intense."

That was good. If there's anything that fifty-two hits of acid screams for, it's "more intense."

"You wanna try this shit?" James whispered.

I looked around the room, trying to find a way out of this situation. I didn't see one.

"Yeah, I guess I'm down." I quivered.

"Not you, you fat fuckin' cop."

"I'm still not a cop." How was I a cop again?

James seemed unfazed by this information. He stared at me as if trying to figure out some equation and then his eyes flashed understanding.

"Well, anyway, I only have one." James turned to Donny like Moebius and Neo offering him a palm with a blue pill resting on it. "You down?"

Donny smiled. "Always."

He swallowed his pill and began his orbit around the moon.

A few hours later Donny started acting strangely. This was not the kind of strangely that we were all used to from dropping acid, the stomach ache, the weird look in the eye; this was something different and off-putting. I noticed he was off when he began batting at things in the air that were not there. As if shooing off a phantom fly, Donny pawed at the air in a sort of cartoon slow motion that gained in speed and intensity until it became quite clear something was very wrong.

Jim began looking a bit concerned when Donny decided to lie down and make snow angels on the sidewalk in front of the coffee shop where we'd been sitting. It doesn't snow in Oakland.

"Jim, is this normal?" I asked, trying desperately not to sound too policey.

"Man, I don't know. No one's ever taken this much at once. This was kind of an experiment." Jim looked scared.

I couldn't believe this shit. "An experiment? You don't experiment with people, you idiot!" Now normally, boldness was not my strong suit unless I was surrounded by friends who were bigger and stronger than me, but this fucking yahoo was going to kill my friend and that gave me courage.

Jim jumped up in my face and snarled, "What the fuck are you going to do about it, fatso?"

"It's not what I'm going to do about it, you suburban white boy, it's what half of North Oakland is going to do to you if you fucked Donny up."

Jim and I had squared off, ready to box, when, as if to break the tension, Donny suddenly stood up, stared at the two of us, and then vomited bright green bile all over the sidewalk as everyone in the Edible Complex Cafe stared in horror.

Donny staggered and then grabbed me and clung to my shoulder. Steadying himself, he whispered, "Don't let anyone see me throw up."

I was confused. "Um, that just happened, like in the past, and you also did it in front of a huge plate-glass window with coffee drinkers and tons of chicks watching, so I'm not sure how much I can do to help hide that."

Donny looked at me quizzically and asked, "Wait, who are you?"

I was now very concerned.

"Jim, what do we..." I looked around but Jim had determined his chemical experiment a failure and slunk off into the night, leaving me to deal with a best friend who didn't know who I was.

"You don't recognize me?" I asked, a bit confused about just what a situation like this called for.

"Man, I don't recognize anything." Donny's pupils were so dilated at this point he looked like a frightened lemur.

He started batting at things again and then suddenly just stopped and stared off into space like he was Commander Data and he had been manually shut down (nerd joke!). I had no idea what to do.

"You sit right here. I'll be right back." I ran inside to try to call Joey and ask him what I should do.

Joey picked up the phone, mad. "What the fuck do you want?"

"Donny's on some weird fucked-up drug, man, he's trippin'. I don't know what to do, he's like freaking out right now."

"Why the fuck are you calling me about this shit?" Joey snarled.

Joey had become increasingly unstable in recent months as coke had flooded into our social group. He'd been snorting for days. Perhaps it was a mistake to have called him.

"Don't be fucking calling me at home with this shit," Joey spat at me.

"Okay, man, okay. Sorry to bug you." Images of Sean The Bomb unconscious on the playground flashed in my mind.

"Where the fuck is Donny now?"

"He's sitting outside batting at invisible mosquitoes, I think."

"Well, go get him, you fucking idiot! Don't leave him by himself." Joey hung up the phone with a clang.

I walked back outside with no more information than when I had entered other than the fact that I now knew I was an idiot.

When I arrived at the spot where I had left Donny, the rumors of my idiocy were confirmed. Donny was gone.

Shit! Shit! Shit! Shit! Shit!

I had lost my best friend who was so out of touch, he didn't even know I was his best friend. This didn't bode well.

I spent the next four hours frantically searching the streets of Oakland calling out his name. I never found him, though. Years later, after his brain had re-formed itself, he told me what happened, as best as he could piece it together:

> *Shit, I disappeared. When I lost track of you, I just started, like, wandering. I was in and out of the world, in and out of touch, man. I don't know exactly what happened but I went over to Corey and DJ's to try and get straight. I don't remember much but Corey told me he knew something was wrong with me. I was peeling wallpaper off of his walls and talking to my hands and*

*shit. We smoked a joint to try and chill but then his
mom came home and fucked everything up. Parents
were always fucking things up back then, huh? It's
like, all I ever wanted, all I ever wanted back then was
to just get them off of my back and be able to hang out
with my friends. It's funny, right? I mean it was such
a small thing, just kickin' it with your homies, but
it was the only thing I wanted. Parents were always
ruining everything. So anyway Corey's mama came
home and started being weird about me, asking like
"what's wrong with him" and shit. Corey told me I
had to leave. At that point I was just a puddle. I didn't
even know who I was. I ended up back at my house
somehow. Shit, I'd lost my identity but retained my
address. Funny what you are able to hold on to, huh?*

*I went into my room and locked it and shut the
lights off. I was determined to just let it pass in the
dark, but my mom insisted on talking to me, trying
to figure out what I was up to. She was like banging
on the door like, "Open this shit up! Let me in!"
I felt like it was the devil banging on the door into
my soul. Fuck that. I cracked the locks open on the
window and jumped down a story and a half onto
the sidewalk and ran over to Terry Candle's place.
At this point, I'm like a full on, demon possession
level madman. Terry was there and his mom, too,
but you know she was chill and we smoked some weed
and they plopped me down onto the couch in front of
the Super Nintendo and I played F-Zero for a couple
hours. Somehow that grounded me. I calmed down.*

I came back into my body and my mind. But I guess Terry's mom called mine because I heard a fuckin', like, police knock on the door and my mom barged into the living room. I tried to bolt out the back door but Sheriff John was there and he grabbed me, bear hugged me so I was trapped. My mom starts scream-ing at me, "You're high! What are you on?!? What are you on?!?" Which is like the worst thing ever to scream at a dude who's freaking out because he's high. I kept muttering something about something slipped in my drink. Is that funny? Even in the middle of a fucking code red psychedelic freakout, I was still worried about getting busted. Of course, I start losing my shit again with the fuckin' KGB interrogation going on. They start saying, "We are headed to the ER to see a doctor," and now I really start flipping out. I almost tore my hair out. Somehow I convinced them to take me home and my mom just sat there with me, holding me, telling me it was going to be okay for like twelve hours. It took that long for me to start believing her. Took me months to feel normal. Actually, scratch that. I never felt quite normal again.

I caught up to Donny, like, two days later, having heard noth-ing from him and fearing him dead. When I saw him, he looked changed, like Moses stumbling back from Mount Sinai or, more accurately, like a fourteen-year-old boy who took fifty-two hits of acid. That shit was scary. For him and for me. But it was nothing compared to what happened next. Even fifty-two hits wasn't as big of a mind fuck as that.

Chapter 12

"Why Do We Live This Way?"
—*Geto Boys*

The mind fuck began with the ultimate Piedmont prize—a girl to drive us wherever we wanted to go. We were still all too young to drive, so DJ and Corey adopted a semi-permanent chauffeur in a Nissan Maxima. A nice Chinese girl from Piedmont who wanted desperately to be a bad black girl from Oakland. Her name was Tina Yee.

Finding a girl from a town like that to come slum it in Oakland was advantageous to us and exciting to her. If you could find a lady friend with a driver's license and a car, you could introduce the wonders of new social vistas into the group. All of a sudden we were driving to San Francisco to parties, and trips to the East Oakland dope spots were easy in-and-out affairs.

Tina was happy to do it, too. Since she was not quite ready to fully commit to having a real Oakland boyfriend—someone scary to drive her around East 14th and show her life in the streets—my friends and I provided Tina with a kind of walk-on-the-wild-side middle ground, a social safari where a rich girl could make her existence seem grittier and more extreme without having to actually experience true dangers. In exchange for that escape from the dreary doldrums of Piedmont life, Tina gave us rides and brought us girls to hang out with.

Tina had a friend named Leah Krauss, who, I suppose you could say, was "fucking nuts." Leah had been in and out of mental institutions since she was a little girl and had the kind of skittish, hypersexual, hyperfrantic energy of a girl who had been exposed to horrors.

There were rumors that she had been thrown out of school the previous year for hurling a pair of scissors at her teacher like a throwing knife. My kinda girl, right? Maybe due to my shame about my own mental health, though, I kept a sort of wide berth and left her to the other guys. Not that that made a difference.

Leah was constantly throwing out suggestive comments, the kind that keep fifteen-year-old boys' attention.

"I sucked twelve dudes off in a day once," she'd throw out into the group as we sat around drinking forties. All of us shot malt liquor out of our mouths at once like an intricate statue in an Italian fountain. Leah grinned at the reaction she got and happily accepted as Corey scooted closer to her and offered her a joint.

"I really think I can fuck that Leah chick," Corey said one day, so excited that we were all made uncomfortable by the erection he undoubtedly had in his pants.

"Congrats," I said. "Your mother must be very proud."

DJ, having the same mother as Corey, and being unable to understand the nuances of my joke, punched me in the chest yelling, "Cave Chest! Don't talk about my mama!"

Cave Chest was a charming game that DJ liked to play. The rules were simple—DJ yelled "Cave Chest!" and punched you in the chest. Presumably to cave your chest in. No one seemed to enjoy this game but DJ.

"I'm a virgin," Corey declared flatly with a humility that was rare for a teenage boy virgin. Corey began a rousing speech that would have made any army grab their rifles and follow him into battle. It went something like this:

"I really think I could finally make this happen. Now I don't know if I can do it alone, but with your help, I hope to take advantage of this crazy girl and to, once and for all, be able to declare myself a non-virgin. It won't be easy. But I can't think of a group of guys I'd rather engage in a sad attempt to fuck a mentally ill girl with!"

As he said this, a Union drummer boy played the fife and drum. We all shed a tear at his courageous speech. We saluted. Of course we would help.

A plan was laid for Corey to get laid. We would all gather back at our safe place, the monastery, and drink and get high with the two girls. Corey, at some point, would pull Leah off to the side and make himself a man.

In typical fashion, by the time that night arrived, the rest of us had busied ourselves with smoking and drinking so much that, by sundown, we were completely tapped.

"Are you guys fucking kidding me?" Corey asked, pissed. "How am I supposed to get with this bitch if I don't have anything to get her high with?"

This alone ought to have been a sign that perhaps this was not a true love connection, but since that was hardly the point, we ignored it.

"Sorry, dog." Donny stepped up to take the blame for it. "We just forgot."

I just stayed silent, knowing anything I said pushed me closer to Cave Chest.

"Well, shit, what am I supposed to do now?" Corey was desperate.

It was seven twenty, and the girls were supposed to arrive any second.

"I'll go back to my house and grab a couple Ritalin pills," Donny volunteered.

Donny had been taking Ritalin to treat the attention deficit disorder he had been diagnosed with during the great ADD epidemic of the early nineties. At that time, essentially any problem you had would be blamed on ADD, and you would be given speed to calm you down, in a sort of Zen opposite-logic pharmacological experiment. No one ever seemed to connect the dots that the very kids who would display the symptoms of ADD were the ones who loved to crush up speed pills and snort them. Donny's parents never quite noticed the fervor with which Donny treated his ADD.

That was really what was going on much of the time back then. People willfully ignored things that were right before their faces screaming, "PROBLEM!" Except my mother, of course. She noticed everything, and when there was nothing to notice, she simply imagined problems. I never got away with shit. Well, maybe I got away with a lot, but I also got busted more than any of my friends. I still can't figure out if it was because I was more of a badass than my friends or if it's because my mother was the biggest badass of us all. It might seem like I got away with murder, but my mother was on me, always catching me in some lie, busting me for some infraction. I spent my life being grounded. Not that it made a difference.

Donny and I ran back to his place to snag a couple pills and to fabricate some fake buds. Such good friends we were. There was no weed to waste on this chick but we'd certainly be willing to create the illusion for Corey.

We'd done this before, usually when we were down on our luck and low on cash. If my mother's purse was ever locked up in such a way that I couldn't get to it, we could make some fake bud and sell it to some marks from the suburbs. It took a sort of taxidermist artistry to make this without arousing suspicion. The idea was for something so realistic-looking that you'd be long gone before they figured out it was fake. We'd gotten quite good at it.

Donny busted out a variety of herbs from the kitchen cabinets and we got to work. I took Elmer's Glue and squeezed a dime-sized puddle into my palm. This reminded me of my phone sex days.

Donny sprinkled thyme and oregano into my palm and I rolled us up a fake bud. With the precision of a Swiss watchmaker, Donny then stabbed the top of the bud with the stripped-down center vein of a dried leaf, providing it with a dry green stem. Beautiful. Then the final touch, while it was still sticky from the glue, we snipped little pieces of purple thread which we embedded into the body of the bud, making it look like purple kush. Yeah, it might be fake but we didn't sell low-quality fake product. This shit was the bomb. Or at least it looked like the bomb.

We then stuffed the bud into a dank baggy that we had used to carry roaches of real joints. The smelly half-burnt butts of our adventures had permeated the bag and infused it with stinky, sour skunk smells. No one would ever notice the difference by looking, and if our suspicions were correct about how rookie this chick was, she might not even notice it when she smoked it.

We put all the stuff into a bigger ziplock bag and headed back toward the monastery to hand it off to Corey and hope he got his way.

As we walked back, we laughed at the idea that the only real drugs we had at that point had been provided to us by Donny's primary care physician. Something was wrong with that picture.

We arrived at the monastery happy and ready to pull a fast one on Leah, not realizing that, in a couple weeks, the joke would very much be on us.

We got to the monastery and met a party in full swing. Leah and Tina had arrived and everyone was drinking forties. Everyone was there that night. All but Joey, who just seemed to never leave his room anymore. We'd called him earlier that afternoon to invite him down but he'd just snapped at us and hung up. Never mind that, there was a party to attend.

Miguel and a Puerto Rican kid named Danny Soto had come through with a case of stolen warm Olde English 800 and, feeling generous, passed them out among the revelers. DJ was there, drunk. Corey, of course, was sitting next to Leah whispering possibly sweet but more likely dumb nothings in her ear.

"Here's that weed you asked for." I plunked my creation down in Corey's hand and he passed it off to his lover to be. What a romantic.

After enough Olde English, the night got hazy for me and for everyone else, I imagine. Corey and Leah stole off to a dark corner and the rest of us sat on the grass and enjoyed a summer night, drunk, laughing, and talking shit. Nothing new or special about it.

An hour later, Corey stormed out after Leah with her frowning and him pleading. "Aww, c'mon, come back, I won't try anything else, okay?"

"We're leaving!" Leah demanded and looked at Tina with a "This is not negotiable" glare.

Tina and Leah left, and I yelled, "Enjoy the weed! It's pretty powerful stuff! Try it with pasta!" Donny and I enjoyed a laugh and Corey socked me in the arm.

"What fuckin' happened?" Donny asked as soon as the girls were out of earshot.

"Ah fuck...I dunno. She let me finger her and everything. Then I whipped out my dick and she just like freaked. She looked at me like I was crazy and just stormed off!" Corey looked pissed.

"You whipped out your dick?" Donny asked, incredulous.

"Well, like, yeah." Corey looked confused.

"Just out of nowhere? Just boom, here's my dick?" Donny was falling apart at the seams trying to hold back laughter.

"I mean, um, yeah, isn't that what you do?"

"Naw, dog, that's what *you* do!" Miguel cackled.

I jumped into the fray. "Never has something so small scared someone so much!" We all lost it. Corey got pissed and told DJ to kick our asses. DJ was too busy laughing at his brother to comply. Just then Donny whipped his dick out for us all to see and yelled, "Isn't this what you do?"

We laughed for what felt like hours and then forgot all about that night.

Two weeks later Corey and DJ were in jail and the police were after us all.

꧁꧂

I got a call one afternoon from a muffled voice. "Hey, it's me."

"Donny?" I asked, confused. "Is that you?"

"Don't say my fucking name!" Something was off here.

"Um, okay?" I was confused.

"Meet me at the corner of College and Hudson at four."

The phone hung up with a clang. What the hell was going on?

I threw some pants on and headed out the door with my mother, as always, standing in the doorway trying to forbid me to leave.

"Where are you going?" she growled.

"Out."

I was always going out. She was always in my way.

I never considered back then what happened those moments when I pushed her to one side and slid out the door.

Never considered that she sighed, wondering if I'd just stolen her money.

Never considered that she cried, wondering if she'd see me again.

Never even thought.

All I knew was that she was in my way and that my friend needed me.

It wasn't until I was an adult that I looked at my mom and the shock of crow's-feet cracking her face and I wondered if I'd caused them.

At the time, though, all I knew was that she was in my way.

"Get out of the fucking way," I'd said to her, unconcerned if she knew what I was saying or not. I was becoming a monster and I didn't even know it.

I sat at the bus stop waiting for the 51A with my mind spinning. What the hell was going on? I'd never received a call like that from Donny before. His voice was shaky, desperate. I realized my hand was shaking.

The bus came, and as the rest of the squares got on the front and paid their fare, I pried the back door open, sliding my fingers beneath the black rubber lip of the thing and pulling. I slipped into the stairwell and immediately flipped the back door mirror up toward the ceiling so that the driver couldn't see me. Then I sat down and collected myself.

As College and Hudson approached, I pulled the cable and dinged the bus to a stop.

I climbed out and Donny was nowhere to be seen. What the fuck?

I lit a Newport and waited.

I heard a whistle from behind me.

I turned to see Donny's red hooded Starter jacket peeking from behind a staircase leading to the basement of the First Presbyterian Church on College Avenue.

"Get over here!" Donny beckoned to me.

I jumped back behind the wall and was surprised to see Miguel, Danny Soto, and Terry Candle back there, too.

"Surprise party?" I couldn't resist.

"Stop cracking jokes." Donny had that fear in his eyes again. "DJ and Corey are in jail. They both got pulled out of class today and arrested."

"For what?" I asked.

"Rape."

The word kinda floated there in the air like a thought bubble.

"Jesus." I didn't know what to say.

"That bitch Leah said they raped her," Miguel said, looking pissed.

"Jesus," I repeated, calling out to the wrong God, "why'd you call me out here? What can we do?"

Terry Candle lit a joint and passed it to me. "She said we *all* raped her."

"Even me?" This couldn't be.

"Even you," Donny said flatly.

"But I'm a virgin!"

This wasn't fair. I hadn't even fucked yet and I was being accused of rape?

"Look, guys, here's the deal." Donny was taking over, establishing control like I'd seen him do so many times before. At least his mind was back with him. "We are all named by our first names only in the police report. At least that's what Corey told me on the phone today."

Terry Candle spoke up. "So what's that mean?"

"It means we aren't in jail already, obviously, but we might get rolled on at any second. As soon as they figure out who we are, we are all fucked. If Officer Joe hears about this, he tells the Piedmont Police, and we are all done for. That prick would get such a fuckin' hard-on if he figured out how to bust us. One call from the cops to him and we are all in jail for raping that girl."

I thought I'd throw in an obvious detail. "But we didn't rape her!"

Donny grinned a sour grin. "You think that matters?"

All of this blew my mind. I was raised by two women in a feminist, bordering on man-hating house. I was raised to assume that all of the things I heard on television relating to men abusing women were spot-on true. My grandmother and mother watched the Clarence Thomas trials with "I believe you, Anita," tears in their eyes. They cursed at the television coverage of William Kennedy at his trial and assumed he was guilty until proven otherwise. I assumed as much, too. It had never occurred to me, until that moment, that women could or would ever suffer that level of indignity for something false. It was like betraying a sacred trust.

My mind was spinning as I puffed on that joint. At least I had that. My thoughts slowed down. My fears numbed out.

That was one of the mightiest medicines of drugs. Their ability to make any crisis, no matter how severe, muted. They never made the problem go away, just the consciousness of that problem disintegrated one grain at a time until all that was left was the moment. It was very Zen. All but the false rape accusation part of it.

To be fair, I couldn't be sure of what had happened between Corey and Leah. I wasn't back there behind that church with them. But I knew Corey. I just didn't think he would have done anything like that. And I knew DJ had been with me the entire time we'd been at the monastery. I had the chest bruises to prove it. And I knew me. And as far as I knew, I was still a measly virgin. I'd hardly even spoken to that crazy broad, much less fucked her, much less engaged in a weird ritual gang rape at a church with her as her friend Tina sat there and said nothing. Okay. Yes. I was pretty sure this whole thing was bullshit and would blow over.

But then, DJ and Corey were in jail. And Donny was freaking out. And my name was on a fucking police report.

Don't be an abuser, remember?

How? How how how how had this shit happened? Why was I always getting in trouble? What the fuck was I going to do?

"What the fuck am I going to do?" Donny said, panicked.

What were any of us going to do? Get high. Check out. Worry again tomorrow.

For weeks, I stalked the streets of Oakland with the weight of a thousand police officers' imaginary eyes on me. The fun stuff seemed gone. I got high at home and stayed out of sight. It was so hard to party when you were afraid of being arrested on sight for a rape you didn't commit.

I stayed in. I became a night rat. Home all day, sneak out to meet Donny at night. Donny would call me with hushed tones and say agreed-upon code words and we would meet in secret at free-way underpasses. One evening, passing a joint back and forth between us, he turned to me and dropped a bomb. "I'm getting out of Oakland for a while. Let the heat die down. I'm going to live with my father."

"The convict?" I asked, the paragon of sensitivity.

"Ha, yeah, I guess. I've been talking to him on the phone like every week. He's real chill, man, not like Sheriff John, you know? He heard about all this bullshit going down and said I could come there for a while to hide out."

I wish I'd been able to say what I was thinking, that I was sad and pissed that he was leaving. That I'd had a best friend leave me before. That I was scared of being alone in the world. But I just said, "Cool, man, good luck. I gotta bounce. I have therapy in the morning."

I left that night, my head swimming from the pot, my heart heavy from Donny moving away, my guts churning with fear that the cops were around every corner. I went home and cried.

Donny was gone, and Corey and DJ were in jail. Terry Candle hadn't been seen or heard from since that day in the church stairs. Miguel, of course, walked around like he wasn't concerned in the least.

Thankfully, Corey and DJ were keeping their mouths sealed shut as to who the other people in the police report were. Leah had only mentioned us by first name since that was all she knew of us.

DJ and Corey, like silent Cosa Nostra enforcers, kept our confidence and kept us free.

There is a kind of feral protectiveness that takes over a family when a kid is in real crisis. Despite all the madness I'd put them through, my mother and grandmother never for one second doubted my account of the story, their love for me taking the place of their fierce feminist instincts. Donny's mom, too. She'd shuffled him onto a plane and sent him to New Mexico without batting an eye. Just like that, he was gone. And there I was, hiding from the cops, lonely as fuck.

"I don't understand why that girl would say that about you," my grandmother told me, grabbing my hand and squeezing it.

"I swear I didn't do anything," I told her, cries of "*abuser*" ringing in my mind's ear.

"Of course you didn't, honey. I know you didn't. You aren't a bad kid; you just act a lot like one sometimes."

Those words washed over me like an absolving bath. But they didn't fully resonate. I knew I hadn't touched that girl, but I'd hurt everyone around me for so long, it was only a matter of time until the karmic wheel ran me the fuck over.

I'd done such a good job of drinking reality away, but it was becoming harder and harder to drink enough to blur its sharpness. I felt cut up and punctured. I didn't know what to do, so I did what I always did. I got high.

After having lain low for months, we got some hope. DJ and Corey were let out of jail. I got the rundown on the police report from Corey and DJ as told to them by their lawyer.

Corey was his normal excited self but DJ seemed hurt and subdued by his experiences. Corey did most of the talking.

"The bitch is fucking crazy! I didn't get to even bust a nut. Just what I told you happened, happened, and anyway, you guys didn't even touch her! Whatever. Doesn't matter what did happen because she's a fucking crazy-ass bitch. My lawyer told me all about her. Nutcase. Loco. I'm telling you for real. She's been to fuckin' mental hospitals and shit." Corey looked at me, realizing.

"Oh, sorry, dude. Anyway, she's like seeing dogs' tails wagging with no dogs attached to 'em and shit. She said, that night after she left the park, she like walks away and right then, I ran up on her, fuckin' all creep style and socked her. Just boom, clocked her in the face and she went down, right? Right, then I guess you guys were like hiding in the bushes or something because she said we all jumped out at her. Just fuckin' held her down and ripped her clothes off. And then . . . well, you know." Corey blushed with the last bit of innocence he had left.

"Anyway, then here's where the story gets weird and don't make no sense. She says we left her there in the dirt and shit. But says, afterwards she got into a change of clothes . . ."

"What, she keeps a spare outfit in case of gang rape?" I asked, mad.

"That's what I'm saying!" DJ broke his silence.

"Right, so that shit doesn't make sense." Corey cracked his knuckles nervously. "Also, she left a person out of her story."

"Who?"

"Fuckin' Tina Yee's ass. Where the fuck was she this whole time? Watching? Why didn't she call the cops? And most of all, where the fuck is she now?"

I was confused. "Okay, where the fuck is she now?"

"Here." Corey stared at me blankly, reset his teeny dinosaur brain, and continued, "But where was she *then*?"

I sighed, "Okay, *then*, where was she then?"

"China."

"Excuse me?"

"Fucking China. Like fuckin' chong chong choi! Tina was in China, and as soon as she got back, we had a person vouching for us, and another thing, here's the weirdest part—she went to the hospital."

"Who, Tina?" I said. Corey sucked at storytelling, I decided.

"No, you idiot! Fuckin' Leah went to the ER and told them she was raped. Not a thing that a girl who was lying would do usually because they can tell by looking at it if there's been like force or something. Like cuts and shit. They checked her out and found some cuts all right but they weren't the right kind. They were exact and like surgical. Like someone had taken a razor blade to it and cut it like that."

I just stared at Corey, confused.

"Bro, she cut up her own fucking pussy."

I thought I was going to be sick.

"She did that to try and fuck us up but it ended up fucking her. The doctors can tell the fucking difference and they were, like, this ain't it. They released the records to the judge and he let us out. My lawyer says the case will ninety-nine percent get dropped."

I didn't understand. "Dropped?"

"Yeah, like done! The whole thing will be over." Corey pulled out the largest joint I'd ever seen and lit it in celebration. We would be free. I felt the weight of a thousand crazy mutilated vaginas ease off me.

"Hey." I looked at DJ and Corey. "Thanks for not telling them our names. That was solid."

DJ looked at me, his lip quivered for a second, then he smiled and punched me in the chest and yelled, "Don't be a fag, Cave Chest!"

We partied that night, celebrating, drinking, smoking, sucking down nitrous. I felt my face vibrating from the gas and the relief.

We all called Donny in New Mexico and yelled and cheered into the phone. It was a beautiful night. The air tasted freer. Still, though, somewhere deep, somewhere beneath the layer of intoxication, beneath the layer of relief, beneath the layer of anger, beneath all those sedimentary levels of delinquency, was a place of quiet pain. A little puddle of realization that, despite the fact that I hadn't done anything to Leah, I had, somehow, placed myself in a world where a girl like that had felt embarrassed enough and angry enough and crazy enough to accuse us of a thing like that. To put it simply, I wasn't living right. That puddle of realization was rising and churning beneath the surface and soon would leak out from its deep place and flow, like veins of lava, into my conscious mind and melt the icy defenses of anger and self-righteousness that I'd built up over the years, fortifying them with drugs and delusion. The doomsday clock was ticking on my ability to defend how I was living.

Perhaps I was just growing up. Or perhaps I was being weighed down by the karmic weight I had accrued. I just realized somewhere that I had created this problem. It was a small shade of the crumbling edifice of my great illusion: that I was the victim of the world's cruelties and the injustices of the adults surrounding me. A tiny little beam of light was trying to break through from that deep place. A small idea that I couldn't hear, couldn't see yet, but that someday would break through, undeniable:

You did this to yourself.

I walked home from Corey and DJ's that night a freer man, but I had a new weight on my shoulders, too. The weight and the ache of cognizance.

I got home, scraped my pipe, smeared a resin ball onto the mesh screen, and smoked it red-hot until I couldn't hold the pipe, until I couldn't feel the ache. Then, my head quiet, I went to bed.

Chapter 13

"That's When Ya Lost"
—*Souls of Mischief*

School was starting again and I was now entering my third year without having successfully passed a grade since the seventh. I was on my way to becoming the cool, older senior with a beard and a Camaro. Every time I'd get thrown back into a school, my new, doomed-to-failure educational plan would be outlined in an IEP.

An IEP, or Individualized Education Program, is created at a meeting that the school administration calls in order to determine the best means of making you successful in school. It never works. At least it never did for me.

"Well, I see here that you have been experiencing repeated failures in all of the placements we have sent you to," the lady assigned to my case said as she handed me a chart that essentially, graphically, explained why I was such a fuckup.

"He just hasn't found the right placement yet. That's your

Alameda County Mental Health Services

GOALS AND OBJECTIVES OF MENTAL HEALTH SERVICES
WITHIN THE INDIVIDUALIZED EDUCATION PROGRAM

Pupil's Name: Mark Kasher   D.O.B.: 7-6-79   Date: 3-23-93

School: Claremont Middle   SELPA: Oakland

For each kind of service recommended and approved, please list:
1. Date for initiation, frequency, and duration of service.
2. Goals of service.
3. For each service goal list specific objectives - procedures and criteria and how they are to be evaluated.
4. Parent/Guardian sign and attach ACMHS consent to treatment.

Service Description: Day Treatment

Frequency: Five days per week.

Duration: At least one year (calendar) with annual review.

Schedule for Initiation: Priority: Next available opening.

Goal 1: Improve interactions with adults and peers.

Objectives: a) Will interact with adults in a calm, cooperative manner 80% of the time.

b) Will express disagreement without becoming verbally abusive 80% of the time.

c) Will approach peers in an age appropriate manner, i.e., without negative, sarcastic or abusive remarks, 80% of the time.

Goal 2: Increase impulse control.

Objectives: a) Will identify consequences for various behaviors when given real or hypothetical problems to solve, 75% of the time.

b) Will identify his part in a conflict or incident and accept responsibility for it 60% of the time.

c) When he begins to be disruptive, agitated or defiant, will cease acting out and substitute constructive behavior, e.g., a self-imposed time out, 50% of the time.

responsibility to find." My mother scolded the school district constantly for what she perceived as their complicit involvement in my educational failures. It was never just that I'd fucked up, it was always that I hadn't been helped right.

Codependent or not, my mother knew the system and wasn't shy about milking it dry.

Mark Kasher
Goals & Objectives - Page Two

Goal 3: Decrease depression and anxiety.

Objectives: ─╳a) Will verbalize feelings and concerns appropriately to teachers,
staff and therapist 60% of the time.

╳ b) Will identify what is causing him to feel sad or anxious 60% of
the time.

Goal 4: Improve attention and concentration.

Objectives: a) Will focus on school tasks at least 80% of the time.

b) Will complete homework assignments at least 90% of the time.

The IEP team including Mark's mother and therapist may modify these goals and
objectives as needed.

Joyce R. Saad, Ph.D.

Joyce R Saad, Ph.D.
AB3632 Evaluator

Approved by: *Susan Dubin-McNeil, Ed.D.*
Susan Dubin-McNeil, Ed.D.
AB3632 Evaluation Coordinator

"Mrs. Kasher, the school board has done all it can do."

My mother upended her purse to reveal the catalogs of fifteen private behavioral modification and special education schools that Oakland contracted through.

"You haven't done enough," she signed.

The entire team assembled by Oakland Public Schools shot eye daggers at my mother. You could almost hear the thoughts of "that uppity deaf bitch" ringing through the room.

My mama.

Whatever, I wasn't thrilled either. Why my mother couldn't just let me be a high school dropout bum in peace was beyond me.

By the way, dropping out wasn't just my idea. Oakland's dropout rate currently sits at 40 percent (Piedmont's is 0.09 percent).

Sorry, I didn't mean to make this a social critique! Back to the destruction!

I was sent, with my mother's blessing, to a school in Alameda called Children's Learning Center. An innocent-enough-sounding name for a school. Well, actually perhaps an innocent name was appropriate as the student body was made up of the most innocent people in the world, the mentally retarded.

I'm not making a joke here. I mean that, literally, the entire student body at CLC, with one notable, adorable, Jewish exception, was straight up retarded.

Some severely so. Autistic children who'd severed their connections to the world in the womb, taking the shortcut on realizing that people disappoint you and retreating inside their own complicated heads where Burger King logos and numerical patterns were *very, very* important.

Some were just mildly retarded, thick-lipped and amiable with enough smarts to make you wonder, "Is he or isn't he?" and then you'd see them picking their nose in front of a cute girl and you'd think, "Ahhh! Of course!"

I was now enrolled in a school with a student body of less than one hundred who all had IQs of less than one hundred.

There are some times when the illusion that you haven't made any wrong turns in life and that you are a victim of circumstance becomes very difficult to believe. Nothing quite defines that feeling as strongly as looking around a classroom and seeing drool dangling from the lip of more than one classmate surrounding you. Being the only non-retarded kid in class, at a certain point you have to ask yourself, "Am I certain I am not retarded?"

I was too weary to ask. I just showed up and did the entire battery of their hardest schoolwork in less than an hour. I'd spend the rest of the afternoon with my Walkman headphones on, feet up on the desk, a pinch of snuff in my lip spitting into a Snapple bottle in defiance. Finally the principal of the school approached me and asked if I'd like to use my sign language skills in the afternoons by helping the autistic preschoolers. I agreed to do it. I still wonder why, in the midst of all that assholery, I would have cared a bit about helping some autistic kids. I must've had something in me that still wanted to be good, to be okay. Also I was fascinated by them. I'd walk downstairs and work with these kids, checked out from reality, and look at them with a kind of envy. There was agony in their existence, no doubt. They would cry and scream in glass-breaking shrieks if even the slightest anomaly blipped outside of their absurdly chosen comfort zones; if snack time didn't have animal crackers, if there was purple Play-Doh and not yellow, it became a fucking crisis. But something about the lack of concern with the real world surrounding them made me jealous. If only I could check out like that. I felt useful down there, the severity of disability at Children's Learning Center ironically providing me an opportunity to actually feel engaged in a school setting. I felt like I was doing something good. The problem seemed to always be that I could never do good for too long.

One day, in the middle of class, I simply got up and walked out. I'd had enough. All this goody two-shoes stuff wasn't for me. I needed to get the fuck out. Thus marked my re-entry into the high school dropout community. I was now three high schools down and no grades successfully passed. This wasn't going well.

CHILDREN'S LEARNING CENTER
(510) 769-7100

1910 Central Avenue, Alameda, CA 94501
Gus Psara, Director
Errol Daste, Assistant Director

Facsimile Transmission Cover Sheet
Fax # (510) 769-1824

Date: 5.12.94   # of Pages (including cover sheet) 2

Transmit to Fax #: 415 695 5843

To: BEA WORTHEN

Company: CESAR CHAVEZ SCHOOL

From: JEFF HAUN

Phone #: 5107697100   Fax #: 510 769 1824

Comments: BEA. MARK LEFT SCHOOL TODAY VERY ANGRY WITH ME. I HAD SEPERATED MARK AND TWO OTHER BOYS IN OUR CLASS FROM THE REST OF THE CLASS/GROUP DUE TO DANGEROUS BREAK ACTIVITIES, THREATS, TEASING ETC. MARK DIDN'T THINK I WAS BEING FAIR AND WAS DISRUPTIVE AND REFUSING TO WORK AND EVENTUALLY WHEN ASKED TO LEAVE THE ROOM HE BECAME ABUSIVE TOWARD ME AND WHEN ASKED TO WALK DOWN TO "TIME OUT" TO CALM DOWN HE REFUSED AND ASKED TO CALL HOPE FOR A RIDE HOME BECAUSE HE WASN'T STAYING AT "THIS FUCKING SCHOOL". HE TRIED TO GET ANOTHER BOY TO LEAVE W/ HIM AFTER HE WAS UNABLE TO

That night I got invited to a kegger at Lake Temescal. Temescal is a lake just up the hill from Rockridge. Far enough from the city to escape the cops' eyes. Close enough to walk if you had to. How I ended up there I don't really know. I was drunk, already having spent the afternoon soaking my high school dropout memories in gin.

I stumbled out onto the field at Temescal, looking for something to do. I found it. A girl I knew from the neighborhood called me over to introduce me to the guy who was hosting this outdoor soiree.

I didn't know this guy and wondered what hell he was doing in my neighborhood, having a party.

It wasn't that it was forbidden, it just wasn't really done. People in Oakland didn't try to own blocks like the gangbangers in L.A. Those guys claimed absolute ownership of neighborhoods, and they'd defend to the death any trespass. We didn't get down like that. It was just, if you blew into the neighborhood, you made yourself a target for the hungry eyes of a group of kids so desperate for cash and drugs that they were robbing each other. And those guys were *friends*. It was *always* preferable to rob a stranger over a friend. That's the kind of questionable closeness the relationships in Oakland yielded.

The party was nice enough. Too bad there was a dirty mole in the mix. Me. I sat down with the birthday boy and chatted him up a bit. Nice kid, a hippie from the hills, he busted out a big brown paper bag and pulled out a handful of buds.

I'm sorry, but you pull out a gallon-sized bag of weed in front of a stranger wearing a Fila hat and you should expect to get jacked.

He kept talking but I stopped listening—that bag was all I had my eyes on.

A big fat brown bag of weed. That would look so nice on my mantel. Or in my lungs. Or converted to cash that sat, plump in my pockets.

Mmmm.

I looked around. There were hippies everywhere. People I could only assume were deadlock connected to Weed-Bag Man. If I tried anything, they would pray to their Avatar Gods, trap me in a Maypole circle, and kill me with kindness.

That bag, though.

It was whispering to me, calling my name. Like a valentine, it said, "Be Mine."

I couldn't take it anymore. I jumped up, muttered something about being right back, and rode my bike, as fast and hard as I could, to Joey's house about a mile away. Donny was gone and I needed help. Tough, Sean The Bomb type help.

I charged into his backyard, back by where his room was, and banged on the window. The blinds opened into a peephole and Joey's angry eye peered through.

"Dude, what the fuck are you doing here!" Joey slid open the door and grabbed me by my shirt.

"Stop! I'm telling you! I've got something for us. An opportunity to split like a pound of weed."

Now, let's be fair here. I had no idea how much weed was in that bag. It might have been a poor man's Russian doll of bags until he got to the little teeny bag in the middle that contained weed.

But I took a gamble. Too big of a gamble, actually.

"A pound?" Joey's rage was ebbing, being replaced by his entrepreneurial spirit.

"Maybe more!" I said, digging my grave deeper.

"Maybe more, huh?" I knew, at this point, Joey was in. Unfortunately, I didn't know that Joey owed hundreds of dollars to Fat Pete for all the coke he'd been snorting lately.

Fat Pete was a thug of gigantic proportions. He was huge. Both in the gut and in the game.

Fat Pete was white, but so dedicated to the wannabe black lifestyle that he had started to actually look ethnically ambiguous. His skin may have been white, but his soul was mulatto.

Pete was the guy who had recruited Terry Candle into his empire of crime and black accents. I feared Fat Pete the way Iraqis feared Saddam Hussein. A leader, but a terrifying one.

Looking back, I realize that Pete was a petty drug dealer, a small-time coke peddler with serious drug and deep-fried food problems. At the time, though, he seemed like the closest thing to Pablo Escobar I could ever hope to meet. A legend of extreme proportions.

Apparently, Joey owed him six hundred bucks' worth of coke that was meant to have been sold but was sniffed into Joey's nostrils instead.

Unbeknownst to me, pounds of theoretical hippie weed was exactly what the doctor ordered to pay off this debt.

Before I had time to protest, Joey was on the phone with Fat Pete making him an offer he couldn't refuse. A bucket of KFC. Just kidding.

"Dude, why'd you tell fucking Pete about it? That was our lick, man!" I was pissed. This shit had nothing to do with Pete, but I could envision my pounds of weed transmogrifying into a snack for him. I imagined him deep-frying the buds and sucking them into his cheeks, cackling as he dangled them just above his mouth, licking his lips like a fat cat holding a proletariat mouse by the tail in a pro-communist propaganda poster.

"Bitch, I told Pete because I fucking wanted to tell Pete. You got something to say about it?"

Joey flinched at me like he was going to punch me in the face but then went too far and, in fact, actually punched me in the face.

"Oh, sorry, dude. I meant to almost punch you, not to punch you."

"Dude, what the fuck? Quit being such a dick!" I held the side of my face, screaming.

"Who the fuck you calling a dick?" Joey reached back and punched me in the other side of the face. This time deliberately.

To this day I have never again been punched by accident, apologized to, and then immediately punched on purpose.

I swallowed my pride and held in my tears. There was business to attend to.

We set out in Joey's bucket, a '92 Toyota Celica jalopy with a modified exhaust that screamed when he accelerated. I didn't even know what we were doing anymore. As we left, Joey grabbed a barbell handle from his drawer, a heavy metal pole just the right size for cracking someone's skull with. I kept staring at it, lying there, gaining violent inertia with every second closer to Lake Temescal we came. The fucking pole was all I could look at.

We burned into the parking lot with some kind of uncanny synchronized timing. Fat Pete and three carloads of North Oakland D-boys pulled in right behind us. Holy fuck. This wasn't supposed to be the deal. First it was just me. Then it was me and Joey. Then Joey invited Fat Pete, and now it looked like all the thugs in North Oakland had heard it was free-plunder night down at Lake Temescal. It wasn't supposed to go down like this.

The cars parked, stacked up right at the entrance of the park, and we all jumped out. It was like an army. It was like a stampede.

There were some twenty dudes, each one more terrifying than the last. I was the weakest link.

As this army of Oakland stormed the field, my hippie locked eyes with me. His hand raised in a hello, his eyes widened in fear. I waved back. Joey ran up on his side and hit him with that pole. He went down, hard. Then there was no more party.

Very quickly, the entire party started streaming toward the parking lot. Suburban white kids came, screaming as the Oakland experience was brought to them. Kids were getting stomped left and right. A huge black dude I'd never met ran up on me, a bat in his hand. I screamed, "I'm with you guys!" and flashed him a North Oakland "N" symbol. He looked unconvinced for a second, hesitated, and ran off to stomp someone else's head in.

All I wanted was some weed. And I had caused all this. The real, scary truth was that I hated it. I didn't like seeing my hippie get hurt. I didn't like seeing these kids in terror. No more than I liked hurting my mother, or seeing her cry. I just needed to feel all right. After all, that was the thing I'd been after this whole time. Just a little comfort. None of this was me. I didn't fully know it yet, but I was cracking. I was coming undone.

I snapped out of it.

No time for pondering my identity, people were getting beaten half to death. Half of the North Oakland Bushrod boys were here. People were getting hurt. People were getting robbed. I was getting the fuck out of there. I never found out what happened to my hippie. I hope he was okay.

I took off into the night, figuring my weed was done for. I had some trouble imagining, realistically, in the wasteland of that party, saying to my big friend with the bat, "You see, Pookie, this was my lick. I planned this. So when you think about it, that's really my weed."

"But of course!" Pookie would reply, hugging me close to him. "It wouldn't be fair to deprive you of your share of the plunder. It's the pirate's way!" Then he would toss me the weed and a jar of Grey Poupon.

More likely I would've whimpered, "Do you think I could pinch a little of that bud? I actually planned this whole thing. I know I don't look like much, but I'm a thinker! Ha ha."

"I *think* you can suck my dick. And stop talking to me before I break your fucking jaw."

Oh Pookie!

Fuck that, I was out of there.

I stole home along the side of the road.

Some hippies pulled over.

"Hey, you need a ride, man? There's some crazy dudes up there at the lake. You oughta be careful. You gotta get away from them!"

I felt like dying.

"Yeah, I know I do. I'll be careful. I'll be all right." I looked straight on into the night. The kids drove on.

What was I becoming?

⚜

As if all the insanity surrounding me wasn't enough, I started to become aware of a more frightening insanity bubbling up from inside me. The years of psychotherapy, psychoactive medicine, and psychedelic drugs were making me psycho. You know, like "Norman Bates" psycho. You know, like "seeing things" psycho. Everywhere I walked, I saw a three-dimensional pancake following me. It lived in the left side of my periphery. It joined me in all of my affairs. Turn to the left? Pancake. Look up? Pancake.

Pancake, Pancake, Pancake.

You know, like "pancake-hallucinating psycho."

I was becoming emotionally brittle and any interaction at all was likely to lead to a full-on rage-filled blowout.

At home all my brother had to do was speak to me and things would sizzle of control. I'd throw baseball bats at his head and freak out the second after at the danger of what I'd just done.

I couldn't look in the mirror without grimacing and making faces at the awful asshole I saw in front of me. I couldn't even look at me. I couldn't even look at me.

Oh, but it wasn't all that bad! It wasn't all just violence and self-hatred! No! There was piss, too! Lots and lots of piss.

Somehow, I'd also become lazy as fuck. Diabetic coma lazy. My room was at least four doors down from the bathroom. At *least* ten feet away. I'd raise my lazy head, my brain swarming from the dance of weed and acid and psychotropics whirling around each other like dervishes, cutting my head to shreds. My bladder cried out like a *Little Shop of Horrors* villain, "Drain me!" I'd begin to get up and then the reality of how far that bathroom was would hit me. Ten feet. Four doors. Too far. Plus if I leave my room, I might see my mom. Might see my brother. Might hurt someone else.

My eyes scan my room, looking for something. Boot, no. *Penthouse* magazine, no. Wendy's cup! Yes. Better than a toilet, it's *right here.*

I grabbed that cup and flipped my little dick into it and began to fill it. Full to the brim. Bye-bye, self-respect.

I didn't even notice, to be honest. See, that's how it happens. When you hustle like I did, you only notice the ups and downs of the day. Do I have money? Do I not? What should I do to get money now? Thoughts like "Where was I at last year at this time?" are rare and easily ignored for the more pressing issues of the day. Every line of moral defense you have is compromised. Every "I will never" becomes an "I might" becomes an "I did." The moment you sink to a new low is the same moment that your conscience becomes compromised to the point that it won't rebel against the indignity you are putting it through. That's why so few addicts get clean. They never seem to even notice there is a problem because, for them, there isn't. You ever wonder how addicts let themselves become such animals? That's how. They forget they were ever human. It wasn't gross that I was pissing in cups and leaving them littered around the room. I simply had to piss and the bathroom was too far away.

Simple, simple.

In that way, I think, the people who *do* get clean are the weakest lot in the addicted bunch. Sure, it takes courage to get clean, but that courage is usually inspired by pain and humiliation. The real hard-core addicts never get sober because they never notice the ache, they never notice the pain. They can't be humiliated, they have nothing left to embarrass. And just like that, they die. So tough they die.

My room quickly became a filth pit of decomposing piss jars. Sometimes, I'd fill a cup too much and rank piss would spill over and splash back onto my belly. Sometimes I'd just piss on the floor, no cup needed. Sometimes I'd bunch up a towel and piss in it. I'd piss in the heater because it made a funny sound. And a funny smell, I found out right afterward.

Oh, fuck you! Don't judge. I told you there was a lot of piss coming. Also I told you I was losing my mind. My mother, usually a bastion of codependent over-involvement in my life, the woman who lived on top of my chest the first fourteen years of my life, suddenly became totally uninterested in coming into my room. Hmm. I wonder why she didn't want to come in. Into my dank, burnt-piss-stank science-experiment room. I finally had my privacy.

I was spitting on the floor. I'd been tagging on the walls in my house. Just like, you know, writing with permanent ink on my house's walls. My mom would look at me like I was an insane person, shake her head, and say, "I know you did it."

I was starting to be desperate for drugs, even as I pretended desperately not to need them.

I got high alone all the time and it had started to bother me.

"Smoking alone, that's dope fiend shit," Jamie told me as we sat together under a bridge one day, smoking out of an apple. "For real, after you start smoking alone, it's a real short hop to sucking dick for crack."

I looked at him, puzzled. "A real short hop? It seems like a longer hop than you are giving it credit for."

"No, dude, I'm telling you. Only a fiend smokes alone." Jamie was so sure of himself, I believed him.

That's one of the odd things about pathological liars. You keep trying to believe them, no matter how fantastical the tale. The idea that they are just lying to you, time after time, seems so counterintuitive that you still try like hell to believe.

"I don't want to be a fiend," I told myself.

I had this bike back then. A bad bike. A junkie bike. I'd bought it for ten bucks from a drunken Indian.

That's the truth.

Everything that could be wrong with it was. The handlebars rotated 360 degrees. The brakes had never worked, and I needed either to put my heel down and scrape my sneakers along the gravel or just leap off the bike altogether and run to a stop. There was no seat. But there was a seat post. A gay joke waiting to happen. Oh, and one day it exploded. Bet you didn't know a bicycle could explode, huh? I was riding along, trying precariously to keep my butt away from the seat post, when the entire bike just poofed into pieces. Just all of a sudden...boom...Legos! The bike disintegrated beneath my weight into a pile of scrap metal. My ass slammed into the seat post and my virginity was nearly taken. The bad virginity.

As horrible as the bike was, ironically, I used it to try and prove to myself that I wasn't an addict.

I'd ride for hours, the weight of the bag in my pocket pulling me down, my bike squeaking beneath me, looking for a friend to smoke with to prove that I wasn't fucked up. When no one was available, I'd ride my shit bike over to Harmonica Guy or some other homeless dude.

Oakland had an array of the oddest homeless people in the world. In the eighties, Ronald Reagan had opened up the California state mental hospitals to save money. "Don't worry!" he said. "We will build community centers to manage these people." Then, after releasing them, he did no such thing.

As a result, we got characters straight out of a comic book. Harmonica Guy was a local homeless guy who sat on a street corner, shucking and jiving for the passersby. He danced around, high on crack, playing the blues. An odd little man.

Then there was Ray, the Vietnam vet who stood on his perch at Rockridge BART like a British Beefeater, never moving, never abandoning his post. His face was burned and mangled from shrapnel. His mind was charred and wasted from trauma. Ray would stand there and scream at the top of his lungs, again and again, shaking the Vietcong demons away. He dressed in rags and scared children away. We loved fucking with him.

There was Hate Man, a famous staple of Telegraph Avenue, a man about whom rumors swirled of a past spent as a professor at the university until he tuned in, turned on, and went mad. Hate Man lived on the streets, downwind of the classrooms where he used to proctor exams. Always wearing a skirt, Hate Man was reliable. If you said hello to him, he would scream, "Fuck you!" Not in anger, but in his cosmology of hate. Don't ask me to explain, I'm sure I couldn't. No one could. He was just Hate Man.

There was Rawr. A man who looked like a Dark Ages barbarian who all day long hollered, "Rawr!" And if you yelled back, "How do you like it?!?" he would always reply, "Hot and wet!" We loved him.

There was a cobbler in Rockridge named Alonzo, who took all of these oddballs under his wing and had their VA checks diverted to his little storefront. Then he would pay them piecemeal, either in cash after taking a percentage for himself, or in cocaine that he stuffed into a shoe and passed to them, like a Brothers Grimm tale gone grimmer. Alonzo was a crooked cobbler. That's life in Oakland.

These messes of humanity were the people I would get high with when I couldn't find my buddies on the street.

All this to convince myself I wasn't an addict. I'd smoke weed out of their crack pipes and look down my nose at people smoking alone. Unless I couldn't find anyone at all. Then I just got high alone and looked down my nose at myself.

My life started to shrink.

The police had come back to my house looking for me. I'd been delinquent from school for months. My mother, exhausted at trying to convince me to go back, brought them into the pee pee nook and sighed, "Here, you deal with him."

They threw me back into school, my first re-entry into an Oakland public school in years. I entered Oakland Technical High School in a daze. Tech, a mildly scary high school that white kids avoided like the plague, held little intimidation factor for me. How could I be scared if I was hardly conscious?

I stumbled into the classroom and all eyes shifted to me like an Apache scalper sauntering into a bar in Deadwood.

"What the fuck is that white boy doing *here*?" I'd hear them mutter.

The mutters went away soon as they realized I was more of a sleeping boy than I was a white boy.

My life at Tech looked like this:

I would wake up to my screaming alarm clock, surrounded by jars of piss, and knock the clock over, falling back to sleep, missing my first two classes. Finally, I'd wake and bake and crawl to school, late for third period.

I was a running joke in the school. The sleeping boy. I'd slop down into my desk and fall asleep to the snickers of my classmates, who I never got to know, anonymous faces laughing at the mess I'd become.

My gym teacher liked to ask me, as I zombie-walked past him from one class to the other, "See you first period tomorrow?"

"Yeah, Coach, see you there. We are doing running drills tomorrow?" I'd roll my eyes, he'd shake his head.

I literally never attended his class. First period, no can do.

I slept, passed out through each class, leaning back in my chair in a haze.

Once, in math class, I leaned back too far and slammed back

onto the floor and woke to the cast of strangers laughing at me. I picked my chair up, flipped off everyone, and fell back asleep.

"Sleeping beauty fell down!" some kid yelled. Fuck him, I thought.

Two weeks later, I woke up with a start and looked at the girl sitting next to me.

"Thought I was gonna fall, huh? Not this time!" I sneered.

She looked at me, puzzled. "You still thinking about that? Nobody else here is."

That bitch, I thought.

That insightful bitch.

Despite all my attempts to shut my thoughts off and numb out, I was stuck in my head, constantly thinking about myself and the way people thought of me. I couldn't seem to get high enough not to care anymore. I think that's why I slept so much. Make it all go away.

Constantly worried, constantly scared. No one thought about me like I thought about me. The real problem was that the drugs I was taking were no longer taking that painful self-awareness away. My medicine was starting to fail me. My painkillers weren't killing the pain.

Addiction is like that. When you first start taking drugs, the thing that gets you hooked is that it takes the pain away. It kills the ache. It makes the wound numb.

Life was the wound. Life seared and stung. The world stung. I was born a mess of paper cuts, the world was a pool of lemon juice I'd been shot into.

So I found drugs, I found a painkiller that made me able to ignore the wound. I could walk upright. I could go forward. I could navigate the acidic reality.

Of course, if you are wounded, and you find a medicine that makes you numb, you don't correct for the wound. I should have been limping, I should have been wincing, holding back, walking tenderly. But in the bag and the bottle, I found a way to walk upright. To fight and scrap and tumble and give life the finger. Not taking it easy, my wound ripped into me. It cut me deep. It rended itself open. The wound ached. Life got worse.

So, of course, I took more of my medicine. I took more handfuls of that painkiller, straightened out, and walked upright again.

Life raked into me. I had to shovel the painkiller into me. I got ripped nearly in two. There came a point where I was all wound. I couldn't see where I stopped and where the wound began.

And, of course, as happens to all addicts eventually, I hit the point where I couldn't take enough medicine to make any pain go away.

So I couldn't make the pain be gone but I needed to keep taking my dose of medicine. If this was how badly I was hurting now, just imagine how I'd feel with no medicine at all.

The great irony of the addict is that the thing he takes, which is the only thing that has ever made life feel good, stops working long before he considers the possibility of life without it.

That first day I'd gotten high, I'd promised myself a life where I'd never stop. I never wanted to *not* feel that way again. The fact that I hadn't felt that good in years hardly registered with me. Eventually my wound ripped so deep I couldn't ignore it.

I didn't know it then but the door had closed on me. I was never again going to find relief in drugs and booze. I was never going to find joy in a bag again. I was only going to feel slightly less misery. My only true friend had turned on me. One more best friend gone, this time without saying good-bye.

What I didn't realize then was that what I needed more than anything was not something to kill the pain, but something new, something to heal the wound. Something to fuse me back to whole. To the whole person I never was. I didn't need to feel good, I couldn't. I needed to heal.

I needed to heal.

Chapter 14

"It's All Bad"
—E-40

Donny moved back to Oakland just in time for me to hit bottom. We were fifteen. He and his father had been drinking together, and he'd been sneaking off to snort coke in the bathroom, and to no one's surprise, that living situation hadn't quite worked out. Donny came back to town beaten up and low.

I went with Donny's mother to go pick him up at the airport. New Mexico had turned him into a new Mexican. During his stint in New Mexico, he had fallen in with some kind of Mexican street gang. They have so many, I can't remember which one it was. His socks were pulled up like a *cholo*'s, his silky locks shaved bald to affect the look of a prison inmate.

The second Donny's mom parked, she turned to the backseat to explain the rules to him. We were already halfway out the car door.

"Where the hell are you two going?" she screamed, frantic that things were about to default right back to where they were before Donny left.

"Out! Give me a night to myself!" Donny screamed at his mom and off we went into the night again. Into Oakland.

This was our city. Ready for us to take it over. But both of us were coming apart, and we knew it.

Fuck it. Ignore the truth and enjoy the dank.

We climbed into an abandoned house on College Avenue and snuck to the top, to a little balcony that overlooked the city.

I pulled out the makings of a blunt I'd brought just for the occasion.

I split a Phillies Blunt cigar down the middle with my thumbnail, cheap brown tobacco spilling out like the stuffing in a sofa. I cracked the leafy shell of the cigar in half and pried it open between my two fingers while I sprinkled bright green bud in place of the crap that had just been there. I packed it full, determined to give my old buddy a royal welcoming ceremony. I ran my tongue down the serrated opening to seal the two sides of the cigar wrapper together and ran my lighter along the wet seam to dry it.

Perfection attained, we smoked.

I coughed, he coughed, we smoked away the night.

When the world swam behind us, and the blunt was cashed, we climbed up to the roof and threw building supplies at cars.

It occurred to me that I'd been doing something just like this with another best friend just a few years earlier.

It felt like a life ago. It felt like a different person's life. I only vaguely identified that as my life. I didn't even know Richard Lilly anymore, but more important, I didn't really know the chubby kid who stood next to him throwing oranges either. I hardly resembled him. I was a different person. I was taller and slimmer, my appetite crippled by years of psychotropic medication and psych-edelic drug use. My eyes were blurry. My hair was slicked back with a thick layer of Tres Flores hair grease, which dripped down onto my face and ringed it with a chinstrap beard of acne. I sagged my pants six inches below my waist as a matter of course. I walked with a pimp limp. I looked like a fool. A dangerous fool.

We climbed down and Donny told me, "There's supposed to be a party tonight, let's roll."

I ran into the Lucky's supermarket and Donny followed behind me about thirty seconds later. All eyes were on us the second we walked into the store. We *looked* like criminals now. There was no sheen of childhood innocence to protect us from prying eyes. More extreme measures were called for. Donny doubled back by the bakery and came out in front of the store. I heard him yell, "I don't feel well!" and he then went down in the grand mal performance of a lifetime, foaming and shaking. The employees stopped what they were doing and ran to help the poor epileptic gangbanger in front of them. They never noticed the blur of a slightly chubby young Jew with a twenty-four pack of Budweiser hoisted on his hip, darting out the front door just feet away from the commotion. The second Donny saw me slip out the door, he straightened up and jumped to his feet.

"I think I'm feeling better now. Thanks, everybody!" Donny waved good-bye, and just like that, we were gone. Another hustle.

We met back at the BART station, jumped the turnstile together, and ran off to the suburbs. By the time we got to Pleas-ant Hill, we were both sloppy drunk, and as we tromped down the escalator, we saw two big BART cops sitting right at our only exit. We just decided to ride straight back to Oakland, tagging up the train cars. It was just like old times.

Back upstairs, at the station, I sat on the bench, waiting for the train, and looked over at Donny.

I sighed.

"This isn't working anymore," I said, cracking a Budweiser.

Donny looked up at me and I knew he knew exactly what I meant.

I sighed. "I mean, is it normal? What we are doing? We are headed no place, doing nothing. I keep waiting for this thing to just change, on its own accord. I keep waiting for the balance to shift in my favor but I'm starting to think it's never going to. I'm starting to think it's never going to change. It's like, is this my life?"

I stared at my friend, my old friend, waiting for a laugh.

It didn't come.

"I feel you." Donny looked close to the edge. Weary. Cracked. Dusted. "New Mexico fucked me up, bro. It's crazy there. I'm all jacked up. I don't know what to do either."

"So now what?"

We were both lost.

DJ and Corey were moving on. Their experiences in jail had fucked them up and scared them semi-straight. Jamie hadn't been seen or heard from in months. We thought he was in jail but there was no knowing.

Everyone had scattered to the wind. Joey was tweaked on coke and hardly human anymore.

"That rehab I went to was a pretty good place. Maybe we could go check in there," Donny muttered, uncertainty marbling his voice.

"Check ourselves *into* rehab?" I was incredulous.

"I don't know, man. I don't know. If nothing changes, nothing changes. You know what I mean?" Donny looked deflated.

"Yeah, I know what you mean. I don't need rehab, though.

That shit never worked for anyone. I'll quit for a while. Get my shit together. I'll stop. We should stop."

Donny looked dubious. "I'm down, I guess."

I finished my Bud and stared at the BART tracks. How the fuck was I going to change?

The next day, I walked into my mother's bedroom and triumphantly announced I would be getting my shit together. An empty promise she'd heard before. The drug addict, the king of the empty promise.

My mom looked at me wearily. She looked old. Tired. Tired of hoping for me. Tired of trying and watching me fail.

To be fair, I was also tired of failing. I truly believed that things were just going to get better on their own. I couldn't imagine I was just going to fail. I looked at my brother and his yellow brick road to success as something that should belong to me, too, but was just out of reach. I couldn't understand how he had faced the same shit as me and always managed to alchemize it to gold.

He was like a little Jewish Rumpelstiltskin, weaving feces into degrees.

I always imagined that things would just flip. That somehow, with no effort on my part, the tipping point would come and my life would right itself. My slimy world would congeal back to normalcy.

I imagined that, any day now, I would be getting a telephone call that would change everything...

RIIIIING!

"Hello?"

"Hello, is this Mr. Kasher?"

"This is he."

"Hi, Mr. Kasher, this is College calling."

"College?"

"That's right, Mr. Kasher, College...College! Listen, we've been tracking your progress for a while now, and while we are aware you've been having some difficulties lately, we think it's obvious that you are far too smart to fail. Maybe even a genius."

"That's what I've been saying!!!"

"Exactly! So anyway, we are prepared to overlook the repeated flunking of ninth grade..."

"That's more complicated than it seems. I have had some serious setbacks, none of which were my fault!"

"Our research proves just that! We are willing to ignore all those difficulties and invite you join us, tuition free, room and board covered...here...at COLLEGE!"

I started to realize that call was never going to come. This wasn't going to change unless I changed it. If nothing changes, nothing changes.

"I've decided to get my shit together," I signed to my mom, walking into her room, triumphant, ready to receive her gratitude. She looked unimpressed. Okay, sure I'd said it before, but I *meant it* this time.

My mom looked up at me with doubt in her eyes. "I wish I could believe that."

"Well, you can." I resented her implication.

"I'm starting to think you'll never change. I wish I had the courage to throw you out. That's what Dr. Susan says I should do. I'm too weak. That's love. Love makes you weak." As my mother signed this to me, her fingers flew in the light, trails streaming from them, playing tricks on my drug-addled brain.

"Well, I'm saying I want to change now. I'm saying I'm *going* to change."

My mom sighed. "So change then."

So I'd lost her, too.

No matter, I'd show her, I'd show everybody who thought I was destined to fail. I'd show them who the fuck I was.

I walked over to Monk's place. He had moved from being a good friend to simply just my drug dealer. Old memories only allotted me a twenty-four-hour credit grace period. I knocked on his door and he slid the privacy screen to the side, identifying me. God, he was just like a real drug dealer.

"Hey, man," I said as I extended payment for yesterday's bag and a fresh one for today, a twenty I'd slipped out of my mom's purse while she was telling me I'd never change. One last twenty. The last one.

"This is it," I told Monk.

"What is *it*?" he asked, hardly interested.

I looked at him seriously. "I quit, man, I'm out of the game. I gotta get my shit together. This is my last bag. I'm done."

Monk looked up. It looked like he was almost impressed as he handed me the bag. "That's cool, man, whatever you need."

So the next day when I went to his house to buy a bag, he came to the door, looked at me, and sneered in disgust.

I smiled and held out my cash. "Hey, lemme hold something, man."

Monk looked at me like he couldn't believe me. He shook his head and held out a bag for me.

"What hell are you doing here?" he snapped at me. "You said yesterday you were out of the game and here you are today. Dude, you've really got a problem."

I am here to tell you that if your drug dealer ever does an intervention on you, it's time to get help. That's when I started quitting. Every night I'd quit. Every night I'd swear I'd never do it again. I had to stop. I had to stop hurting people. I had to get my shit together. I had to get out of high school before I was thirty. I had to stop pissing anywhere other than the toilet. Every night I quit. And every morning I woke up and forgot about the promises I'd made to myself the night before. The thought to get high would hit me and I'd be at my dealer's house or at Safeway with a bottle of gin in my pants before I even had a chance to argue with myself. It wasn't how you would imagine it to be. I didn't crumble. I forgot. I didn't have a wrestling match with my conscience, struggling back and forth until I gave up on it. Rather, it seemed like I didn't have a conscience at all. It wasn't a struggle of good over evil. I didn't have an angel pop up on one shoulder . . .

ANGEL

Remember your declarations! Come with me
and walk toward the light. This way to salva-
tion! This way to high school graduation. This
way toward contemporary Christian rock music!
Come toward the light.

No devil popped up on the other shoulder.

DEVIL

Fuck that square-ass angel! Come with me! Let's
get high and fuck shit up! Fuck high school. Let's
go to HIGH school! Cisco! Gin! Malt liquor!
LET'S FUCK SHIT UUUUUUUUUUP!!!!

There was no struggle to decide.

ANGEL

Come to me. I have kittens.

DEVIL

Come to me. I have pussy!

ANGEL

Follow me, I'll make your family proud.

DEVIL

Follow me, I'll make pissing on the carpet seem
fun again.

ANGEL

Walk with me, be a better man.

DEVIL

Walk with me, and let's go jerk off while we
smoke weed.

That's how logic would dictate that the addictive thought process would work. Temptation stacked against prudence. Prudence crumbles. Temptation conquers. That's how it should work. How it actually does work is much scarier. When it came right down to it, there was no moral struggle. There was no struggle at all. There was simply an empty space in my brain where the night before there had been a firm declaration never to do this again. When the thought to take a hit, hit, I simply forgot I was planning on quitting. I just forgot. It went more like this:

I'd think:

ME

I should get high.

Then I'd think:

ME

I'm gonna go get high.

No struggle. How are you supposed to combat that?

That went on for months. Every night I quit. Every morning I forgot.

Another thing.

Another thing.

Another thing.

Every day was like the last one. Groundhog Day. Wake up. Get up. Steal money. Get high. Steal booze. Get drunk. Wake up. Get up. Steal money. Get high. Steal booze. Get drunk. Wake up. Get up. Steal money. Get high. Steal booze. Get drunk.

This.

Day.

Never.

Seems.

To.

End.

No end in sight.

I'm defeated.

Chapter 15

"Who Am I?"
—*Snoop Dogg*

I hadn't expected this. I'd been telling myself for years what every addict will identify as a familiar trope: "I could quit if I wanted to, I just don't want to." Then came the day that I wanted to. Then came the realization that I couldn't. The moment you need control is the moment you realize you've lost it.

Donny was having similar results.

We'd meet up and discuss our plans to sober up while drinking forties of St. Ides.

"Maybe we *should* check back into that rehab," I said, scared.

"You can't stop either?" Donny laughed a sick laugh.

"Naw." I stared at my hands, wrapped around that thick bottle, beer sweat dripping down over my fingers. I finished that forty off and made up my mind.

I told my mother the plan, and a flicker of hope flashed in her eyes.

"I'm going to go to Kaiser and check in," I told her.

"That's great. I'm really happy to hear that."

Donny and I traveled out to the Kaiser Outpatient Adolescent Chemical Dependency Program in Walnut Creek and told them the truth for a change.

We were admitted immediately.

I realized the second I got there that I hated them just like I had hated the people in the last place, just like I hated every fucking adult with power over me.

Oakland Public Schools had also noticed I'd dropped back out of school. Not that it mattered. I was a nuisance to them. More trouble than I was worth.

My mother caused a stink and got me on the waiting list for another school called Spraings Academy, which she was convinced would be the answer for me. Oakland agreed to one more year of funding therapy for me. I'd have another fucking counselor to go to. Oh joy.

I walked into group at Kaiser that first day and realized I'd made a huge fucking mistake. The kids seemed cool enough but then group started. The door opened and a voice from the back of the room boomed, "Hey, everyone. Great to see you all."

I knew that voice. I knew it from somewhere. I turned and looked.

Tim Fuckin Hammock. New head counselor of the Kaiser program. My nemesis from New Bridge. The guy who hated me and baited me back at my old rehab was now the freshly minted head counselor of my latest one, conveniently transferred to Kaiser just in time to ruin my attempt at getting my shit together. I couldn't ever catch a break.

He winked at me. He smiled big.

That fucking bitch, I thought.

This was going to suck.

Nonetheless, I was interested in trying. I was trying every night. And failing every morning. Rehab couldn't take away that hunger. I was starting to get really scared.

I sat in group, wondering what the point of all this was. Tim walked into group every day and sneered at me. He sat down and lectured us about how to change. No one listened.

Donny and I spent our hours in group fucking around, mocking Tim for the wart he'd grown on his cheek in the years since I'd seen him at New Bridge.

We'd take turns, Donny and I, circling around the room making eye contact with the other kids in group and fucking with them. We'd convince them that they had something on their face and laugh as we watched them rubbing away imaginary stains.

Whenever the group psychiatrist, Dr. Dale Dallas, would enter the group and sit in to observe Tim's leadership skills, Donny and I would yell, "Wokka Wokka Wokka!" at him.

What? He looked exactly like Fozzie Bear.

We'd yell about injustices Tim had never committed.

"Dr. Dallas, is it normal for Tim to be holding my penis while I give a urine sample?" I snickered.

"That's not a funny accusation at all." Dr. Dallas squirmed uncomfortably.

"Okay, fine, Tim never held my dick, but can you tell us one more time what life was like with Kermit and Miss Piggy?" I'd ask as Donny cackled one last "Wokka Wokka Wokka!!"

We died laughing.

Tim turned red. Dale Dallas left the room shortly thereafter.

I was trying. I was, I just didn't really know how to try. Kaiser, like New Bridge, chanted, "Get rid of your friends, you'll never get better surrounded by those guys."

How could I do that? No way. I'd just be strong.

Every night after group, I'd go back to Oakland with Donny and we'd go catch up with DJ and Corey and whoever else was around.

Again and again I'd declare to the boys, "I'm not drinking tonight, guys!" I said it earnestly, nudging Donny for his assent. It never came.

"More for us!" DJ would slur and take a slug of the booze.

We sat in a circle, the bottle being passed, person to person.

Each notch closer to me it got, the less clearly I could grab hold of my resolve not to drink.

It was coming to me next.

Ahh, forget it. A drink and oblivion. The pain didn't go away but at least it quieted down. I get hazy memory when I look into a bottle of gin.

I stumbled home, glowing drunk, stinking of gin, close to the edge.

I fell into the house and hobbled my ass toward the bathroom.

My mother was waiting, standing sentinel at the top of the stairs. "Is this what it looks like when you get sober?" she said, angry at her hopes being betrayed again. "You're drunk."

"A bit!" I laughed and pushed her out of the way, making my way to the bathroom for a nice drunken shit.

She chased after me, screaming, but I stopped listening and slammed the door in her face. I plopped down on the toilet and began the drunken defecation. That's when my mother kicked the bathroom door open like an angry police officer.

"I'm sick and tired of you pushing me around!" she screamed, charging me like a linebacker.

"Mom, I'm shitting!" was the only reply that made sense.

She didn't slow a tick. She ran straight for me, screaming like a madwoman, "FUCK YOU!!!!!"

My eyes widened in terror.

Contact.

She slammed into me and wrestled me off the toilet, pulling me down onto the bathroom floor, a tail of feces still hanging from me.

With my pants around my ankles and shit everywhere, I threw her off me and her hands scratched and slapped at my face. I grabbed her hand and bit down, hard. Her skin popping under my teeth, her blood shooting into my mouth. I slapped her. I shook her.

She crawled out of there, crying.

Here I am on the bathroom floor with shit and blood and tears and anger covering me. I was just like that baby shooting down the birth canal. Once again, my mother was asking, "What *is* he?" I didn't even know. I'm not human anymore, am I?

I'm a fucking animal. I'm a monster.

The police came. My mother called them. Aw, fuck. I'm too drunk for it. I fell asleep and hoped everything would go away.

I woke up early the next day, my head buzzing. That flush of the memory of what I did came flooding back to me.

"Hey, Mom," I whimpered.

My mother turned and looked at me. Cold and pissed. Emotions gone. No disappointment left.

The police report that my mother had filled out was sitting beside her.

"They are sending us a date for you to go to trial. They said it would be a few months," my mom signed to me, matter-of-factly.

"A court date? Ma, what'd you do?" I couldn't believe this.

"I didn't do anything. The police did. They are sending us a date for you to go to trial," she repeated, turning her back on me and flipping the TV on.

I could tell that the discussion was closed.

My mother had entered me in some kind of juvenile first-offense court program, which was the limit of the trouble she could get me into that night. Fed up and convinced that I needed to be taught a lesson, she pressed charges, and months later, I went to trial.

It was a kind of kangaroo court, where every single defendant was declared guilty and sent to anger management classes and community service weekends, humiliated and wearing a bright neon safety vest.

Head down, I entered the workspace with my vest hanging on me like a dunce cap, declaring me unfit for human consumption.

A thousand-yard walk to the work furlough check-in. My fellow juvenile delinquents sized me up.

"Ay, man," one kid said to another. "Whachu in here for?"

A pimply black kid replied, "Grand theft auto. What about you?"

"I robbed a liquor store."

Pimples looked at me up and down. "What about you, white boy?"

"I bit my mama," I growled. "Better watch out before I bite you, too."

The kids pretty much left me alone after that.

I did my work, minding my own business. The last thing I wanted to do was make friends. One more time I'd landed myself in some dumb shit quite without my own consent.

❧

Before that trial, though, I had to go back to Kaiser and in front of all my peers there face the music of what I'd done.

Tim was waiting for me, armed with the information he wanted. He knew just what I'd been up to. He looked delighted at the prospect of calling me out in front of everyone.

"You wanna tell us about what happened last weekend?" he asked me, pretending to sound concerned.

"Not really, Tim. No, not really." What was this dickhead trying to buddy up with me for? Trying to connect with me? Fuckin' yeah, right.

"Well, after an incident like the one your mother told me about, we can't continue here without you discussing it. It's a pretty big deal." Tim crossed his arms.

"I thought we weren't supposed to cross our arms, Tim. Don't you know that's a sign of defensiveness?"

"Making smart-ass comments isn't going to get you out of this," Tim said flatly.

"Look, just please leave me alone. Just stop fucking pushing me."

I was getting desperate, close to tears. I was so fucking ashamed and confused. But I wasn't telling this guy that. He's trying to get me to admit this shit in front of a group of kids? No way.

"Well, then, we might need to ask you to leave the group." Tim sighed and crossed his legs.

"Yeah, you'd like that. Here I am finally trying to quit and nobody gives a fuck. Nobody wants me to get better, they just want to talk about how fucked up I am. Kick me out then. I don't care anymore."

We sat in silence for thirty seconds. A standoff.

"Let's take a break, guys." Tim looked at the group like they were all in on something I wasn't. Only Donny was on my side but he was high as fuck. I knew *that* for a fact. "Take five and we'll regroup for family session."

Family session. Ugh. My mother would be there, bandaged. Everyone's parents would be there, staring at me, disgusted. I couldn't fucking deal with it.

Donny and I climbed into the elevator ready to go have a smoke and calm down. I was shaking.

Right as the elevator doors inched to a close, a hand darted in. Nails flashed the sensor and the door opened back up.

Pantera Neck. We called this chick Pantera Neck because of the shaved high back, rocker hairstyle she sported. She jumped into my elevator giving me the stink eye.

"The fuck are you staring at me like that for?" I snarled at her.

"I don't like you. You give Tim too much attitude," she said, frowning. Hadn't she just been flirting with me last week?

"Lucky me, I don't give a fuck about your opinion of me." I turned to Donny to ignore this bitch.

"Fuck you, don't turn your back on me." She grabbed my shoulder and spun me toward her.

I shoved her away from me, yelling, "Hands to yourself, ho!"

She leapt at me, her hands spinning furiously at me like a feral cat's. Her manicured nails slid down my face, raking a red streak down my cheek.

Did she just cut me?

I felt a trickle of blood dripping down my face like a tear, calling back to mind the memory of the blood I let from my mother's hand. I snapped. You see, somehow, the impotence I felt at the hands of all the women in my life, my mother, my grandmother, Dr. Susan, played itself out in overcompensation in the rest of the world. I would lash out at the few girls in my life at any slight disrespect. I'd yell and mock them mercilessly, hoping for tears, hoping for a breakdown. I had no idea at the time that I was just wresting from them the power I never had over the real women in my life, my mother and my grandmother. I didn't think about the deeper implications of all this of course—I just snapped.

I pounced on Pantera Neck, snapping, throwing her up against the elevator wall screaming, "Don't ever fuckin' put your hands on me, you tweaker bitch!" I shook her, grabbed a handful of hair, and yanked her head back. She spat at me.

Donny lunged over to stop me, and just then, the elevator hit the ground floor and the doors opened to all of my peers staring at me with this chick in my hands, their mouths agog.

They rushed in and pulled me off her.

Time for family session!

Ten minutes later, Tim shuffled into group having just debriefed with Dr. Dallas in the hallway. The elephant in the living room was me. I could feel the tension in the room. I'd felt it before. I'd lived my life as the "identified patient." I was used to being the subject of conversation wherever I was. Used to being the problem. Every eye in that place was on me, silently accusing me of being the worst of the worst. Shit, maybe I was.

"What? I'm the one who's cut!" Blood was dripping down my face. I dabbed it away with my sleeve.

Pantera Neck and her entire family glared at me from across the room with death in their eyes.

I shrugged, like, "Sorry?"

I was embarrassed.

I'm sitting here looking like a brute. How did I get here?

Worst of all, my mom's interpreter that night was this guy I'd always looked up to. Mike Hicks. A cool interpreter. Might not mean much to you, but interpreters were a ubiquitous feature in my life by then. I was the subject of so many meetings, there were so many reasons to need an interpreter. They sat in the back like the silent third party. A passive conduit of the information that bore my sins. They knew all my secrets. Bound by a code of ethics that swore them to secrecy and nonjudgment like the Federation of Planets from *Star Trek*, but I knew better. I knew I was a hell gig for them. I was nasty and unforgiving to interpreters. Nobody liked me. Except Mike. I knew he liked interpreting for me. Mostly because he didn't quit like all the other interpreters who'd come to family session. Mike was like me, the child of two deaf parents. He wore leather ties and signed like he knew what he was doing. He had long hair and a chimney sweep, E-Street mustache. A cool guy. An ex-drinker himself, he didn't seem to be judging me like every other adult in my clinical malaise. He was almost like me.

Everyone else's eyes accused me. Even Donny looked at me like, "I can't help you."

Ahh, nobody could.

Tim spoke up.

"After today's group, and especially after the incident in the elevator, I'm afraid we are going to have to ask you to leave the program. I'm sorry." I almost believed Tim just then. He looked disappointed. Was that possible? I sighed.

"I'm the one with a fucking gash on my face. Why don't you kick her out?"

Pantera Dad lunged at me, his eyes popping out of his head. His wife held him back or I might have been the first fatality in the Kaiser Adolescent Chemical Dependency Program.

A sign in the break room would've read, IT'S BEEN ONE DAY SINCE OUR LAST WORKPLACE ACCIDENT (MURDER!).

"All right, I get it. I really tried this time." I got up and made my way to the door.

Tim looked up at me. This time he didn't wink. He turned to my mom. "If you'd like, you can stay in family session without your boy and we can discuss a plan for his future."

My mother. To her ever-loving credit, she stood up, raised her bandaged hand, and signed to the group, with Mike speaking for her, "If you won't help my son, who clearly needs that help more than any of these kids, you can't help me."

She grabbed my hand in hers and we walked out of group together.

I squeezed her hand gently, and signed, just to her, "Thanks."

Two rehabs down.

Me, Mike Hicks, and my mom took that elevator to the ground floor.

My mom, crying again, got in the car and started it up. I had opened the door when Mike called me over to him.

"Hey, man, you got a second?" He smiled.

"Ha, I got all the time in the world. I've literally got nowhere to be."

"Listen, bro, I just wanna tell you, man—I get it. I get what's going on with you. I'm not trying to lecture you, I just want you to know that. Just want you to know I get it. I drank for twenty-five years and smoked my life away. I couldn't stop. I hurt people. I get it." He stopped smiling and looked at me in my eyes. Looked at me like he got it. Looked at me like I was his equal. An adult hadn't spoken to me like that ever.

"I'm not supposed to be telling you this. You know? We aren't supposed to interject our opinions. Ha, I could be fired for this, but your mom isn't gonna snitch on me."

He signed to my mom in the car, "You aren't gonna snitch on me, are you?"

My mom laughed her tears away and signed back, "No."

"Look, man, I just need to tell you, you aren't a bad kid. Sorry, you aren't a bad *guy*, shit, you aren't a kid anymore. You aren't bad. You're sick. I was real sick once. But I got well. My mom died this year and she died at my place. I was with her. She forgave me, you get what I'm getting at?"

I didn't, but I did.

He pulled out a ten-year AA chip.

"I stopped drinking a while ago and got my shit back together. Just don't let these people tell you you're a bad guy, because you aren't. You're lost. But if you want help, it's there. You can call me, we can hit a meeting, whatever. I'm only telling you this because someone told me the same thing once upon a time. Saved my life."

I was shaken up, close to matching my mom's tears tit for tat. "Cool, man, I appreciate it, thanks." I turned to jump in the car. Mike grabbed my shoulder. Grabbed me right where Pantera Neck had. I let him.

"Remember, though, you're gonna have to take a right turn someday. You're gonna have to decide, you know? There comes a time. You're gonna have to walk alone. Someday, you'll have to turn right. You'll have to walk alone."

"Yeah, well, thanks."

He hugged me. Why was he hugging me?

"You don't need to get good, you need to get well. Later, bro."

I didn't know what to say. "Yeah, later."

I jumped in the car. We drove away.

My mom put her hand on my leg. I looked down at her hand. My mom still loved me. That made one of us.

Chapter 16

"Free"
—*Goodie Mob*

It was a Wednesday six months later. Or maybe it was a Tuesday a month later. It was a day. In the afternoon. The fog was playing on the ground, unrolling itself onto Oakland like an old gray rug. The fog was everywhere, it was in me too. I'd just been thrown out of the newly minted Oakland branch of the Kaiser Adolescent Chemical Dependency Program. I'd joined right after Walnut Creek Kaiser kicked me out. They kicked me out and shuffled me to a nearly identical program closer to home. You know the comfort you feel when you are out of town or in a foreign country and you go to a chain restaurant that you might resent back home but, in that moment, the familiarity brings you comfort?

This was like the exact opposite of that.

I knew every trick. I'd heard every word. The walls were decorated with the same "Don't leave before the Miracle happens" crocheted wall art. I'd managed to gather a few weeks of sobriety but I couldn't keep my mouth shut. I got kicked out again.

Another rehab. I was a flagship member. First to be enrolled, first to be kicked out.

Three rehabs down.

This was my life. Nothing had changed. Nothing ever changed.

I laughed about it sometimes. I cried about it, too.

The boys and I were gathered at Rockridge BART again, trying to drum up a plan. One more afternoon in Oakland.

Donny was there. He'd been kicked out of Kaiser right after me for spitting on Pantera Neck in retaliation for getting me kicked out.

That's my boy!

DJ was there, penny rolls in his fists.

His brother Corey was there, scheming.

Jamie was there, lying.

Miguel was there, being weird.

Even Joey was there that day.

We were all there, all together. The remains of the Pure Adrenaline Gangsters. The remnants of us all.

The lost boys. Kids without a compass.

I knew.

That day, I knew.

Why that day was any different, I don't know. There comes a time. The pain of existence transcends the fear of change. There comes a time.

DJ looked up and I could almost see the lightbulb going off above his head. Electric currents shocking an idea into his atrophied brain.

"Hey, let's go to Brodricks!"

Brodricks was a bar we'd found that, in the rush of after-work madness, never seemed to card for beer. No matter how young the commuter ambling up to the bar seemed to be.

"Let's go get ripped up!" DJ was stoked.

Everyone was. Everyone agreed. Everyone. Everyone but me.

"I can't go, guys." I surprised myself as the words came out of my mouth. I looked at the confused faces of the guys. These guys. The guys I loved. My other family.

There comes a time.

"Huh?" DJ was confused. He'd had an idea. It was a good one.

"I can't do it today. I gotta go."

Donny looked at me. He looked at me in the eyes. Every scene of every moment we'd ever been through together was playing, fast-forwarding in them. He saw it. Saw the change. Saw that something had died in me. My will had died. My childhood had died. He saw that I was done fighting. He saw it.

He smiled.

He grabbed my hand and slapped a half hug on me.

"Right on, man, we'll holler atcha later." Donny held my gaze. I looked away.

"Yeah, f'sho. Holler later."

There comes a time. When you have to walk alone. Take a right turn.

"All right then, let's bounce." I could hear Corey salivating for beer. Hell, I was, too. All of my friends, all of them, turned and walked away.

I turned right and walked home alone.

I never looked back.

Part Five:
Exodus

Six months sober, age sixteen, I entered the Spraings Academy, another non-public school designed for people for whom every other educational modality had failed. I sat in the waiting room for another ridiculous dance. I'd done this so many times before. They'd talk to me, test me, attempt to fix me, and then label me: Broken. Damaged. Done.

They called me in. I took a seat.

I sat across from Dr. Violet Spraings, and she asked me a question no one in the educational world ever had.

"So, what do you want to do?" She smiled.

I thought about it.

"Well, I've been a freshman for going on forever. I've never passed a grade since seventh. To be honest, I'm just not willing to stick it out. I'll just drop out if I have to but I'd rather find a way not to. So I guess, what I want to do is have someone help me get my GED and get me out of here."

Dr. Spraings leaned forward and looked me in the eyes. "Okay."

"Okay?"

"Okay. Let's do that. You give me the rest of this school year and I'll set you up to be tutored all day with the specific goal of you getting your GED."

"Are you serious?"

"Totally." She frowned. "Are you?"

"What do you mean, am I?" I asked.

"I mean, are you going to work your ass off for me? Even when you want to quit again, are you going to stick it out? I need you to tell me you are serious, too."

"I'm serious. I promise." For the first time since I could remember, I knew my promise meant something.

"Okay, then we will do it. It will take me a while to arrange a schedule where I can get you a tutor to work one-on-one with you all day. In the meantime, you're just going to have to sit in my office and read this book. But read it deep, try and study it. I think you might really get something out of it if you do. Deal?"

I smiled big. "Deal!"

She passed me a beaten-up crimson-covered book, and I started my first day at my last high school.

I opened the cover and looked at the title page.

The Catcher in the Rye, by J. D. Salinger.

⁂

Three years passed. I'd gone back to school and entered community college when I was eighteen, only six months behind when I might've started college had I been a normal kid who graduated high school on time. Two years later I was ready to apply to transfer to a university. I applied to only one. The University of California at Santa Barbara. I'd been doing well. I had a strong GPA with only one weak spot.

I'd taken pre-algebra four times and failed four times. Apparently seventh grade is a lousy time to stop studying math if you are to acquire those algebra skills that will come in so handy later in your life as a stand-up comic. I hadn't been able to fulfill the requirements to transfer because of those damn math classes.

I applied anyway, thinking, "Whatever, algebra, no big deal; they'll let it slide."

Apparently the admissions office did not share my "let it slide" philosophy. I was denied entry.

I appealed the decision. I wrote the school explaining my past, explaining my weakness. Explaining myself. Explaining why.

And in the last paragraph of my appeal, I explained one more thing: "I'm clean and sober. Have been for five years. Your school is filled with active alcoholics. Drunken surf bums who drink 40's of Mickey's malt liquor before class (white boy drink, remember?). And you need me at your school. Just to be me. Just to be sober. You need me."

And they said: "Okay!"

I walked the stage two years later. They called my name and then said, "Graduating with honors."

This isn't amazing. Lots of people graduate college. It's amazing for *me*. I looked down at my mom, smiling at me. Crying for me. Crying good tears now. I signed to her, "I love you." She signed back, "I love you, too." That makes two of us.

One seat was missing. My grandmother was too sick to make it. I drove home to Oakland, where she lay, dying.

I took her hand in mine and whispered, "I graduated college, Grandma."

She squeezed my hand and whispered back, "Of course you did."

⁂

In the book of Judges, we meet Samson. The ultimate Jewish man. He knocked down temple walls with his bare hands. He slew an army with the jawbone of an ass. His long flowing hair provided him with supernatural strength and turned him into a Jewish Superman. And let's be frank, the Jews don't have many Supermen. Despite all the resentment and anger I had, my Samson was my father. Everyone's is.

But, of course, Sampson's power was gone when he lost his hair. His potent hands rendered flaccid. Every Superman has a kryptonite.

In February of my twentieth year, my father was diagnosed with cancer. He died in May. I was there. This isn't amazing. Lots of people are there when their parents die. It's amazing for *me*. I was never there.

I walked into the hospital room and saw my father in the full repose of his weakness. My hero was broken. My anger was, too. All the anger I might have ever had seemed useless. He was skinny. So skinny. My dad the dynamo was a wreck, stuck in bed. The tumors in his head had swollen, pushing into his ocular nerve, forcing one eye closed. A little one-eyed skeleton. The blood left my face. The lightning struck my heart. I couldn't breathe. I walked out of the room after waving a pathetic hello. I had to catch my breath.

"Is he afraid of me?" my dad signed weakly to my brother.

I pulled myself together and walked back into the room. Back to my father, the one we'd left in New York, so many years ago. "I'm here, Daddy," I signed to him.

"Of course you are," he signed back.

"You feeling okay?" I asked, the answer written all over his body.

He smiled. Lifted his hands up and mimed playing a sad little guitar.

A joke for me. One last joke.

I took his hand. Held it tight. Felt him there.

A week passed. My father was worse. Skinnier. Closer.

I'd been meaning to try and talk to him. To tell him how sorry I was for so many things. To make things right. I'd prepared some kind of formal speech, laced with recovery aphorisms and apologies. I sat down next to him and told him I needed to speak to him. My affect was frank. My motives were pure. My methods were shit.

My poor, weak dad tried his best as I launched into a speech about my past and the mistakes I had made. But he was weak from cancer and chemo, and five minutes into my grand attempt at making amends, I was interrupted by the sound of him snoring. My father had fallen asleep.

I sat, silently, next to him, laughing at myself a little. Crying to myself a little. I got up to go. Just then my dad rustled awake. He meekly raised his hands and signed to me. A full sentence. It had been days since he'd had the strength to say more than one or two words at a time. "Water." "Bed up." "Bed down."

All of a sudden he signed to me a string of words that must've sapped him. His body was so broken, his hands so weak, I couldn't make out what he was saying.

"I don't understand," I signed back.

He repeated himself.

"I'm so sorry, I don't understand." I felt like an asshole. For him this was running up to a marathon runner at the finish line and saying, "Sorry, didn't see it, start over."

He did. I understood. "I'm so lucky that you are my son."

"I'm lucky you're my dad," I signed back. Tears falling down my face. It was the last conversation we ever had. It was perfect. It said everything.

I was in the room when he disappeared. The King's reign had come to an end. Days earlier, he'd slipped into a coma—lifeless. I remember staring at him, asking God to take him, thinking: "He's dead already." When his heart stopped and something *else* left, I realized how wrong I was. I sat there, next to my father, as he breathed his last. I looked back at him and saw that he'd left the room. I was happy I hadn't.

I clawed my shirt in two in that moment, according to the rites of Jewish grief. The sound of the cloth ripping in two, slicing through the room, scraping the roof of my mind. My dad was dead.

I sat, the next week, close to the ground, receiving visitors along with the rest of my family as we sat shiva. Shiva is a kind of psychedelic experience where you sit, high on grief, as a parade of your loved one's history comes to pay respects. You just sit. All day long you sit and hear tales of how much people loved the person you loved.

I got to hear all the stories my mother never told me about my father. To hear what an amazing guy he could be. What an artist. What a man.

We sat and did nothing all day. When you sit shiva, you aren't even allowed to cook for yourself. If you are hungry, someone cooks for you. They don't want you distracted. You just sit. You sit with your grief.

Three times a day, local men gather at the house of grief to make sure ten men are present. You need ten men to make what's called a *minyan*, a quorum that forms a kind of express channel of communication to God. You need a minyan to be able to say Kaddish, the Aramaic prayer for the soul of the dead.

Three times a day, you are interrupted in your sitting to stand and speak to God. To tell the stories you've been hearing about your loved one back to the Lord. To stand and pray.

The time for the afternoon prayer had come one day and I stood, in a daze, to pray once again. Mordechai Ben David, the Chassidic rock star from my Bar Mitzvah, was the tenth to arrive. He took his fancy black coat off and assessed the scene. Me, my brother, my father's deaf best friend Billy, and six local penguins made ten. Well, at least we thought it did.

"We have to wait for one more man," Mordechai Ben David yelled to us.

"Why would we do that?" my brother asked. "There's ten men here."

"There's nine officially," the Pig spoke. "The deaf one doesn't count."

In my dead, deaf father's house this peacocking asshole refused to acknowledge another deaf man as a man at all.

I needed to say something. I needed to scream, "Get the fuck out of my father's house," but I couldn't. I was broken by grief, and the remnants of my childhood terrors still danced in my head. Screaming was hardly being invisible. Me, the one who always had something to say to the adults who wronged me, simply sat there impotent and ashamed. We waited for one more man. We prayed to what must have been a very disappointed God. I just sat there and thought, "If I ever write a book, I'll be sure to include in it what an asshole Mordechai Ben David is."

A week after sitting down, we got up. During shiva, the soul is said to be lingering in the room, hearing all the stories about itself. My dad, maybe hearing for the first time. A week later, you stand, open the door, and walk around the block, setting the soul of the dead free, letting it go.

Grief in the Jewish religion is very structured.

A week of sitting.

A month of no shaving, no music, no parties.

For a year you say the Kaddish prayer every day.

It's very comforting, actually. At a time when, more than any you can remember, you are at a total loss for what to do and how to do it, there is a structure that tells you, "Don't worry, here's how."

A year passed. Three hundred sixty-five days since my father died. Almost time to stop grieving every day. Almost time to stop saying Kaddish. I flew back to Sea Gate one last time. Back in time. My family was gathered there for the last time we would say Kaddish that year. All we had to do was go to the synagogue led by Rabbi David Meisels, my ineffective savior who'd referred me to Chabad so many years ago.

There was one problem. In the previous year I'd grown my hair out, long. I had huge frizzy curls and really looked like a freak. Back home in Oakland, I loved it. Here in Sea Gate, the prospect of going back into synagogue like this sent bolts of fear into my scalp. I didn't know what to do. I ran around the house, frantic, trying to stuff my hair into a comically undersized fedora that belonged to my younger half brother when he was thirteen. With my hair spilling out of it, I looked like the Scarecrow stuffing my brains back into my head. Shame was swirling around me a thousand turns a second. I became twelve again, ashamed of who I was and how I looked. Painfully aware that I wasn't, that I never would be, right.

Then I took a breath.

Realized I wasn't twelve.

Realized I wasn't ruled by those demons from my past.

Realized I was a grown-up.

Realized it didn't matter if they knew I was different.

Hell, I *was* different.

I took off my hat.

My hair spilled down onto my shoulders like Samson's.

I got my strength back.

I knocked down the walls of my past with my bare hands.

I walked to shul.

I became a man.

❧

Every time Donny's mom's number popped up on my caller ID, I held my breath, waiting for her to say, "Donny's dead."

One night she almost did.

The phone rang.

"Hello?"

"Donny fell asleep at the wheel. Crashed into a guardrail. Almost lost his leg. Almost died."

He'd been up for days, smuggling speed in from Juárez, Mexico, and woke up in the hospital.

He'd be okay.

A year later Donny called me collect from New Mexico. I recognized the area code, expected the worst.

But he wasn't dead. He wanted to live.

"I'm broken, bro," he whispered.

"I know, man. Come home."

I picked him up at the airport.

He was sucked up and stank. He'd been living out of a duffel bag for weeks. His only companion was an emaciated and slightly violent pit bull appropriately named Capone.

Donny took a right turn that day.

Last year I got a call from him again.

"Come to the hospital."

I rushed over.

I lifted his baby girl out of his arms. His wife was asleep in the hospital bed. His mother was sitting next to her. I held his daughter, hours old.

"She's beautiful. But you sure you don't want to go with the name *Moshe*?"

❦

Joey. Big Joey. Big Tough Joey. My hero. The guy who knocked Sean The Bomb the fuck out. The stud of studs. Joey Zalante. What a man. He fell off his motorcycle one day, jacked up on coke, riding like a madman. Ass scraping on the gravel, disintegrating beneath him. His tailbone gnarled, jutting out forever. Pain that would never go away.

He was in the hospital for months.

He was laid up in the hospital right across the way from the therapist that I went to, the final round of therapy that was paid for by the funding from Oakland Public Schools, which lasted just long enough to ensure I was serious about getting better.

I visited Joey every week after therapy and talked to him about my new life, convinced that my proximity to him was a divine signal, God's finger putting us together. I was going to save him. I never considered he wouldn't let me. Or that it wasn't my business to.

Just like a newly saved Christian, I bored him to tears with saccharine tales of my new life. He smiled. He appreciated me being there. My old hero.

Joey got out of the hospital half a year later. He sat on a donut and limped around.

He drank the pain away. He sucked down pills. He suffered greatly.

Years later, his doctor told him if he kept drinking, he was going to die.

Joey left the doctor's office, locked himself in his apartment, and did just that.

They found his body frozen in an easy chair in the living room.

The pain gone forever.

Big tough Joey.

I sat in a meeting, bored. I'd been going to these things for years. At some point you've heard it all. No bother, I was there mostly to see friends and maybe remind myself of where I came from.

A voice spoke from the back of the room. The guy they'd just called on.

"I'm afraid. I've been sinking into a deep depression for years now. I feel so scared and broken. I know I shouldn't be this screwed up, I've been sober for twenty years now. I just need some love from the group right now."

I know that voice. I know it from somewhere.

I turned and followed the voice back. I recognized him, and when I did, he melted from a resentful memory into a human being.

After the meeting I walked up to him.

"Tim? Tim Hammock?"

"Yeah, that's me, do I know you?"

"You don't recognize me? I guess that's a good thing. You were my counselor once upon a time at Kaiser, and New Bridge, too, actually. It was really good to hear you. I really related. I'm sorry you're having a tough time. Oh, and I'm sorry I was such a dick back then!"

Tim smiled. "You *were* kind of a dick. It's nice to see you."

He winked at me. Then he hugged me.

⚘

At twenty-five, I'd been a freelance sign language interpreter for years. I moonlighted as a stand-up comic but I was new in the game and it wasn't paying the bills yet. Imagine, my deaf mom and my big mouth, the two things that seemed to stack the chips against me, were now getting me paid. Joke's on you, Oakland Public Schools.

I got a call one day from the agency that sent me out on jobs.

"We have a six o'clock assignment for you at Kaiser Walnut Creek, in the Adolescent Chemical Dependency Program. I'll e-mail you directions."

"That's okay," I said, "I know my way there."

"Oh, okay then. The appointment is for something called family session."

My heart pounded as I sat in my seat at my old rehab, interpreting for a deaf family and their fourteen-year-old son. A kid falling into addiction. Maybe a touch of attitude, too.

The parents spoke and I listened, passive, a conduit for their communication, a fly on the wall.

Everybody assumed I was just another adult, sitting right where I needed to be. In my mind, I had shrunk back to a fifteen-year-old kid, lost, shattered, desperate. No one knew who I was. No one even suspected.

I listened to the parents complain and make excuses and I realized, like a lightning bolt, "Whoa, these guys are just as fucked up as their kids."

I listened. I signed. I healed a little bit more.

The group ended.

I looked around and realized I was free to go. I was free.

The elevator dinged.

The doors opened.

Just as they slid closed, a hand darted in and set the sensor off, sending the doors back open.

That kid stepped into the elevator with me.

I turned and looked at him.

"Can I help you, bro?" He sneered at me like an enemy.

He thinks I'm an adult. I *am* an adult!

"No. It's just ... Well, I want you to know you aren't bad, you're sick. But you can get better. Once upon a time I did, too."

"This is a really inspirational story, mister. Should I tell my dad the interpreter was giving me advice on getting better? Wouldn't that get you fired?"

I laughed. "Yeah, probably. But you aren't going to snitch on me, are you?"

"Not if you leave me the fuck alone, starting...now."

"I gotcha. No problem, man. Sorry to bug you."

I smiled to myself.

The door opened.

The kid stepped out.

As I saw that kid walk away angry, attitude in his step, I saw myself in him. Saw myself back then, pissed off, young, shattered. The elevator closed shut and I looked at the reflection staring back at me from the mirrored doors.

It was that kid again.

No. I shook it off. I looked again. I saw the real me looking back. That big wound had sutured up. It had healed. All the pain was gone. I was whole. I wasn't all broken and bad like the last time I'd stood here staring at myself, wondering what I'd become. But then, maybe I hadn't been so broken. Maybe I wasn't such a bad kid back then after all. If I was, how had I turned into what I was looking at now? A good guy.

A good guy, that's what I'd become.

Violet Spraings, Ph.D.
Director

Diane Angel Emberlin
Assistant Director
Chief Financial Officer

Tammy G. Weisberg
Administrative Assistant

SPRAINGS ACADEMY

February 6, 1995

To: Mrs. Bea Worthen

From: Violet Spraings, Ph.D., Director, Spraings Academy

The faculty is working diligently with Mark and getting to know who he is, trying not to overwhelm him with work.

Reading <u>Catcher in the Rye</u> was Day 1 assignment. Each day he will be given more responsibility in accord with his tolerance level.

A major concern of our faculty is to bring about an attitude change in Mark. He is getting quite a bit of one-to-one attention.

I think after he has seen Dr. Calendar and has medication appropriate to his attention deficit disorder, there will be considerable improvement in Mark's willingness to work without one-to-one and to take on responsibility in accord with his high level of ability.

Please be patient and allow our faculty to use their expertise with Mark.

cc: Mr. Jeffrey Pollock, Chief, Secondary Division, Spraings Academy

About the Author

Moshe Kasher is an award-winning stand-up comedian and writer. He has been featured on Comedy Central, NBC, Fox, MTV, E!, VH1, Showtime, and a million other places. He makes his living telling jokes. His mother loves him very much.

www.moshekasher.com